This book is available in quantity at special discounts for your group or organization.
For further information, contact:

Triumph Books LLC
814 North Franklin Street
Chicago, Illinois 60610
Phone: (312) 337-0747
www.triumphbooks.com

Printed in U.S.A.
ISBN: 978-1-63727-257-2

The Athletic

Editors
Nando Di Fino, Brandon Funston and Adam Hirshfield

Andrew DeWitt
Carly Dubois
Mike Harris
Nunzio Ingrassia
Craig Lancaster
Jessica Lenchner
Danny Santaromita
Courtney Shultz
Monica Thomas
John Vogl

Special Thanks
BetPrep
TruMedia

Design by Patricia Frey

All interior photos courtesy of AP Images

Contents

Introduction

Hello Friends!

Welcome to another year of fantasy football!

These welcome letter things tend to be boring. We used to skip past them to get to the good stuff — they're like old Nintendo game instructions. But allow us to throw this curveball at you: We grew up reading the "Tales from the Crypt" reprint comics in the early '90s. Intros are supposed to be fun (and maybe a little macabre, but hold that thought for now). Not pedantic and sales-y.

So here's what you have in your hands — the key to unlocking your full fantasy potential and steamrolling over your leaguemates with ease. We have a neuroscientist in here! And not just any neuroscientist — Dr. Renee Miller, who has a Ph.D in neurodegenerative disease research, won the 2019 Fantasy Sports Writers Association award for Best Fantasy Football Series. She's awesome, and she'll tell you, in these pages, how to not let your brain get in the way of … well, your brain.

Jake Ciely has accomplished so much as one of fantasy's preeminent rankers that when we asked him to send some of his high points in accuracy challenges for this letter, he emailed a spreadsheet, with multiple tabs. And thought that was normal. Over the last decade, he's been more accurate than hundreds of other fantasy football experts, which allows him the freedom to make weird "DuckTales" references in his columns and get away with it. That is true power.

One of the best parts about working at The Athletic is the access to our team beat writers. And they're all generally nice people, so we take advantage of that and ask them questions about players when we need to make trades in our own leagues. But we wanted to bring some of that flavor to this bookazine, so we took the questions we had for every team, asked the writers and published them here. For you. For us. For everyone! And then we assume they loved it so much we asked them to help with a second column and give us a breakout candidate, too. We cannot stress how great this information is. And how wonderful each one of the writers are. Some even wrote deep dives on players in our Rankings section, to give a little more insight into what to expect in 2022.

We have brilliant scouting minds who have unique takes on players and advanced analytical tables and graphs that'll ignite the inner nerd in you. And columns that will make you think twice about taking a running back in the second round. Looking for injury analysis? Inside Injuries is like no other company out there — the doctors who founded it crafted an algorithm based on past recovery time and diagnosis (and a bunch of other things) and have created measures that will more accurately predict a player's return — or how poorly he'll play and how much of an injury risk he is if he returns too soon.

This is our first fantasy football guide at The Athletic. We wanted it to be awesome. With everything we considered here, we asked ourselves, "would we want to read this?" And then stared a little more deeply into our eyes in the mirror, leaned in menacingly, and asked "but really, you can tell me … would we really want to read this?"

We don't mess around with fantasy football here. If we weren't going to create the greatest fantasy football bookazine, then our time could be better spent elsewhere.

So away we go. Get that title. And strap in, boils and ghouls, for what should be a frighteningly fun ride!

Hugs and kisses,

Nando Di Fino, Brandon Funston and Adam Hirshfield

QUICK NOTES:

1. Love that Jake Ciely comic? It was done by Alex Miller, better known as @smudgeandfrank on Instagram/Twitter

2. Love the graphs and tables? They're courtesy of BetPrep (famous for their virtual sportsbook, for the bettors out there) and TruMedia

3. Wondering why Chris Vaccaro didn't write a column? He decided to go to the Jersey Shore instead. But you should still show up at his bar the next time you're in NYC: the Greenwich Street Tavern has the best wings in New York. For real.

4. If you're more of an audiophile, we have The Athletic Fantasy Football Podcast on pretty much any platform you need

5. You'll see QR codes throughout this book — it's because we wrote this bookazine in July and stuff has probably changed by now (wild prediction — D'Onta Foreman has 400 preseason yards in two games). That QR code will take you to a page of updated columns found in here, with pertinent new info. ▬▬▬

A

I. 2022 Player Rankings (Overall)

Jake Ciely's
2022 overall rankings

RK	OVERALL PLAYER	POS RK	BYE	FPS
1	Jonathan Taylor	RB1	14	323.5
2	Christian McCaffrey	RB2	13	310.1
3	Derrick Henry	RB3	6	304.2
4	Cooper Kupp	WR1	7	299.5
5	Ja'Marr Chase	WR2	10	279.8
6	Najee Harris	RB4	9	277.4
7	Austin Ekeler	RB5	8	269.5
8	Justin Jefferson	WR3	7	252.6
9	Joe Mixon	RB6	10	246.8
10	Deebo Samuel	WR4	9	243.1
11	Saquon Barkley	RB7	9	239.8
12	D'Andre Swift	RB8	6	239.2
13	Stefon Diggs	WR5	7	239.4
14	Davante Adams	WR6	6	238.6
15	Dalvin Cook	RB9	7	237.7
16	James Conner	RB10	13	237.2
17	Nick Chubb	RB11	9	230.9
18	CeeDee Lamb	WR7	9	230.6
19	Leonard Fournette	RB12	11	229.6
20	Aaron Jones	RB13	14	224.4
21	Cam Akers	RB14	7	219.3
22	Javonte Williams	RB15	9	219.1
23	Mike Evans	WR8	11	219.2
24	Alvin Kamara	RB16	14	218.0
25	Antonio Gibson	RB17	14	217.2
26	Tyreek Hill	WR9	11	217.5
27	Tee Higgins	WR10	10	216.6
28	J.K. Dobbins	RB18	10	215.7
29	Josh Jacobs	RB19	6	213.5
30	Josh Allen	QB1	7	421.9
31	Travis Kelce	TE1	8	218.6
32	A.J. Brown	WR11	7	208.1
33	Ezekiel Elliott	RB20	9	204.0
34	David Montgomery	RB21	14	201.7

RK	OVERALL PLAYER	POS RK	BYE	FPS
35	Keenan Allen	WR12	8	201.4
36	Diontae Johnson	WR13	9	200.8
37	Jalen Hurts	QB2	7	393.3
38	Michael Pittman	WR14	14	199.4
39	Amari Cooper	WR15	9	199.3
40	Mike Williams	WR16	8	195.2
41	Mark Andrews	TE2	10	199.7
42	Justin Herbert	QB3	8	384.8
43	Jaylen Waddle	WR17	11	194.0
44	Kyle Pitts	TE3	14	197.8
45	Allen Robinson	WR18	7	190.4
46	DK Metcalf	WR19	11	189.2
47	DJ Moore	WR20	13	188.6
48	Brandin Cooks	WR21	6	188.3
49	Rashod Bateman	WR22	10	187.1
50	Travis Etienne	RB22	11	184.2
51	JuJu Smith-Schuster	WR23	8	184.3
52	Damien Harris	RB23	10	183.6
53	Terry McLaurin	WR24	14	183.4
54	Gabriel Davis	WR25	7	182.6
55	Patrick Mahomes	QB4	8	384.4
56	Lamar Jackson	QB5	10	381.8
57	Breece Hall	RB24	10	176.9
58	Tyler Lockett	WR26	11	176.4
59	AJ Dillon	RB25	14	175.3
60	Elijah Moore	WR27	10	175.5
61	Hunter Renfrow	WR28	6	175.3
62	DeVonta Smith	WR29	7	175.3
63	Elijah Mitchell	RB26	9	173.2
64	Courtland Sutton	WR30	9	172.3
65	Darnell Mooney	WR31	14	171.0
66	Jerry Jeudy	WR32	9	170.2
67	Amon-Ra St. Brown	WR33	6	169.6
68	Drake London	WR34	14	169.5

RK	OVERALL PLAYER	POS RK	BYE	FPS
69	Chris Godwin	WR35	11	167.9
70	Marquise Brown	WR36	13	167.6
71	Allen Lazard	WR37	14	167.3
72	Darren Waller	TE4	6	169.3
73	Christian Kirk	WR38	11	162.5
74	Cordarrelle Patterson	RB27	14	161.4
75	Joe Burrow	QB6	10	361.7
76	Tony Pollard	RB28	9	159.6
77	Treylon Burks	WR39	6	159.2
78	Adam Thielen	WR40	7	158.6
79	Clyde Edwards-Helaire	RB29	8	157.3
80	George Kittle	TE5	9	161.5
81	Russell Gage	WR41	11	157.4
82	Kyler Murray	QB7	13	353.6
83	Tom Brady	QB8	11	352.0
84	Michael Gallup	WR42	9	154.0
85	Devin Singletary	RB30	7	151.9
86	Dalton Schultz	TE6	9	155.9
87	Tyler Boyd	WR43	10	151.7
88	Garrett Wilson	WR44	10	151.6
89	Michael Thomas	WR45	14	150.7
90	Aaron Rodgers	QB9	14	337.0
91	Matthew Stafford	QB10	7	334.8
92	Brandon Aiyuk	WR46	9	148.4
93	Dallas Goedert	TE7	7	151.2
94	Kareem Hunt	RB31	9	146.6
95	Dak Prescott	QB11	9	334.4
96	Rashaad Penny	RB32	11	144.7
97	Kenneth Walker	RB33	11	144.4
98	Melvin Gordon	RB34	9	142.7
99	Trey Lance	QB12	9	324.0
100	Robert Woods	WR47	6	142.2
101	Miles Sanders	RB35	7	141.0
102	Russell Wilson	QB13	9	321.3
103	Chase Edmonds	RB36	11	139.0
104	Jameson Williams	WR48	6	138.4
105	Tim Patrick	WR49	9	137.1
106	Trevor Lawrence	QB14	11	318.1
107	Marvin Jones	WR50	11	136.1

RK	OVERALL PLAYER	POS RK	BYE	FPS
108	Mecole Hardman	WR51	8	135.0
109	Chase Claypool	WR52	9	135.0
110	T.J. Hockenson	TE8	6	137.7
111	Justin Fields	QB15	14	309.5
112	Chris Olave	WR53	14	131.6
113	Irv Smith	TE9	7	134.5
114	Derek Carr	QB16	6	302.1
115	Kenny Golladay	WR54	9	131.1
116	Kirk Cousins	QB17	7	301.9
117	Alec Pierce	WR55	14	130.3
118	DeAndre Hopkins	WR56	13	129.9
119	Van Jefferson	WR57	7	129.6
120	Tua Tagovailoa	QB18	11	298.1
121	Jarvis Landry	WR58	14	128.8
122	George Pickens	WR59	9	128.6
123	Zach Ertz	TE10	13	131.3
124	Kadarius Toney	WR60	9	127.0
125	Robbie Anderson	WR61	13	126.8
126	Cameron Brate	TE11	11	129.1
127	Jakobi Meyers	WR62	10	125.5
128	Nyheim Hines	RB37	14	123.9
129	Gus Edwards	RB38	10	122.9
130	Jahan Dotson	WR63	14	123.3
131	Dawson Knox	TE12	7	126.4
132	Carson Wentz	QB19	14	279.6
133	David Njoku	TE13	9	125.5
134	J.D. McKissic	RB39	14	122.0
135	Skyy Moore	WR64	8	122.1
136	Christian Watson	WR65	14	121.1
137	Kenneth Gainwell	RB40	7	120.5
138	Rondale Moore	WR66	13	120.5
139	Rhamondre Stevenson	RB41	10	119.6
140	Pat Freiermuth	TE14	9	122.7
141	James Cook	RB42	7	119.1
142	Cole Kmet	TE15	14	121.7
143	John Metchie	WR67	6	118.7
144	Ronald Jones	RB43	8	118.1
145	Matt Ryan	QB20	14	276.8
146	Zach Wilson	QB21	10	276.6

2022 Player Rankings (Overall)

RK	OVERALL PLAYER	POS RK	BYE	FPS
147	Hunter Henry	TE16	10	119.2
148	Isaiah Spiller	RB44	8	115.9
149	Alexander Mattison	RB45	7	115.3
150	Byron Pringle	WR68	14	113.5
151	Curtis Samuel	WR69	14	112.9
152	Mike Gesicki	TE17	11	114.8
153	DeVante Parker	WR70	10	111.8
154	Mark Ingram	RB46	14	111.2
155	Brevin Jordan	TE18	6	114.0
156	Noah Fant	TE19	11	113.8
157	Darrell Henderson	RB47	7	109.0
158	Jamaal Williams	RB48	6	108.9
159	Joshua Palmer	WR71	8	108.7
160	Albert Okwuegbunam	TE20	9	111.2
161	Michael Carter	RB49	10	108.1
162	Donovan Peoples-Jones	WR72	9	107.5
163	Daniel Jones	QB22	9	272.3
164	Ryan Tannehill	QB23	6	271.1
165	Robert Tonyan	TE21	14	109.1
166	Logan Thomas	TE22	14	108.4
167	Cedrick Wilson	WR73	11	105.3
168	James Robinson	RB50	11	104.2
169	Marquez Valdes-Scantling	WR74	8	104.1
170	Dameon Pierce	RB51	6	103.3
171	Tyler Higbee	TE23	7	105.3
172	Tyler Allgeier	RB52	14	102.4
173	Khalil Herbert	RB53	14	102.4
174	Marlon Mack	RB54	6	101.9
175	K.J. Osborn	WR75	7	102.1
176	James White	RB55	10	101.5
177	Gerald Everett	TE24	8	103.6
178	Rachaad White	RB56	11	100.3
179	Evan Engram	TE25	11	102.9
180	Jameis Winston	QB24	14	259.3
181	Jalen Tolbert	WR76	9	99.3
182	Jamison Crowder	WR77	7	99.2
183	Jared Goff	QB25	6	258.1
184	Mo Alie-Cox	TE26	14	100.7
185	Austin Hooper	TE27	6	100.1

RK	OVERALL PLAYER	POS RK	BYE	FPS
186	Hayden Hurst	TE28	10	100.1
187	Deshaun Watson	QB26	9	255.9
188	Nick Westbrook-Ikhine	WR78	6	97.1
189	D.J. Chark	WR79	6	95.8
190	Kendrick Bourne	WR80	10	95.2
191	Sterling Shepard	WR81	9	94.7
192	Devin Duvernay	WR82	10	94.5
193	Nico Collins	WR83	6	94.3
194	Rex Burkhead	RB57	6	93.8
195	Darrel Williams	RB58	13	92.9
196	Randall Cobb	WR84	14	91.1
197	Sammy Watkins	WR85	14	90.7
198	Damien Williams	RB59	14	89.3
199	Raheem Mostert	RB60	11	89.0
200	Mac Jones	QB27	10	243.3
201	Davis Mills	QB28	6	238.2
202	Jalen Guyton	WR86	8	85.5
203	C.J. Uzomah	TE29	10	87.1
204	Corey Davis	WR87	10	83.4
205	Terrace Marshall	WR88	13	83.2
206	Zay Jones	WR89	11	82.4
207	Kenyan Drake	RB61	6	81.9
208	Kenny Pickett	QB29	9	217.7
209	David Bell	WR90	9	75.6
210	Chris Evans	RB62	10	74.2
211	Marcus Mariota	QB30	14	209.1
212	Wan'Dale Robinson	WR91	9	73.1
213	Velus Jones	WR92	14	72.9
214	Sony Michel	RB63	11	71.5
215	A.J. Green	WR93	13	70.7
216	Parris Campbell	WR94	14	70.3
217	Olamide Zaccheaus	WR95	14	69.2
218	Dan Arnold	TE30	11	69.4
219	Tommy Tremble	TE31	13	69.2
220	Matt Breida	RB64	9	66.4
221	James Washington	WR96	9	64.7
222	Sam Darnold	QB31	13	182.4
223	Dee Eskridge	WR97	11	63.9
224	Adam Trautman	TE32	14	64.8

RK	OVERALL PLAYER	POS RK	BYE	FPS
225	Boston Scott	RB65	7	61.6
226	Bryan Edwards	WR98	14	61.4
227	Laquon Treadwell	WR99	11	60.7
228	KJ Hamler	WR100	9	60.5
229	Laviska Shenault	WR101	11	59.8
230	James Proche	WR102	10	59.8
231	Braxton Berrios	WR103	10	59.2
232	Isaiah McKenzie	WR104	7	58.6
233	Drew Lock	QB32	11	161.3
234	Jauan Jennings	WR105	9	56.2
235	Ricky Seals-Jones	TE33	9	57.5
236	Dontrell Hilliard	RB66	6	55.9
237	Calvin Austin	WR106	9	55.6
238	Anthony Schwartz	WR107	9	55.5
239	Zamir White	RB67	6	53.7
240	Jonnu Smith	TE34	10	55.1
241	Brian Robinson	RB68	14	53.1
242	Brandon Bolden	RB69	6	51.3
243	Geoff Swaim	TE35	6	52.7
244	Giovani Bernard	RB70	11	51.1
245	Donald Parham	TE36	8	52.3
246	Tyler Johnson	WR108	11	50.8
247	Chuba Hubbard	RB71	13	50.2
248	Harrison Bryant	TE37	9	51.2
249	Samaje Perine	RB72	10	47.8
250	Cade Otton	TE38	11	48.2
251	Hassan Haskins	RB73	6	45.8
252	O.J. Howard	TE39	7	46.1
253	Demarcus Robinson	WR109	6	44.8
254	Marquez Callaway	WR110	14	43.9
255	Jordan Akins	TE40	9	44.1
256	D'Onta Foreman	RB74	13	42.7
257	Tony Jones	RB75	14	42.3
258	Geno Smith	QB33	11	106.8
259	Kyle Juszczyk	RB76	9	40.1
260	Tyrion Davis-Price	RB77	9	39.9
261	Anthony Firkser	TE41	14	40.2
262	Tyler Conklin	TE42	10	39.6

RK	OVERALL PLAYER	POS RK	BYE	FPS
263	Foster Moreau	TE43	6	39.0
264	Pharaoh Brown	TE44	6	38.7
265	Jacoby Brissett	QB34	9	96.9
266	John Bates	TE45	14	37.9
267	Kylen Granson	TE46	14	36.5
268	Eno Benjamin	RB78	13	35.4
269	Ian Thomas	TE47	13	34.6
270	Desmond Ridder	QB35	14	87.4
271	Will Dissly	TE48	11	33.9
272	Derrick Gore	RB79	8	30.4
273	D'Ernest Johnson	RB80	9	30.0
274	Greg Dulcich	TE49	9	30.5
275	Trey McBride	TE50	13	30.3
276	Matt Corral	QB36	13	76.0
277	Kyren Williams	RB81	7	29.3
278	Phillip Lindsay	RB82	14	28.1
279	Jeff Wilson	RB83	9	27.9
280	Duke Johnson	RB84	7	27.7
281	Demetric Felton	RB85	9	27.2
282	Joshua Kelley	RB86	8	26.1
283	Ke'Shawn Vaughn	RB87	11	25.0
284	Jashaun Corbin	RB88	9	24.9
285	Benny Snell	RB89	9	24.3
286	Rico Dowdle	RB90	9	23.7
287	Snoop Conner	RB91	11	22.2
288	ZaQuandre White	RB92	11	20.6
289	Dare Ogunbowale	RB93	6	20.4
290	Pierre Strong	RB94	10	20.1
291	Darrynton Evans	RB95	14	18.7
292	Keaontay Ingram	RB96	13	18.5
293	Mike Davis	RB97	10	18.1
294	Jermar Jefferson	RB98	6	17.5
295	Zack Moss	RB99	7	16.9
296	Tevin Coleman	RB100	10	16.6
297	Mitchell Trubisky	QB37	9	54.1
298	Taysom Hill	QB38	14	43.7
299	Tyrod Taylor	QB39	9	28.0
300	Gardner Minshew	QB40	7	18.3

2022 Player Rankings (Overall)

A

Fantasy Football 101: Best league settings, scoring tweaks, rules for trading and more!

By Jake Ciely

So you want to play fantasy football? Awesome. It's fun, it's challenging, and you even get to name your team — and be as tame or NC-17-ey as you like! You don't get that brand of freedom with Cribbage.

I've put together what is basically an encyclopedia of knowledge for fantasy players of all shapes and sizes. Obviously the newbies may benefit most here, but even the most grizzled fantasy veteran can take something away to help improve your league setup or even your chances of winning.

Drafting

Whether you're doing a snake (where you pick in order, then the rounds reverse) or an auction (you have a budget to obtain a certain amount of players and fate is in your hands), a few rules apply to everyone. First, don't go in with a preset strategy. Too often, I see people ask, "Who should I take 10th?" or "Should I start RB-WR-RB?" The problem is that no matter how well you think you know your league, you never know how the draft will go. If I tell you to take a running back first, and the best wide receiver falls to 1.10 (the 10th pick in the first round), the wise pick is the receiver. If I say go RB-RB-WR-WR and then, after that, go "BPA" (Best player available), that could overlook values, as well.

The same goes for auctions. People want to know if they should allocate a specific amount to a position — for instance, "Grab two running backs for $50 each." Auctions are even more volatile than snakes. People get crazy and start bidding wars. You might find a league overpaying for the top 10 running backs, another auction might flatten the wide receiver prices with none nearing $50 but all of the WR3/4s hitting double-digits when everyone realizes the good ones

are all unavailable. You need to adapt to every draft, and trying to plan your roster goals ahead of time could burn you.

Second, too many managers waste their bench. If you have the thought, "At least he'll be a decent bye-week option," you're wasting value and reducing your upside. Don't waste your time with replacement-level players, who you could find every week on waivers. Yes, there is value in an RB3/4 or WR4 who you will need to start some weeks and even put in for a great matchup over a fringe starter. But there is no value in a player who may reach double-digits maybe one or two times a year and doesn't even have a path to greatness with an injury, etc. So, instead of drafting the also-rans of fantasy, draft high-end backup running backs, wide receivers who could take off if one or two things break right, etc.

There is one strategy that holds true no matter when you draft: positional value. I often tell people to ignore overall rankings, even though we get asked about them constantly. It's not because we're lazy or hate you; it's because overall rankings aren't going to give you the best team if you just go straight down the list.

Draft for value, and pay attention to the value drop-off at each position. An easy example of draft and positional value is how quarterbacks should never come off the board in the first two rounds, despite being top scorers. See where the runs are (runs = when a bunch of players at the same position are taken in a row), how your team is developing, where your potential weaknesses are, etc.

With early rounds, I always recommend coming out of the first three with two running backs ... as much as possible. I've drafted two receivers when drafts have gone RB-crazy, and a top 10 wideout was still there in the third. However, if possible, getting two running backs does two things. First, you can avoid the pitfall (aka "dead zone") running backs in Rounds 4-6, as many of those end up busting every year. Second, and this ties in, by avoiding the need to get running backs in those rounds, you can load up on receivers and/or even grab your quarterback or tight end.

Those rounds are littered with top 25 receivers, most all of whom have the upside to finish inside the top 10. Conversely, those same running backs have very few with that upside and most others with floors to be bench players just weeks into the season ... or worse.

Mid-rounds (7-10), I'd look to get your quarterback and tight end if you haven't already, and then you grab running backs and receivers with upside but also who are still solid plays. You can find top-end running back backups and undervalued receivers. This value/upside mix of players should be your targets.

Late rounds are all upside. Again, if the thought, "I could use him during my bye," enters your mind, Do. Not. Draft. Him. You want RB/WR options who could finish top 25 at their positions or a QB/TE who has top 10 potential.

Lastly, stacking isn't too meaningly in standard redraft leagues. It's mainly for DFS and Best Ball, especially if you're looking to stack a playoff run in Best Ball. You don't hurt yourself much with a pair of teammates, but when you get to three or more, it's a bit risky in redraft. Yes, the ceiling is high, but a one-off week (or several) will destroy your team.

TL;DR ("too long; didn't read") — Don't try to predict the draft and/or have a preset plan, and don't waste your bench.

Auctions

Back to auctions — it's my preferred way to build a roster because of the strategy, fun, thrill and ability to be in or out on every player. It is wild and I suggest practicing as much as you can ahead of time. Many people try auctions for the first time each year, so here are a few tips.

Auction prices are a suggestion/guide ... think of them as a speed limit sign. People are going to speed, and keeping up with the traffic means you need to as well.

It's not a guarantee, but be ready to jump in early, as others are often hesitant to bid heavily at the start. Many like to see the market set or are debating whether to let a high-priced player eat up their budget early. Some of the best values are the first several players.

If you are done somewhere (tight end, high-end running back, etc.) start nominating similar players. Get others to spend their bank so more values are available later.

If you are starting to aim for the cheap option (and have the wiggle room), throw a player out for $2, not $1. If it's a sleeper or sneaky cheap pick, someone might jump you at $2, and then you're not going to spend $3 (same for a top-end DST you might want).

Mix up your tendencies. Price enforce (bid on a player you don't want, but who is worth more money, so other GMs will spend their budgets), toss players out for $1 or $15, don't bid at all until the very end, bid throughout and dip at the end, etc. Treat it like poker, and don't have an obvious tell.

TL;DR — Auction prices are like speed limits, jump in early, nominate positions you don't need, be careful of $1 nominations and don't be predictable.

League size, regular season and playoff format

With any fantasy sport, you want to find that delicate balance between going deep enough to test every GM's ability and intelligence but not so deep that you add significant luck (injuries, specifically). Going too deep and losing a top-end player or two leads to eliminating a team's chances.

Having a 12-team league is a perfect balance, for two reasons. First, we're already near the player-depth area of testing skill (16-player rosters, 192 players rostered before IR). But second — and just as important — it lends itself to the best playoff setup. With 10 teams, you either have four playoff teams for two weeks or six (with two teams getting byes). If you use six teams and byes, more than half the league makes the playoffs, and it ruins the regular-season value. So, with 12 teams, you can award the top two teams byes and have three rounds of playoffs. Getting a bye gives a little extra something to fight for during the season.

Also, the final playoff team should be the one with the most points scored that didn't have a top 5 record. Fantasy football is extremely luck-dependent. I always say fantasy football is made of three equal parts: drafting, in-season management (waivers, trades, etc.) and luck. There is simply nothing you can do or anything that's in your control when a player randomly scores three touchdowns and you lose 130-120 while the rest of the league averaged just 100 points (more on that in a bit). A team that is continually one of the best in scoring shouldn't miss the playoffs due to the (bad) luck of the weekly matchup draws.

Now, I didn't mention my favorite playoff setup, which adds an interesting twist.

Of course, it's hard to avoid some luck in the playoffs since it's just a one-week matchup, especially that first week, for some reason. How many times have you seen the sixth seed easily win the first round and advance? So, here's what my home league did: The first week of the playoffs is a five-team, best-three-scores-advance setup. Yep, only one team gets a bye, and there are no matchups for the first round. This eliminates a good amount of luck, as there are no matchups and the top three scores (plus the No. 1 seed on bye) simply advance. You could tweak it and still have two byes (maybe one top record and the other top-scoring team) and then the top two scores advance. No matter how you want to cut it up, though, the scores advancing in the first round (as opposed to winners) have often been a much-loved change in my leagues.

Now, back to that "I scored the second-most points and lost" scenario. During the season, you need to start playing doubleheaders. I have pounded the table for this change almost as much as #BanKickers. The great thing about doubleheaders is that it helps mitigate some of the luck factors while still not having an egregious impact on the game. If you score the second-most points, the worst-case scenario is that you go 1-1 because the second part of the doubleheader is based on the league's scoring that week. The top six scoring teams get a win and the bottom six get a loss. Simple, yet effective. In my home league last year, the third-highest-scoring team had a losing record due to the luck of the draw, but when you looked at his doubleheader record, he was the fourth-place team — and deservingly so.

TL;DR — 12-teams, 16-players rosters; One bye and high scores advance for playoffs first round; Doubleheaders.

Rosters

Now, let's go into the 16-player rosters and what that entails. First off, and once again, #BanKickers. This isn't the article for all of the reasons why (particularly luck). Second, make sure you replace that kicker starting spot with a SuperFlex (where you start a QB/RB/WR/TE). Quarterbacks have lost their value in fantasy with the increase in scoring and the knowledge that you should wait, wait and wait some more to draft them.

Bring in the SuperFlex and add value back to the quarterback position. Then, you can legitimately have those early-round quarterback debates again. Additionally, the reason it's SuperFlex and not 2QB is because at 12 teams, you already come out of the draft with four teams not having a bye-week option. It just doesn't make any sense. Not to mention, if you're in a 2QB league with 12 teams and lose a quarterback to injury, especially if you spent high draft capital on the said player to gain an advantage there, you're basically up that ol' poop creek.

Here's another radical idea, and you obviously don't have to do it unless you think it would be fun too, but I've thoroughly enjoyed it. Roster: 1 QB, 1 RB, 1 WR, 1 SuperFlex, 5 Flex, 1 DST. Five Flex? What, are you mad, Jake?

Hear me out. Honestly, even NFL teams don't have a running back or wide receiver on the field 100 percent of the plays — and I don't mean punts, etc. Five wide and goal-line formations can often go without a back or receiver.

Sure, that's real football, so let's talk fantasy. This setup opens you up to a world of strategies, flexibility, debates, etc. You want to argue that loading up with running backs is the best method? Do it. You want to argue that running backs are worthless? Do that too. Want to take three stud tight ends? Heck, go right ahead (and tight end cost isn't inflated by scarcity now). You do you and create the best roster you think you can.

However, that's outside the box and away from the norm, so for a typical league, my recommendation with the SuperFlex is: 1 QB, 2 RB, 3 WR, 1 WR/TE Flex, 1 Flex, 1 SuperFlex, 1 DST (if you don't want a SuperFlex spot, at least add a second Flex). Yes, there is one extra wrinkle here, and that's the WR/TE Flex instead of a flat TE spot. If a tight end scores a touchdown, it's a near guarantee that he's a TE1 for the week, and that's a ton of random-weighted value. The tight end position is miserable and a wasteland. Instead of forcing people to pray for a touchdown, add a bit of flexibility to the position. And before people argue that no one will want tight ends, I've seen managers regularly start one in the "standard" Flex because he reaped the reward of breakout flier pick/waiver pickup. Changing TE-only to WR/TE doesn't kill tight ends. It kills the meaningless ones and allows for flexibility/debates of high-end TE2s versus a WR5/6.

TL;DR — SuperFlex; WR/TE Flex; 16-players rosters.

FAAB/FAB and waivers

Side note before anyone asks, yes, we need to do away with "FAAB" and use FAB. Two reasons: Free Agent Acquisition Budget is just redundant. Of course, you're trying to acquire the player if he's a free agent. Second, how do you pronounce the car brand SAAB? With an "AH" not a short "A" like in cab … or … like the soda, Tab! So, FAAB would be FAAHHB, and FAB is FAB!

I know you're thinking, "Sir, this is an Arby's," so let's move on.

Okay, for those moving from rolling waivers (picking up players and dropping them based on the order of standings or claims) to FAB, congrats! Those who haven't moved yet, do it now! Rolling waivers is antiquated/archaic. Just like auctions versus snake, FAB allows for everyone to be in on all free agents every week. Plus, there's more strategy when it comes to how much you spend, when (early or late in the season), what level of importance the potential player carries, etc.

What is FAB? Each team starts with a set budget ($100, $1000, etc.) to spend on pickups for the entire year. So instead of having a free-agent queue, you're blind bidding against your leaguemates. Think another manager will go $40 on a high-end backup running back getting the lead role after an injury? You submit a bid for $41. Maybe, you even panic before the midnight deadline and up it to $48. The bids are all run through the system and at 12:01 a.m. you discover you have won ... and the next highest bid is $17. But such is life. And this is what makes it fun.

When it comes to FAB, it has similarities to auctions and knowing your league. If you're new to it or don't know your leaguemates, that makes it a bit tougher, but some leagues might go as high as $60-70 for a backup running back taking over in Week 3, and some might never reach $50. Heck, I've finished seasons with $70-plus left in FAB money. What you can figure out is how important the pickup is to you. Here's an example:

Let's say a top 10 running back suffers a season-ending injury in Week 3, but no one has the backup, who will reportedly see a bell-cow role. In this case, the bids would likely reach $50-plus even in conservative leagues. But the "next man up" isn't always a guarantee. If you are the one losing the high-value running back, you likely need to go into the $50s or even higher, due to need. However, because there is a chance reports are wrong or the backfield is clouded, you might not need to be as aggressive if you are already deep at running back. You can toss out a modest bid for about half that and hope you get him at a discount, and if not, then you still have the budget for another need later or a clearer replacement elsewhere. You still want to bid because if you do win at a discount and find a top 20 running back, you have more depth and trade capital.

The last note with FAB is early versus late-season spending. There is a case to save some of your budget for late in the year, but it's a slim one. Think of it this way. Let's take the above example, and you get RB2

value from the replacement. Which is more valuable? The replacement from Week 4 through the end of the season or getting him for Weeks 14-17? Yes, it might feel more valuable or exciting to get amazing value that late in the year, but the value is with more games. Even if you missed the playoffs, 10 weeks is better than three. Be aggressive early in the year, but maintain a bit of sensibility.

TL;DR — FAB (not FAAB) is better than rolling waivers; spend early, factor in team need. (Editor's note: Most of us here still prefer "FAAB," so don't be swayed by Jake's weird aversion to the second "A").

Scoring

As for scoring, I have always loathed full-PPR scoring. PPR started as a reactionary scoring method back when running backs monopolized drafts — and fantasy football in general. For the past several years, not only have wide receivers evened the playing field, they have surpassed running backs, which has skewed things back in the other direction. Not to mention the failed logic of this: a 5-yard loss on a blown-up receiving play (screen, etc.) equals a positive 0.5 points. Huh? Anyway, Half-PPR is not only the happy medium, it's becoming the default in more places than not. We're not stopping there, though, as scoring overall needs a fix, in my opinion.

While awarding six points makes sense for a touchdown because it mirrors real life, why does it need to be six if we're going to pick four for a passing touchdown? On that same note, while one point for 10 yards is pretty and clean math, why pick one for 25 yards passing? Or really, why does it have to be easy and clean when every site we play on tracks scoring to the second for us? It's not as if we're still grabbing the Monday paper and doing the math ourselves.

Now, we know the quarterback numbers are different than RB/WR/TE to create a more balanced scoring system, but four (TDs) and 25 (yards) are still "made up" numbers. So, I'm going to share my home league setup, which gives yards more value. After all, a 1-yard catch for a touchdown equaling 66 yards receiving or rushing is pretty absurd when you think about it.

Instead of six points for RB/WR/TE touchdowns and four for a QB, it's five across the board. Additionally, every 10 yards rushing or receiving is 1.25 points, as is 25 yards passing. Not only do we have a better balance between yards and touchdowns, but scoring will now see an uptick (you could even push it to 1.5 if you like to truly reward yards over touchdowns). What's even better is that (with the roster settings from above with SuperFlex) a very low score is just under 100 points, and for an incredible/everything-went right score, you might get someone hitting 200. It's happened only once in the past several years in my home league, and it's a blast to see. It's kind of like a grand slam in baseball.

Let's now talk about DST scoring because people want to rid themselves of DST or push for IDP. But that's because DST scoring has always been broken, in my opinion, and as much as the IDP crowd would love for it to be the norm, that's never happening because the casual knowledge of football is what makes fantasy football so popular. No random office league is going to have IDP players; it's not going to happen. So as with quarterbacks, the DST scoring "default" has more randomness than aspects of it that truly make sense. Speaking of randomness, DST touchdown scoring is extremely frustrating when you're on the receiving end of the random week where the Titans happen to score two, or, heaven forbid, three DST touchdowns.

Starting with touchdowns, they are five points, just like everything else, instead of six. Second, a sack and interception are both just one point. The same goes for a fumble recovery, as a forced fumble is 0.5 with another half-point for the recovery. All of these things equaling two easily makes a random DST outscore a powerful defense by random luck — only safeties and blocked kicks get two points. And speaking of powerful defenses, reward them (and penalize) for points allowed, but also reward them for limiting yards. We count yards for all of the other starters, so why not the DST? So, 7 = 0 points allowed with a waterfall down/up to -5 = 46+ points allowed, plus, 5 for holding a team under 200 total yards, 3 for fewer than 300 yards, 1 point for under 400, -1 for 400-499 and -3 past that. Top DST scores rarely reach 20 points with this setup, and the top teams average around 8-10 FPPG, or a Flex-level player.

TL;DR — Half-PPR; 5-point TD everywhere, 1.25 for 10 or 25 yards; DST retooling.

Keepers and trades

If you really want to maximize the fun, move to a keeper league. I prefer a four-or-five-keeper setup to a dynasty format because you can go after a different mix of players every year instead of only rookies.

Auction leagues make the keeper pricing rules easy. If you drafted a player, his keeper price is the auction value plus $5. If you picked the player up off waivers, his price is $10 to keep (so there is a bit of an extra reward if you were smart enough to stash a guy for $1-$2 versus picking him up). You can add a three-year keeper maximum (or longer/shorter), which prevents holding on to a player forever, and that increases trading. An additional point with keepers: If you drop a player during the season, his keeper price is still the auction price plus $5 to keep the following season. This is key because people will try to drop and re-add injured players or veterans who suddenly developed a second wind.

If you are playing in a snake draft, I still recommend keepers, as it adds more intrigue and trading, but it's a bit different. I usually play with four to five keepers per team, and if you keep a player, his round cost goes up one round each year and waiver players start at Round 12. Additionally, I recommend allowing the trading of draft picks, because more trading equals more fun!

Lastly, when it comes to trading in general — and this is huge — vetoes should never happen ... outside of collusion (which, yes, is extremely hard to prove). Everyone is free to value players and manage their team the best way they see fit. It's not your job to decide if someone is making the correct moves for their team. The main reason anyone tries to veto is bitterness: a team in contention got better, they could have made a "better offer," etc. Additionally, every year ... Every. Single. Year ... there are trades where people disagree about player values that, come season's end, end up looking unreal in the opposite direction that people originally thought. Again, vetoes are the worst!

TL;DR — Keepers! 4-5 per team; Auction cost, plus $5; $10 or 12th round for waiver adds; Dropped players keep auction price; Vetoes shouldn't exist.

Dynasty

I'll start this section short and quick ... Don't overrate youth! Too often, fantasy managers bypass proven young talent to get the player who might become as good if he hits his peak just because he is two or three years younger. Yes, dynasty leagues mean you want to build for the future and contend for years, but you still want to contend now. Nothing is guaranteed years from now, heck, even just next season. This is especially true for rookies, who rocket up dynasty boards because people think they are getting the next

Michael Thomas, when the truth is that players hit way less frequently than perception would suggest.

The one area where I would suggest getting youth and even attacking a bit earlier in your draft is quarterback. You don't have to get a top 3 quarterback who is young, but there is a distinct advantage in having a top 10 quarterback who you don't have to worry about for at least five to six years versus rostering four to five quarterbacks, hoping even just two of them carry value for three seasons. I'd also look to roster three quarterbacks or more, as they often carry the most draft value/capital in future seasons.

Another tip is to load up on receivers. They have the longest value length, both in career and peak performance seasons. Don't ignore running backs, and handcuffing — if there is a clear "next man up" — carries a bit more importance than redraft leagues (aka "non-dynasty leagues"), but building a top-end receiving corps will have you in contention for years, even if you have an off-year at running back or tight end.

One last bonus tip. If you're in a dynasty startup, field offers for draft picks. Similar to the rookie/youngster love, people will overpay for future picks. There is no guarantee that first-rounders will hit, let alone second-rounders and later. In fact, too many managers will rate second- and third-rounders higher than WR2/3s who are 28 years old because of the imagined potential.

TL;DR — Don't overrate youth, boost quarterback value, load up on receivers, exploit youth love in trades.

Advanced: Hype/ADP/SOS

You have to be careful about inhaling too much of the preseason helium each year ("helium" = players who rise in ADP — "Average draft position" — like little balloons as we get closer to drafting), and not just because you could pass out and hurt yourself, but you could hurt yourself fantasy-wise. The fantasy helium comes from various sources, including everyone here at The Athletic. Reports from practicing and camps offer intel, but they aren't foolproof. The fantasy industry will often overlap on underrated players, creating a group-think helium boost. That can lead to players going at such a high cost, positive ROI becomes impossible. If camp reports and the fantasy industry were 100 percent accurate, you wouldn't need waivers because we'd all tell you exactly how the season will play out. Pay attention all offseason, soaking in all of

the important information you can find. Just be careful not to overreact to a random highlight catch in practice.

Where ADP comes into play is using it as a tool to see where players are undervalued and finding a reasonable price to make sure you grab that player without going overboard. This is quite simple — even if you are right in predicting a breakout, that doesn't mean you need to draft the player at his peak cost/value. Now, you've simply bought all the risk. Never do that! Use ADP as a guide, and if your favorite breakout has an ADP in the 10th round, there is no problem taking him in the eighth, but pushing him up to the 4-5th rounds because you believe that's his potential is losing your potential ROI and losing the player value who you could have taken there instead.

Strength of schedule is meaningless! You know how much parity is in the NFL and how defensive quality changes yearly. Don't look at a team's win-related schedule and play into it. Now, strength of opponent by position (SOP?) carries some importance, but don't go crazy. Checking a running back's early-season schedule for rush defenses can help break ties. Seeing which wide receivers face top corners or favorable secondaries can help too. But again, this is to break ties, not rocket or torpedo players in the ranks, and please, please, don't concern yourself with the playoff schedules, even by position. Every year we see injuries, performance, etc., flip the best matchups to worst and vice versa.

TL;DR — Be an info sponge, find the values in ADP, don't overdoes on helium; SOP not SOS, and moderately. ▬▬

Brandon Funston's Big Board:
The Preseason Top 50

The Big Board takes into consideration past returns, current performance and expected future gains in determining who should be included among The Top 50 fantasy football players. Essentially, the Big Board is a cheat sheet designed for a GM who is planning to participate in a draft today. Half-point PPR scoring settings are used as the baseline for the Big Board, which is updated on a regular basis (in-season).

Rank	Player Name	Team	POS	Cheatsheet
1	Jonathan Taylor	IND	RB	Checks every box for what you look for in a No. 1 overall pick
2	Cooper Kupp	LAR	WR	2021 was elite on an all-time scale, and his week-to-week consistency was unprecedented at WR
3	Christian McCaffrey	CAR	RB	The biggest gamble of 2022 drafts: league-winning upside vs. season-ending injury downside
4	Austin Ekeler	LAC	RB	In PPR formats, highest Fantasy Points per Touch mark among RBs over past 3 seasons (min. 30 games)
5	Justin Jefferson	MIN	WR	No player has amassed more catches (196), receiving yards (3,016) through their first 2 NFL seasons
6	Najee Harris	PIT	RB	Volume, versatility are the selling points, while the QB situation is the biggest question mark
7	Joe Mixon	CIN	RB	Bell cow for one of the league's skyrocketing offenses, and he's still only 25
8	Derrick Henry	TEN	RB	Top RB in half-PRR FPPG over past 3 seasons (min. 30 games), but coming off serious foot injury at his size, age (28) is cause for pause
9	Dalvin Cook	MIN	RB	Ceiling scales as high as any RB ahead of him, but he's never played more than 14 games in a season
10	Ja'Marr Chase	CIN	WR	Joined Randy Moss as only WRs since the AFL/NFL merger to top 300 PPR FPPG in a rookie season
11	Stefon Diggs	BUF	WR	Averaging 165 targets, 115 catches, 1,380 rec. yards, 9 TDs in 2 seasons as Josh Allen's go-to WR
12	D'Andre Swift	DET	RB	Top 10 RB in PPR FPPG over his 2 seasons, and now poised for workload boost in arrowing-up DET offense
13	Davante Adams	LV	WR	Move from GB to LV should be considered only slight downgrade — a little less target share, a little less QB talent
14	Travis Kelce	KC	TE	At 32, posted 3rd season with at least 90 catches, 1,100 receiving yards, 9 TDs — no other TE in NFL history has done that more than once
15	CeeDee Lamb	DAL	WR	No. 17 WR in half-PPR formats in 2021 was a letdown, but bigger things expected in '22 with Amari Cooper's 103 targets vacated
16	Deebo Samuel	SF	WR	No. 2 WR in half-PPR FPPG, but sans his rush output, would have been WR25, making reports of plans to dial back his carries concerning

Rank	Player Name	Team	POS	Cheatsheet
17	Mark Andrews	BAL	TE	Became only TE ever to reach thresholds of 100 catches, 1,300 receiving yards, 9 TD catches in same season
18	Alvin Kamara	NO	RB	Top 5 among RBs in PPR FPPG in first season sans Drew Brees, so only question is availability — suspension or injury (7 DNPs in past 3 seasons)
19	Saquon Barkley	NYG	RB	With O line, head coach upgrades it's worth a look back at his rookie numbers as a reminder of what a healthy Barkley is capable of
20	Aaron Jones	GB	RB	6th-most catches among RBs over past 3 seasons (148), and is in line for career-high receptions to help fill Davante Adams void
21	Mike Evans	TB	WR	Stat line has been nearly identical in each of 2 seasons with Tom Brady at QB, averaging 72 catches, 1,025 yards, 13.5 TDs in that span
22	Nick Chubb	CLE	RB	RB1 in half-PPR formats each of past 3 seasons, and is only RB in NFL history to average 5.0 YPC in each of first 4 seasons (min. 100 carries)
23	Javonte Williams	DEN	RB	63 Missed Tackles Forced was only 3 behind leader Jonathan Taylor despite 129 fewer carries
24	Keenan Allen	LAC	WR	Tied to one of the elite arm talents in the NFL, and has delivered WR1 PPR profits in 5 consecutive seasons
25	James Conner	ARI	RB	Notched 18 TDs in 15 games in 2021 and, while regression expectations are fair, volume increase a likelihood with Chase Edmonds gone
26	Kyle Pitts	ATL	TE	Rarified rookie TE air with 1,026 rec. yards, 20% TeamTarget share, which could rise with WRs Calvin Ridley, Russell Gage out of the picture
27	Tee Higgins	CIN	WR	Finished 2021 with a flourish, reaching 96+ yards in 8 of his final 13 games (including playoffs)
28	Tyreek Hill	MIA	WR	Had 38 catches of 30+ yards from Patrick Mahomes in his time in KC — big question is how many of those throws could Tua have made?
29	Leonard Fournette	TB	RB	4 seasons of 15+ PPR FPPG in past 5 years — only Alvin Kamara has more among RBs in that span
30	David Montgomery	CHI	RB	Volume a big driver of his value, but with new coaching regime, expected run scheme changes, expect backup Khalil Herbert to be more involved
31	A.J. Brown	PHI	WR	Philly should be mostly a lateral move — should still see plenty of big-play opportunities working off play action in run-heavy system
32	Jaylen Waddle	MIA	WR	Hard to ignore 100+ catches as a rookie and chemistry with Tua Tagovailoa, but also hard to ignore Tyreek Hill reaching in for his slice of the pie
33	DK Metcalf	SEA	WR	Caught 4 TD grabs in 3+ games with Geno Smith at QB in 2021, so at least not all hope is lost with Russell Wilson now in Denver
34	George Kittle	SF	TE	Averaging 76.4 receiving YPG over past 4 seasons — only Travis Kelce is better (81.0)

Rank	Player Name	Team	POS	Cheatsheet
35	Elijah Mitchell	SF	RB	RB1 upside leading one of the top run games in the NFL, but also piled up injuries (knee, finger, concussion) — are you glass half full or half empty?
36	Diontae Johnson	PIT	WR	Heavy target volume has been, and should continue to be, a constant, but the flip side is QB and durability concerns
37	Michael Pittman Jr.	IND	WR	In Year 3, with an upgrade in competency behind center, it's easy to believe Pittman can improve upon last year's WR18 finish
38	Josh Allen	BUF	QB	No. 1 fantasy QB in each of past 2 seasons — QB whisperer Brian Daboll is with the Giants now, but Allen can take care of himself at this point
39	Josh Jacobs	LV	RB	RB17 and RB8, respectively, in first 2 seasons, and little reason to think he won't be Top 20 RB again with Raiders' offensive upgrades
40	J.K. Dobbins	BAL	RB	Returning from lost season (ACL), worth a reminder that he averaged 6 YPC and rushed for 9 TDs in 134 carries as a rookie in 2020
41	Ezekiel Elliott	DAL	RB	Toughed out nagging injuries for RB7 finish in 2021, but hard to be overly bullish given his odometer reading and emerging Tony Pollard behind him
42	Travis Etienne Jr.	JAC	RB	Could see in the neighborhood of 200 carries, 50 catches unless James Robinson makes unexpectedly strong return from Achilles injury
43	DJ Moore	CAR	WR	Consistently a back-end Top 20 WR despite being tied to sub-par QB play — any kind of upgrade/improved QB play should treat Moore well
44	Darren Waller	LV	TE	Likely to lose target share with Davante Adams now in the Raiders' fold, but that could be offset by seeing less double-teams
45	Breece Hall	NYJ	RB	RB22 on this board, which may be conservative considering the top RB selected in each of past 7 NFL drafts has finished no worse than RB21
46	Cam Akers	LAR	RB	Miraculously returned from blown Achilles after half-year of rehab, but lacked previous explosiveness — will the offseason help him regain it?
47	Terry McLaurin	WAS	WR	Carson Wentz will be the best QB he's worked with yet, giving McLaurin Top 20 WR upside (assuming contract issue works itself out)
48	Antonio Gibson	WAS	RB	No. 10 at RB in PPR fantasy points over the past 2 seasons — can afford to cede touches to rookie Brian Robinson and still easily deliver RB2 returns
49	Mike Williams	LAC	WR	Elite big-play threat tied to one of top arm talents in the NFL — 7 games with 80+ receiving yards was 5th-most in 2021
50	Allen Robinson II	LAR	WR	Surprisingly finds his ADP at the lowest level since his rookie season despite being paired with an elite passer for first time in his career

III. The Quarterbacks

Jake Ciely's
2022 QB rankings

The depth of the quarterback position means you wait … and wait some more to draft yours — unless value with the top 6-7 guys slips into the 4-6th rounds. Of course, if you're in a SuperFlex league (give it a try; it brings value back to quarterbacks and adds more strategy), grabbing two top-16 quarterbacks will give you an advantage.

Jalen Hurts ranks higher in these projections than even I would have thought (but history has taught me to have faith in these numbers), and this feels a lot like Lamar Jackson's breakout season; he's back inside the top-5.

If you don't get a top-tier quarterback, waiting until the end game to take a boom/bust option (like Justin Fields) with a solid option (sayyyy, Kirk Cousins) or even doubling down on boom/bust picks is a smart move. You can get into the high-20s of quarterbacks and still find players with a QB1 tier ceiling (Daniel Jones, James Winston, etc.).

Rank	Player Name	Team	BYE	PASS ATT	PASS CMP	PASS YDS	PASS TDS	PASS INTS	RUSH ATT	RUSH YDS	RUSH TDS	FPS	AUC$
1	Josh Allen	BUF	7	652	420	4659	37	10	121	701	6	421.9	$30
2	Jalen Hurts	PHI	7	572	355	4247	27	9	135	763	9	393.3	$25
3	Justin Herbert	LAC	8	683	453	5155	38	10	56	273	3	384.8	$23
4	Patrick Mahomes	KC	8	678	445	5000	38	9	64	361	2	384.4	$19
5	Lamar Jackson	BAL	10	495	321	3615	30	9	174	1026	5	381.8	$18
6	Joe Burrow	CIN	10	619	420	5130	37	10	40	140	2	361.7	$13
7	Kyler Murray	ARI	13	605	403	4485	28	9	96	487	5	353.6	$11
8	Tom Brady	TB	11	701	472	5064	38	9	21	52	2	352.0	$11
9	Aaron Rodgers	GB	14	587	399	4425	36	5	32	119	2	337.0	$9
10	Matthew Stafford	LAR	7	601	402	4800	38	11	26	70	1	334.8	$9
11	Dak Prescott	DAL	9	627	421	4633	33	8	51	187	2	334.4	$8
12	Trey Lance	SF	9	532	331	4056	24	14	120	601	5	324.0	$6
13	Russell Wilson	DEN	9	579	380	4353	32	7	51	232	2	321.3	$5
14	Trevor Lawrence	JAX	11	648	410	4540	28	11	68	334	2	318.1	$4
15	Justin Fields	CHI	14	556	347	3881	20	10	117	620	6	309.5	$3
16	Derek Carr	LV	6	617	418	4614	30	10	31	109	1	302.1	$3
17	Kirk Cousins	MIN	7	595	394	4404	31	7	27	106	1	301.9	$2
18	Tua Tagovailoa	MIA	11	611	406	4291	27	10	53	170	3	298.1	$2

Rank	Player Name	Team	BYE	PASS ATT	PASS CMP	PASS YDS	PASS TDS	PASS INTS	RUSH ATT	RUSH YDS	RUSH TDS	FPS	AUC$
19	Carson Wentz	WSH	14	597	377	4194	25	8	48	196	1	279.6	$0
20	Matt Ryan	IND	14	557	369	4176	26	8	36	110	2	276.8	$0
21	Zach Wilson	NYJ	10	581	353	3917	23	9	42	242	4	276.6	$0
22	Daniel Jones	NYG	9	544	341	3733	22	8	64	337	3	272.3	$0
23	Ryan Tannehill	TEN	6	535	356	3710	23	9	48	241	4	271.1	$0
24	Jameis Winston	NO	14	524	327	3838	23	7	27	155	2	259.3	$0
25	Jared Goff	DET	6	614	401	4152	25	11	23	92	1	258.1	$0
26	Deshaun Watson	CLE	9	360	237	2945	21	4	86	390	4	255.9	$0
27	Mac Jones	NE	10	515	346	3786	24	9	36	127	0	243.3	$0
28	Davis Mills	HOU	6	569	374	3945	22	9	21	78	0	238.2	$0
29	Kenny Pickett	PIT	9	528	323	3402	20	8	28	113	1	217.7	$0
30	Marcus Mariota	ATL	14	453	286	3290	17	8	30	182	1	209.1	$0
31	Sam Darnold	CAR	13	437	270	2904	12	8	41	178	3	182.4	$0
32	Drew Lock	SEA	11	349	216	2476	13	6	30	140	2	161.3	$0
33	Geno Smith	SEA	11	233	151	1672	9	3	15	61	1	106.8	$0
34	Jacoby Brissett	CLE	9	194	122	1312	10	2	13	54	1	96.9	$0
35	Desmond Ridder	ATL	14	194	117	1323	7	3	18	83	1	87.4	$0
36	Matt Corral	CAR	13	187	116	1223	6	3	12	55	1	76.0	$0
37	Mitchell Trubisky	PIT	9	119	76	766	4	1	17	60	0	54.1	$0
38	Taysom Hill	NO	14	6	3	36	0	0	40	210	3	43.7	$0
39	Tyrod Taylor	NYG	9	60	37	397	2	1	6	28	0	28.0	$0
40	Gardner Minshew	PHI	7	30	19	231	2	0	7	29	0	18.3	$0
41	John Wolford	LAR	7	32	19	193	1	0	1	5	0	12.8	$0
42	Tyler Huntley	BAL	10	15	10	102	1	0	10	59	0	12.5	$0
43	Kyle Allen	HOU	6	30	19	213	1	1	1	4	0	12.5	$0
44	Cooper Rush	DAL	9	26	16	177	1	0	4	12	0	12.3	$0
45	Teddy Bridgewater	MIA	11	19	12	136	1	0	5	18	0	11.8	$0
46	Trevor Siemian	CHI	14	29	18	195	1	0	1	3	0	11.5	$0
47	Jimmy Garoppolo	SF	9	16	11	136	1	0	3	11	0	10.7	$0
48	Mike White	NYJ	10	24	15	168	1	1	4	4	0	10.4	$0

The Quarterbacks

Rank	Player Name	Team	BYE	PASS ATT	PASS CMP	PASS YDS	PASS TDS	PASS INTS	RUSH ATT	RUSH YDS	RUSH TDS	FPS	AUC$
49	Malik Willis	TEN	6	17	10	115	1	0	3	20	0	10.1	$0
50	Taylor Heinicke	WSH	14	13	8	93	1	0	5	24	0	9.1	$0
51	Andy Dalton	NO	14	22	15	168	1	1	0	0	0	9.0	$0
52	Colt McCoy	ARI	13	19	12	129	1	0	1	6	0	7.9	$0
53	Tim Boyle	DET	6	19	12	123	1	0	1	4	0	7.5	$0
54	Brett Rypien	DEN	9	12	7	79	1	0	1	3	0	5.6	$0
55	Nick Mullens	LV	6	13	8	82	1	0	1	2	0	5.2	$0
56	Brian Hoyer	NE	10	11	7	74	1	0	1	2	0	4.9	$0
57	Nick Foles	IND	14	11	6	74	0	0	0	0	0	4.4	$0
58	Jordan Love	GB	14	6	4	39	0	0	3	12	0	4.1	$0
59	Kyle Trask	TB	11	7	4	44	0	0	2	5	0	3.7	$0
60	Case Keenum	BUF	7	7	4	46	0	0	1	3	0	3.4	$0
61	Mason Rudolph	PIT	9	13	8	70	0	0	0	0	0	3.4	$0
62	Chase Daniel	LAC	8	7	4	46	0	0	1	5	0	3.4	$0
63	Chad Henne	KC	8	7	4	44	0	0	2	4	0	3.4	$0
64	C.J. Beathard	JAX	11	7	4	43	0	0	1	6	0	3.2	$0
65	Brandon Allen	CIN	10	6	4	38	0	0	1	4	0	2.9	$0
66	Kellen Mond	MIN	7	6	4	36	0	0	1	7	0	2.8	$0

Who are the 2022 NFL fantasy football breakout quarterbacks? Trevor Lawrence, Trey Lance and more

By Jake Ciely

Finding the next breakout quarterback in fantasy football brings a special kind of joy. Nobody enjoys paying a premium cost when you can find mid-to-late round picks who finish inside the top 10, or even top 5. So, who makes this year's cut? Well, I have the top-5 breakout quarterbacks for the 2022 NFL season, which includes several second-year options.

A

Rookies and non-qualifiers

- **Jalen Hurts, PHI** — Hurts doesn't qualify for two reasons: 1) Hurts was last year's top breakout pick and 2) He broke out last year with a QB9 finish (QB7 in FPPG). Hurts still makes questionable decisions, but let's remember his top wideout was a rookie who missed development time due to his preseason injury (MCL sprain). Jalen Reagor failed as the No. 2, eventually losing time to Quez Watkins. Now, Smith is in his second season, and most importantly, Reagor is further down the depth chart with the addition of A.J. Brown. Don't be surprised if Hurts is breakout-ier this year. If there is a quarterback who could surprise as the No. 1 quarterback in fantasy, it's 2022 Hurts.

- **Joe Burrow, CIN** — Burrow was the No. 2 breakout pick from 2021, and he was QB8/QB10, so another breakout in the books. It's possible Burrow pushes the top 5 in 2022.

- **Jameis Winston, NO** — I thought about Winston, but he's more of a rebound, or last year's (or couple of years) trash. Winston had two nice seasons to start his career and a top 5 finish in 2019, so the breakout happened. But, you can expect to see Winston's

name in an upcoming Last Year's Trash piece, as the Saints go all-in on helping him succeed.

- **Kenny Pickett, PIT, et al rookies** — As I mention each year, I don't see rookies as "breakout" qualified since they don't have any NFL performance to break out from. Some might believe rookies should make the list, but whether or not you do, it's hard to see Pickett or any quarterback cracking the QB1 tier given their talent or situations (Malik Willis and Desmond Ridder could be waiting until 2023 to start).

A

Top-5 breakout quarterbacks

1. Trevor Lawrence, JAX — If nothing else, Urban Meyer's exit should vault Lawrence into the top 5. Okay, jokes aside, Lawrence showed improvement once Meyer left town. I'm not claiming it was a vast improvement, but let's not forget the mess in Jacksonville with Travis Etienne missing the year, James Robinson getting hurt late in the year, D.J. Chark missing most of the season, Laviska Shenault failing to launch, Marvin Jones aging and struggling with top coverage, and Laquon Treadwell becoming a significant receiving option given the rest of the choices.

Lawrence is still supremely gifted, and let's also not forget the "generational talent" tag nearly everyone cast on him during the 2021 NFL Draft. The Jaguars, while vastly overpaying, brought in an accomplished wideout in Christian Kirk to give Lawrence an arsenal of Kirk, Jones, Zay Jones (another free agent), Treadwell, Shenault and many others who could help as the No. 5 receiver. Plus, Evan Engram — a great receiving tight end who's dealt with injuries and Jason Garrett — is also a new arrival, and then Etienne and Robinson return from injuries (Robinson is still a bit of a question, but Snoop Conner arrives from the draft).

Lawrence also carries rushing upside with a rushing line of 334/2 as a rookie, and he could reach 500-plus yards as he gets more comfortable scrambling to the level he did at Clemson. Burrow had an amazing Year 2 leap into the Top 10, and that came with just 118/2 rushing. No, Lawrence didn't get a Ja'Marr Chase to help and shouldn't be expected to throw for 4,611/34, but 4,200+ yards, near 30 touchdowns, plus around 400/4 rushing is well within his abilities, especially with head coach Doug Pederson in charge. Those numbers would have put Lawrence at QB5 last year and might sound aggressive, but even 4,000/25 through the air and 300/3 on the ground would give Lawrence 308 fantasy points, which is two more than

Hurts (QB9) last year. Sign me up for Lawrence to be the quarterback everyone thought he could be.

2. Derek Carr, LV — Carr would rank at the top of this list if looking for the safest, best bet. After all, we're talking about a quarterback who has five top 14 finishes in his career ... though, somehow, never higher than QB13. Even so, Carr threw for a career-high 4,804 yards last year thanks to 626 attempts. There might be concern that Carr will see a downtick in attempts, but he still had three of his top four single-game attempt totals after Jon Gruden left, including 54 against the Bengals in the playoffs. Of course, that was without the biggest factor in Carr finally reaching the QB1 tier, and that's the arrival of Davante Adams via trade.

Carr was already primed for regression (if he threw for 4,800 yards again), as his 23 passing touchdowns were shockingly low. Adams, Hunter Renfrow, a Darren Waller rebound and the collection of options behind them, plus Josh Jacobs getting more passing-game work means Carr's 2021 numbers could be his floor. Even if he drops a bit in the yards, the talent in Vegas is too good to keep Carr from reaching 30 touchdowns, and 4,500/30 passing is better than 4,804/23 and would have ranked Carr as QB10 in 2021. A top-10 finish is finally within his grasp.

3. Justin Fields, CHI — There is already talk about whether the Bears are sold on Fields as their future, and it would appear they don't care to help him have more success in Year 2. Fields draws plenty of comparisons to Hurts, and if he has a second season anything like Hurts, well, that'd be good for QB10. Hurts had just 3,144/16/9 passing but added 782/10 rushing (15 games), which is where Fields' fantasy value lies. Fields ran for 386 yards and a touchdown in 10 starts with upside for more, as he had 361 of those yards in his final seven games. Push that rate to 16 games and Fields finishes with over 800 rushing yards and likely 5-plus touchdowns.

As mentioned, the weapons are far from amazing with Darnell Mooney as the No. 1 receiver, Cole Kmet primed for a breakout (more on him in the upcoming tight end piece), Byron Pringle arriving via free agency and the drafting of Velus Jones, plus various other depth receivers. Nevertheless, Hurts' passing numbers came with less than great weapons, so asking Fields to pass for 3,000 yards and near 20 passing touchdowns isn't absurd. Fields could have a mediocre season and still be a QB1 in fantasy.

4. Trey Lance, SF — We've already seen the rushing upside of Lance, which helped him score double-digit fantasy points in both starts while rushing 16-for-89

and 8-for-31, respectively. Lance chipped in another 7-for-41 while replacing Jimmy Garoppolo in Week 4. There were comparisons to Josh Allen when Lance came out of college, and while I wouldn't put him in the conversation with Allen — even 90 percent of Allen — currently, the path to success and fantasy upside are similar. Lance has a great trio of weapons, though the Kyle Shanahan offense will limit some of Lance's passing upside, which could be turnover-filled already in 2022. I would consider Lance over Fields if we knew he'd be the starter all year and Shanahan wouldn't turn to Garoppolo due to struggles and/or chasing a playoff spot.

5. Zach Wilson, NYJ — Wilson draws Daniel Jones similarities, and while that isn't overly inspiring and is worrisome from an NFL success level, there is fantasy appeal. Sure, Wilson's rookie season was rough, as Davis Mills averaged more FPPG, throwing 16 touchdowns to Wilson's nine (both in 13 games). But again, there is hope. Wilson will run a bit, adding a potential 200-300 rushing yards and a few touchdowns. The greater hope lies in his weapons, as Wilson wasn't able to get a great rapport with Elijah Moore due to Wilson and Moore missing time to injuries. Even so, Moore flashed his terrific upside, and now Corey Davis (also missed time) is down to third on the depth chart with the addition of supremely-talented rookie Garrett Wilson. Breece Hall was the draft's best running back and forms a terrific duo with Michael Carter in the backfield, while C.J. Uzomah and Tyler Conklin will push to give the Jets value at tight end. Wilson is a great last-round flier for a quarterback who could push for the top 15. ▬▬

A deep dive on
Trevor Lawrence

By Larry Holder

If you're pondering drafting Jaguars quarterback Trevor Lawrence onto your fantasy football roster, you're probably in desperation mode. I get that completely.

Many managers probably felt the same way when they drafted Joe Burrow leading up to the 2021 season. And no, I'm not saying Lawrence will guide the Jaguars to the Super Bowl like Burrow pulled off in his second season with the Bengals.

What I am saying is that Lawrence could be primed for a sharp increase in production in Year 2 considering the additional pieces and the rough circumstances surrounding him during this rookie campaign.

Despite their struggles last season, the Jaguars ranked 18th in rushing DVOA (defense adjusted value over average, via TruMedia) and early-down rushing success rate (37.9 percent of their early-down runs were successful, based on down and distance). Not great, but not especially dire.

Making matters worse was the fact Jacksonville's defense was rotten as well, ranking 31st in DVOA. Sixteen of Lawrence's 17 interceptions occurred while the Jaguars trailed.

When tied or ahead, Lawrence threw 10-plus yards downfield (air yards) on 24.8 percent of his attempts — last among 31 qualified quarterbacks. When trailing by at least a touchdown, 35.4 percent of his attempts were 10-plus air yards — the ninth-highest rate among 31 qualified passers. This could be an indicator that he was being riskier when the situation necessitated it, thus the picks.

"That was my first time really dealing with checking in and out of things, getting us in the right play — good matchup, route, whatever it was," Lawrence said in June. "Last year it was tough to think about all of those things, to have all those options, to figure what was best.

"Now that I've had that experience ... it helps a lot. I have a few things. You can't do everything, so you have a checklist in your mind: 'These are some things I want to get to. If we get the right look, get to them. If not, do the best with what you've got and do the next-best thing.' That's something I've been trying to work on, and I think it has helped a lot."

Lawrence performed relatively well in avoiding sacks as a rookie. Opponents pressured him on 33.1 percent of dropbacks, slightly above the league average of 32.4 percent. But he finished with the NFL's ninth-lowest sack rate (5.0 percent, which led all rookies).

The bigger issue last season was the team's receiving corps. Lawrence had 37 of his passes dropped, behind only Justin Herbert of the Chargers. It's probably part of the reason Jacksonville spent big bucks on its new wideouts.

New Jags receiver Christian Kirk ranked 23rd in yards per route run from the slot (1.78) last season. Maybe not impressive enough to merit his big contract, but still an upgrade over Lawrence's top slot options last year. Marvin Jones and Laviska Shenault ranked 53rd and 54th in yards per route run from the slot (1.3 for both). Zay Jones, another new Jags receiver, ranked 35th in yards per route run from the slot: 1.6 on 113 such routes.

Plus, Kirk led the Cardinals with 77 receptions for 982 yards and five touchdowns in 2021. That would have led Jacksonville last season in all three categories. There's no doubt the Jaguars have provided Lawrence more to work with in his second season.

Lawrence also adds value as a runner. His rushing success rate of 51.5 percent — which excludes scrambles — ranked seventh among 13 quarterbacks with at least 50 carries last season. In the red zone specifically, he ranked fourth among the same 13 passers in rushing success rate (70 percent). Seven of his 12 red zone carries went for first downs, and another two were touchdowns.

Sure, you're staring at his 12 touchdown passes, 17 interceptions, a 59.6 percent completion percentage and a 71.9 passer rating from last season. But a late-round flier on Lawrence as a backup quarterback might pay off more than you expect. ▬▬▬

A deep dive on
Lamar Jackson

By Jeff Zrebiec

There's little ambiguity about what the Ravens tried to do around quarterback Lamar Jackson this offseason.

In signing veteran right tackle Morgan Moses and using a first-round pick on center Tyler Linderbaum, the Ravens prioritized rebuilding an offensive line that struggled throughout 2021. Even with the expectation that running backs J.K. Dobbins and Gus Edwards will return from injury and make strong contributions this year, the Ravens signed veteran Mike Davis and drafted Tyler Badie. And they gave standout tight end Mark Andrews some help with the selections of Charlie Kolar and Isaiah Likely.

Although team officials may not admit it, the roster fortifications point to the Ravens trying to recapture their offensive recipe from 2019, when Jackson was at his best and most dangerous while armed with a dynamic running game and a versatile tight end group — and was protected by a strong offensive line.

On his way to being named just the league's second unanimous Most Valuable Player, Jackson led the NFL with 36 touchdown passes and finished sixth in the league with 1,206 rushing yards. He was a gift to fantasy football GMs everywhere.

Jackson has not been a one-year fantasy wonder. His 19.76 fantasy points per game rank seventh among all quarterbacks dating to 2000. However, he has never been as prolific as he was in 2019.

Ravens officials believe that the first step to Jackson getting back to that level is improved health. The 25-year-old was one of the front-runners for the league MVP award around midseason last year despite the offensive line and backfield being wracked by injuries. However, bouts with illness forced him to miss significant practice time and one game, then a bone bruise in his ankle knocked him out of the Ravens' final four regular-season games.

As he vowed to do, Jackson took a few weeks off to give his foot more time to heal, then got back to work the day after the Super Bowl. While Jackson stayed away from Baltimore's workout program and organized team activities, which drew plenty of attention given his contract status, the Ravens were pleased with the work he put in this offseason. Jackson spent extensive time with quarterback guru Adam Dedeaux, who has trained a number of NFL quarterbacks, including Matthew Stafford.

Meanwhile, the Ravens went to work bolstering a roster that plays more to Jackson's strengths. In 2019, the Ravens had one of the top offensive lines in football, which included three Pro Bowl selections in Ronnie Stanley, Orlando Brown Jr. and guard Marshal Yanda. Jackson was sacked just 23 times in 15 games.

Last season, Jackson was sacked 38 times in 12 games. Ravens general manager Eric DeCosta said that any time he has asked Jackson about what he needs, the quarterback usually mentions improving the offensive line. On paper, the Ravens have done that with two new starters in Moses and Linderbaum joining guard Kevin Zeitler and Stanley, who the team believes will be ready for Week 1 after he missed all but one game last season.

When the Ravens have been at their best offensively in recent seasons, they've gouged teams with their run game. And Jackson has been the ringleader. With Dobbins and Edwards out last year and the Ravens

relying on aging vets Devonta Freeman and Latavius Murray, Jackson was afforded little space, and his yards per carry dropped to 5.8 yards per attempt, more than a full yard less than his 2019 average. The return of Dobbins and Edwards should open things up for Jackson, and Davis and Badie should diversify the backfield.

Plenty has been said about Jackson's wide receiving corps, which lacks experience and proven options. The Ravens traded Marquise Brown, Jackson's closest friend on the team and his favorite target behind Andrews, to the Arizona Cardinals. They didn't replace him in the draft or sign a coveted free agent, leaving 2021 first-round pick Rashod Bateman, Devin Duvernay, James Proche and Tylan Wallace as their top four receivers. Instead, the Ravens doubled down at tight end, drafting Kolar and Likely, accomplished pass catchers in college.

The lack of moves at receiver appeared to be a nod toward 2019, when three of the Ravens' top five pass catchers were tight ends as Jackson worked the middle of the field and spread the ball around. Brown was the Ravens' most productive receiver, finishing with 46 catches for 584 yards.

He's not around any longer, and it would be hard to make a case that the Ravens receiving group is better for it. However, the Ravens appear to have gotten better up front, in the backfield and at tight end. Those elements have brought out the best in Jackson before. ▬▬

A deep dive on
Jalen Hurts

By Zach Berman

The Eagles are still determining if Jalen Hurts is the quarterback who can lead them deep into the postseason. That's less of a question among fantasy football GMs. Hurts isn't just capable of being a fantasy team's top quarterback; he's capable of being one of the best in the league.

Hurts ranked No. 6 in Jake Ciely's post-draft quarterback rankings — ahead of Joe Burrow, Tom Brady, Aaron Rodgers and Russell Wilson. That shows the type of fantasy asset Hurts proved to be in his first year as a full-time starter, and there's still potential for growth in 2022.

Start with what makes Hurts stand out as a fantasy quarterback: his running ability. Hurts rushed for 784 yards and 10 touchdowns in 15 games last season, with most of the production coming before a late-season ankle injury. There have been 28 quarterbacks with at least 100 carries since 2000, and Hurts ranked eighth in that group in total rushing EPA on all dropbacks. Hurts' production was not buoyed by a few big rushes or even a few big games. His 2021 season ranked eighth in that group in rushing success rate, showing that he was consistently effective.

Even if the Eagles pass the ball more in 2022, Hurts' running likely won't take a sharp dip. Hurts' rushes accounted for 12.9 percent of the Eagles' offensive plays last season, while rushes by the running backs made up 38.3 percent. The Eagles neither drafted nor added a veteran running back, so there won't be a newcomer who commands a bigger share of the offensive touches. They did not re-sign Jordan Howard, who had 86 carries. If there are plays that are going to be distributed elsewhere, start there.

Unless Hurts rushes like 2019 Lamar Jackson, though, it's hard to see a major jump from nearly 800 yards and 10 touchdowns. That's why, if you're looking for growth from Hurts this season, focus on what he does through the air.

Hurts was inconsistent as a passer last season, completing 265 of 432 attempts (61 percent) for 3,144 yards, 16 touchdowns and nine interceptions. The Eagles were a pass-heavy team early in the season, with Hurts ranking 22nd in the NFL in yards per attempt (7.09) during the first seven weeks, 20th in adjusted net yards per attempt (6.39) and 20th in EPA per dropback. When the Eagles shifted to a run-first offense down the backstretch of the season, Hurts became more efficient. He ranked eighth in yards per attempt (7.52) from Week 8 through the end of the season, 11th in adjusted net yards per attempt (6.3) and 11th in EPA per dropback.

The effectiveness of the Eagles' running game helped. Hurts' natural development and comfort in the offense were also factors. And a softer schedule contributed to the jump, too.

Inside the Eagles' building, there's confidence that Hurts will be a better passer in 2022. For the first time since high school, he's in the same scheme with the same play caller for a second consecutive year. He spent his offseason in California refining his mechanics.

And the Eagles upgraded the weapons around him. The addition of A.J. Brown gives Hurts an established No. 1 receiver to join with DeVonta Smith and Dallas Goedert. Brown excels at yards after the catch, and only 46.5 percent of Hurts' yards last season came after the catch. That ranked 22nd in the NFL.

Hurts already showed a willingness to throw the ball downfield — he ranked fourth in the NFL last season in air yards per attempt (8.99), and 25.7 of his passes traveled at least 15 yards downfield. Only Russell Wilson had a higher rate. Hurts was second in the league in passes that went at or past the stick (48.4 percent). With Brown, Smith and Quez Watkins, the Eagles have receivers who can be vertical threats. The attention they command can help keep safeties away from Goedert.

"Jalen is, in my opinion, more comfortable in the offense," coach Nick Sirianni said. "That's just part of the process for the second year. He knows where the receivers are going to be versus different looks. He knows where to go with the football a little bit quicker."

The Eagles hope those improvements are enough to lift them into title contention. There are fewer questions for fantasy GMs. ▬▬▬

A deep dive on
Justin Herbert

By Daniel Popper

In one year, the framing around superstar quarterback Justin Herbert of the Chargers has changed.

Heading into the 2021 season, the question was: Can Herbert do it again, or was his rookie year a flash in the pan?

Now, heading into his third year, there is only one question left for Herbert to answer: How good can he be?

No one has an accurate answer to that question — not even the people in the Chargers' organization who spend every day with Herbert. And that is because there is truly no limit to what he can achieve. Herbert has otherworldly physical tools. He has ultra-elite processing, intelligence and acumen. What happens when you marry those attributes, surround the player with personnel and coaching continuity and let him learn and grow from more and more on-field experiences? We are about to find out.

So from a fantasy perspective, the analysis for Herbert is simple: buy, buy, buy.

He has accomplished historic feats in his first two NFL seasons. Among the 47 quarterbacks who have attempted at least 600 passes over their first two seasons since 2000, Herbert ranks first in passing yards (9,350) and touchdown passes (69). Herbert has averaged 22.3 fantasy points per game in his career. Since 2000, the only quarterback to produce more fantasy points per game in his first two seasons is Patrick Mahomes.

And there is good reason to believe Herbert is only going to get better.

Chargers receivers led the league in drops last year with 38. Herbert had 15 interceptions last year — a number bloated by tipped balls on some of those drops. That total should decrease in 2022.

The Chargers' protection up front should be improved. They drafted an offensive lineman in the first round in Zion Johnson, who will start at right guard. The elite left side of left tackle Rashawn Slater, left guard Matt Feiler and center Corey Linsley is returning. They did not upgrade at right tackle, but with the other four spots on the line solidified, the Chargers feel like they can target their help to that right tackle spot — whether it is Storm Norton or Trey Pipkins starting — to alleviate some of the pressure that came from that side last season.

By adding Johnson to the right side, the Chargers should have a more balanced rushing attack in 2022. They were much more effective rushing the ball to the left than the right last season. That balance will create a more efficient ground game overall, and that will take some of the pressure off Herbert, potentially creating more opportunities down the field.

Above all, though, Herbert will be able to fully master Joe Lombardi's offense. For the first time in his NFL career, Herbert will have continuity. He had to learn a new system as a rookie. He had to learn another new system in his second year when Brandon Staley was hired as head coach. This year, Herbert does not have to start over. As Lombardi said earlier this spring, the Chargers can start moving on to "Football 202"-level concepts and discussions with Herbert. He has the same offensive coordinator. He has the same quarterbacks coach in Shane Day. He has the same offensive quality control coach in Chandler Whitmer, a former quarterback at UConn who is a de facto assistant quarterbacks coach. He has the same backup quarterback in Chase Daniel.

He also has a familiar group of skill players returning in Keenan Allen, Mike Williams, Josh Palmer, Jalen Guyton, Austin Ekeler, Donald Parham and Tre' McKitty. The only new face is tight end Gerald Everett, who was signed to replace Jared Cook. The Chargers feel like Everett's athleticism will give them an even more explosive yards-after-the-catch dynamic to their offense — even after Herbert had the third-most YAC for any quarterback in the league last season.

We have not seen the fully realized version of Herbert yet. He is still ascending. Fasten your seatbelts, sit back and enjoy the flight. ▰▰

Quarterback
Injury Updates

By Virginia Zakas, Inside Injuries

Jameis Winston, NO

The Injury: Torn left ACL and MCL (October 2021)

What It Means: Winston suffered his season-ending knee injury last October. The torn ACL is what has been making headlines, but it's important to understand that he also damaged the MCL and might also have some meniscus damage. We often see these three things damaged together, called the "unhappy triad."

Scan here for up-to-date content on TheAthletic.com

When there is damage in addition to the ACL, it can delay surgery (meaning a delayed comeback) and lead to a more complicated recovery. The risk of future complications also increases.

Injuries to Look Out For: Muscular strains (hamstring, quad, groin), future arthritis

Expectations for 2022: Winston is progressing in his recovery and appears to be right on track. He is participating at OTAs, although he does still have a bit of a limp, which isn't surprising at this point in his recovery. Winston has a good shot at being ready to start in Week 1, but he won't be 100 percent. His lateral movements and running outside of the pocket are going to suffer early on. Our projections show a slow start to the season for Winston as he will still be within a year from his surgery date. He could enter the QB1 conversation in the second half once his leg is feeling stronger and he gets back to fully trusting that knee.

Dak Prescott, DAL

The Injury: Cleanup procedure to left shoulder (February 2022)

What It Means: Prescott underwent a minor surgery on his non-throwing shoulder early in the offseason. This is a minimally invasive procedure that can address a variety of issues. This could be anything from impingement to removing a torn piece of cartilage to a small rotator cuff tear. If this was to his throwing shoulder, I would be much more concerned but, because it's to his left shoulder, the recovery should be fairly straightforward.

Injuries to Look Out For: Weakness and soreness in left shoulder

Expectations for 2022: I don't see this injury impacting Prescott this season. He is expected to be fully cleared ahead of training camp and is already throwing. Last year, Prescott spent the offseason rehabbing the ankle fracture-dislocation, and then he dealt with a shoulder strain during training camp. Prescott also suffered a calf strain during the season, an injury related to the previous ankle injury. For the first time in a few years, Prescott is going to enter the season healthy, and our projections indicate more consistency coming in 2022. ▰▰▰

IV. The Running Backs

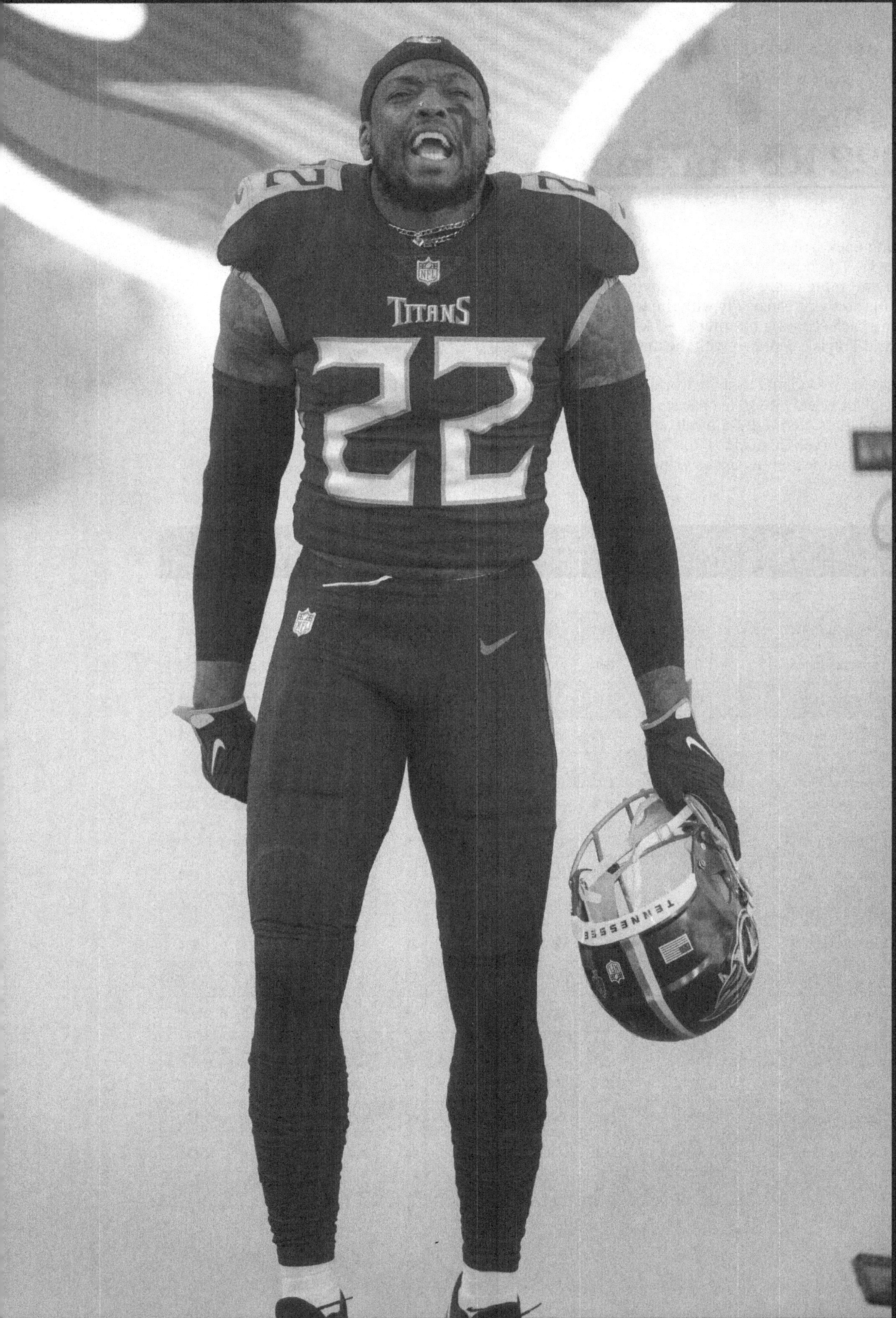

Jake Ciely's
2022 RB rankings

Running back bellcow depth has been thinning for years, and things look more precarious than ever. There are about seven true bellcow options before questions of workload, role, health and more come into play. Leaving Round 3 with two running backs is going to be a tempting strategy, especially with the wide receiver depth this season. There are three young running backs coming off injury — J.K. Dobbins, Cam Akers (who already returned late last year) and Travis Etienne — with the upside to reach the RB1 tier.

More teams are looking to share workloads, damaging the lead's value a bit but increasing the potential for weekly RB3/Flex plays: AJ Dillon, Tony Pollard and the pass-catching specialists (Nyheim Hines, Kenneth Gainwell, etc.) all fit this description. Rounding out your team with backups set for top-20 upside if the lead misses time is the best strategy. Don't waste your time with the backups topping out as a timeshare piece no matter what situation arises.

Rank	Player Name	Team	BYE	RUSH ATT	RUSH YDS	RUSH TDS	TGTS	REC	RECV YDS	RECV TDS	FPS	AUC$
1	Jonathan Taylor	IND	14	321	1655	16	52	41	344	2	323.5	$66
2	Christian McCaffrey	CAR	13	261	1159	11	110	87	698	3	310.1	$62
3	Derrick Henry	TEN	6	380	1701	15	36	30	232	1	304.2	$60
4	Najee Harris	PIT	9	314	1260	10	92	69	432	3	277.4	$51
5	Austin Ekeler	LAC	8	192	845	8	92	74	677	6	269.5	$48
6	Joe Mixon	CIN	10	270	1134	10	56	44	320	3	246.8	$41
7	Saquon Barkley	NYG	9	224	991	6	90	62	498	4	239.8	$39
8	D'Andre Swift	DET	6	198	862	7	94	74	542	3	239.2	$38
9	Dalvin Cook	MIN	7	269	1239	9	61	43	306	1	237.7	$38
10	James Conner	ARI	13	207	886	11	64	52	407	3	237.2	$38
11	Nick Chubb	CLE	9	242	1293	10	39	27	233	1	230.9	$36
12	Leonard Fournette	TB	11	206	917	10	74	59	387	2	229.6	$35
13	Aaron Jones	GB	14	193	893	6	72	56	475	4	224.4	$33
14	Cam Akers	LAR	7	257	1083	9	49	35	280	2	219.3	$32
15	Javonte Williams	DEN	9	215	953	7	67	53	364	3	219.1	$32
16	Alvin Kamara	NO	14	206	846	7	74	52	431	4	218.0	$31
17	Antonio Gibson	WSH	14	253	1082	10	45	34	254	2	217.2	$31
18	J.K. Dobbins	BAL	10	212	1048	10	42	31	249	1	215.7	$31

Rank	Player Name	Team	BYE	RUSH ATT	RUSH YDS	RUSH TDS	TGTS	REC	RECV YDS	RECV TDS	FPS	AUC$
19	Josh Jacobs	LV	6	232	970	9	64	47	330	1	213.5	$30
20	Ezekiel Elliott	DAL	9	220	925	9	61	43	267	2	204.0	$27
21	David Montgomery	CHI	14	228	900	7	69	50	356	1	201.7	$26
22	Travis Etienne	JAX	11	167	719	5	63	51	411	2	184.2	$20
23	Damien Harris	NE	10	203	929	11	26	20	144	0	183.6	$20
24	Breece Hall	NYJ	10	200	866	6	55	39	297	1	176.9	$18
25	AJ Dillon	GB	14	183	808	6	43	35	278	2	175.3	$17
26	Elijah Mitchell	SF	9	244	1048	8	23	16	109	1	173.2	$17
27	Cordarrelle Patterson	ATL	14	114	446	4	67	51	474	3	161.4	$13
28	Tony Pollard	DAL	9	148	718	4	57	44	327	1	159.6	$12
29	Clyde Edwards-Helaire	KC	8	155	694	5	48	37	265	2	157.3	$11
30	Devin Singletary	BUF	7	164	737	6	46	34	201	1	151.9	$10
31	Kareem Hunt	CLE	9	105	502	4	62	46	370	2	146.6	$8
32	Rashaad Penny	SEA	11	144	693	6	40	29	204	1	144.7	$7
33	Kenneth Walker	SEA	11	183	806	7	24	16	114	0	144.4	$7
34	Melvin Gordon	DEN	9	157	700	6	34	25	167	1	142.7	$7
35	Miles Sanders	PHI	7	173	858	3	34	26	173	1	141.0	$6
36	Chase Edmonds	MIA	11	127	538	3	68	49	341	1	139.0	$5
37	Nyheim Hines	IND	14	61	292	2	66	55	445	2	123.9	$0
38	Gus Edwards	BAL	10	129	623	6	19	14	119	1	122.9	$0
39	J.D. McKissic	WSH	14	47	205	2	74	55	485	2	122.0	$0
40	Kenneth Gainwell	PHI	7	72	312	3	66	46	355	2	120.5	$0
41	Rhamondre Stevenson	NE	10	155	696	5	16	12	92	0	119.6	$0
42	James Cook	BUF	7	93	391	3	57	41	327	2	119.1	$0
43	Ronald Jones	KC	8	140	602	6	26	17	122	0	118.1	$0
44	Isaiah Spiller	LAC	8	134	566	4	36	24	186	1	115.9	$0
45	Alexander Mattison	MIN	7	124	501	4	40	31	211	1	115.3	$0
46	Mark Ingram	NO	14	148	574	4	26	20	138	1	111.2	$0
47	Darrell Henderson	LAR	7	109	494	4	32	24	158	1	109.0	$0
48	Jamaal Williams	DET	6	125	502	4	33	25	167	1	108.9	$0

The Running Backs

Rank	Player Name	Team	BYE	RUSH ATT	RUSH YDS	RUSH TDS	TGTS	REC	RECV YDS	RECV TDS	FPS	AUC$
49	Michael Carter	NYJ	10	98	417	3	54	36	277	1	108.1	$0
50	James Robinson	JAX	11	94	436	4	37	26	193	1	104.2	$0
51	Dameon Pierce	HOU	6	126	508	4	32	22	156	1	103.3	$0
52	Tyler Allgeier	ATL	14	135	540	4	27	17	121	1	102.4	$0
53	Khalil Herbert	CHI	14	99	415	3	37	29	218	1	102.4	$0
54	Marlon Mack	HOU	6	137	549	4	24	18	122	0	101.9	$0
55	James White	NE	10	38	151	1	62	49	393	2	101.5	$0
56	Rachaad White	TB	11	81	347	3	45	32	232	1	100.3	$0
57	Rex Burkhead	HOU	6	72	285	2	49	36	267	1	93.8	$0
58	Darrel Williams	ARI	13	102	433	4	22	17	133	1	92.9	$0
59	Damien Williams	ATL	14	85	347	3	35	27	184	1	89.3	$0
60	Raheem Mostert	MIA	11	98	418	3	25	17	137	1	89.0	$0
61	Kenyan Drake	LV	6	69	282	2	37	25	216	1	81.9	$0
62	Chris Evans	CIN	10	66	274	2	33	22	171	1	74.2	$0
63	Sony Michel	MIA	11	108	401	3	12	8	59	0	71.5	$0
64	Matt Breida	NYG	9	65	275	2	29	20	143	1	66.4	$0
65	Boston Scott	PHI	7	64	271	4	16	11	70	0	61.6	$0
66	Dontrell Hilliard	TEN	6	28	148	1	40	30	178	1	55.9	$0
67	Zamir White	LV	6	62	267	2	14	9	71	0	53.7	$0
68	Brian Robinson	WSH	14	56	241	2	16	12	87	0	53.1	$0
69	Brandon Bolden	LV	6	34	143	1	30	21	179	1	51.3	$0
70	Giovani Bernard	TB	11	37	158	1	30	19	137	1	51.1	$0
71	Chuba Hubbard	CAR	13	58	214	2	21	15	92	0	50.2	$0
72	Samaje Perine	CIN	10	30	124	1	30	21	147	1	47.8	$0
73	Hassan Haskins	TEN	6	55	227	2	14	10	69	0	45.8	$0
74	D'Onta Foreman	CAR	13	44	180	1	17	12	94	0	42.7	$0
75	Tony Jones	NO	14	53	200	2	12	7	50	0	42.3	$0
76	Kyle Juszczyk	SF	9	6	21	0	34	23	180	1	40.1	$0
77	Tyrion Davis-Price	SF	9	22	95	1	30	19	133	1	39.9	$0
78	Eno Benjamin	ARI	13	38	145	1	15	11	85	0	35.4	$0

Rank	Player Name	Team	BYE	RUSH ATT	RUSH YDS	RUSH TDS	TGTS	REC	RECV YDS	RECV TDS	FPS	AUC$
79	Derrick Gore	KC	8	25	112	1	14	9	64	0	30.4	$0
80	D'Ernest Johnson	CLE	9	26	135	1	12	8	61	0	30.0	$0
81	Kyren Williams	LAR	7	32	139	1	7	5	40	0	29.3	$0
82	Phillip Lindsay	IND	14	45	174	1	6	4	35	0	28.1	$0
83	Jeff Wilson	SF	9	34	134	1	7	5	31	0	27.9	$0
84	Duke Johnson	BUF	7	26	108	1	11	8	60	0	27.7	$0
85	Demetric Felton	CLE	9	1	3	0	21	15	128	1	27.2	$0
86	Joshua Kelley	LAC	8	37	149	1	10	6	46	0	26.1	$0
87	Ke'Shawn Vaughn	TB	11	21	92	1	13	8	50	0	25.0	$0
88	Jashaun Corbin	NYG	9	25	105	1	12	8	53	0	24.9	$0
89	Benny Snell	PIT	9	35	132	1	7	4	23	0	24.3	$0
90	Rico Dowdle	DAL	9	26	106	1	9	7	44	0	23.7	$0
91	Snoop Conner	JAX	11	22	92	1	11	8	50	0	22.2	$0
92	ZaQuandre White	MIA	11	19	78	0	11	7	49	0	20.6	$0
93	Dare Ogunbowale	HOU	6	19	68	0	11	8	57	0	20.4	$0
94	Pierre Strong	NE	10	26	106	1	6	4	31	0	20.1	$0
95	Darrynton Evans	CHI	14	16	64	0	9	7	51	0	18.7	$0
96	Keaontay Ingram	ARI	13	20	95	0	6	5	37	0	18.5	$0
97	Mike Davis	BAL	10	17	86	1	8	5	33	0	18.1	$0
98	Jermar Jefferson	DET	6	20	89	1	3	2	14	0	17.5	$0
99	Zack Moss	BUF	7	15	61	1	6	4	32	0	16.9	$0
100	Tevin Coleman	NYJ	10	19	76	0	10	6	40	0	16.6	$0
101	Isaih Pacheco	KC	8	16	66	1	8	5	39	0	16.5	$0
102	Tyler Badie	BAL	10	10	45	0	10	7	56	0	16.1	$0
103	DeeJay Dallas	SEA	11	14	58	0	9	7	46	0	15.1	$0
104	Ty Johnson	NYJ	10	10	38	0	11	7	57	0	15.0	$0
105	Kylin Hill	GB	14	19	74	0	6	4	31	0	14.8	$0
106	Kevin Harris	NE	10	21	90	1	0	0	2	0	14.4	$0
107	Qadree Ollison	ATL	14	15	56	0	8	6	41	0	14.4	$0
108	Abram Smith	NO	14	14	63	0	5	3	27	0	14.3	$0

The Running Backs

Rank	Player Name	Team	BYE	RUSH ATT	RUSH YDS	RUSH TDS	TGTS	REC	RECV YDS	RECV TDS	FPS	AUC$
109	Craig Reynolds	DET	6	12	52	0	7	5	32	0	14.0	$0
110	Ty Chandler	MIN	7	17	76	1	3	2	16	0	13.7	$0
111	Travis Homer	SEA	11	13	72	0	6	4	31	0	13.6	$0
112	Mike Boone	DEN	9	16	70	0	4	3	17	0	12.4	$0
113	Kene Nwangwu	MIN	7	11	48	0	5	3	22	0	11.4	$0
114	Trestan Ebner	CHI	14	7	27	0	7	5	41	0	11.4	$0
115	Larry Rountree	LAC	8	11	41	0	7	4	21	0	10.0	$0
116	Jaret Patterson	WSH	14	5	21	0	9	6	38	0	9.8	$0
117	Trey Sermon	SF	9	11	43	0	4	2	17	0	9.2	$0
118	Jerome Ford	CLE	9	8	35	0	4	3	24	0	8.3	$0
119	Kennedy Brooks	PHI	7	10	42	0	4	2	16	0	7.9	$0
120	Jake Funk	LAR	7	10	40	0	3	2	13	0	7.9	$0
121	Anthony McFarland	PIT	9	4	18	0	6	4	26	0	7.3	$0
122	Gary Brightwell	NYG	9	7	28	0	5	3	18	0	7.2	$0
123	Ryquell Armstead	JAX	11	1	3	0	6	4	25	0	5.0	$0

Who are the 2022 NFL fantasy football breakout running backs? Travis Etienne, Cam Akers and more

By Jake Ciely

Now we're on to the running backs. As always, breakout "rankings" carry a bit of "how big is the jump from the previous value?" So a jump from RB12 to RB5 is of greater value — in this piece, particularly — than leaping from RB3 to RB1. It's not where you end up, it's the journey! Got it? Ready to dive in? Let's get this thing going!

———————— A ————————

Rookies and non-qualifiers

- **Damien Harris, NE** — After finishing RB11 in his rookie season, there isn't much room to improve, and that's before we start the yearly worry about a full-on Patriots committee. The early offseason hype seems to be romanticizing what Rhamondre Stevenson did in his rookie season. Yes, he looked quite good, but Harris was the better player, doing more on fewer touches, regularly. The concern lies with James White (or if Pierre Strong takes that role as a rookie), as White had six receptions in his two healthy games. Harris, Stevenson and White (or, more specifically, The James White Role) prevent anyone from reaching the Top 10, and even Harris only reached 11th due to 15 touchdowns. I'm taking Harris over Stevenson, but I'm not taking either to break out (more) in 2022.

- **Javonte Williams, DEN** — Williams had a great rookie season, finishing as RB16 despite sharing the load with Melvin Gordon and only getting 246 touches. If Gordon hadn't re-signed — and the Broncos didn't add a significant piece similar to Gordon — Williams would have been atop the breakout list, as a top 5 finish was in the cards. As it stands, Williams will command a bit more of the work in 2022, but being a fringe RB1 isn't as exciting … or breakout-ish.

- **Devin Singletary, BUF** — Yes, Singletary saw bell-cow work late in 2021. No, I don't expect that to continue, especially with the drafting of James Cook. If the Bills used any running back as a bell cow, there would be RB1 upside, as evidenced during Singletary's Week 15-18 run, but again, Cook will eat into the workload given 1) his passing game ability, and 2) Singletary isn't built for 300 touches. When you share a backfield with Josh Allen, the ceiling is already capped, and more of a split means less likelihood for Singletary to build off last year.

- **Breece Hall, NYJ; Kenneth Walker, SEA; Dameon Pierce, HOU; Tyler Allgeier, ATL; and other rookies** — As mentioned, rookies don't qualify for my "breakout" definition, but a few could reach the top 20. Hall is the most obvious and best talent in the draft. Walker likely sees a Broncos-like (near 50/50) split for the Seahawks with touchdown reliance. Pierce and Allgeier should be the early-down options for questionable teams/offenses. Don't overlook Isaiah Spiller, as Austin Ekeler could use a lighter workload to stay healthy, and if he doesn't, Spiller has RB1 potential as Ekeler's replacement

———————— A ————————

Top-5 breakout running backs

1. J.K. Dobbins, BAL — The first of two returnees from 2021, Dobbins barely lasted (article-wise) before suffering a season-long injury and being cut from the 2021 version of this piece. Dobbins was coming off a rookie season with 6.0 YPC, posting 805 yards and nine touchdowns on the ground. He chipped in just 12-for-120 receiving, but that still led the backfield. The truth is, there won't be heavy passing-game value in a Ravens backfield, but 2020 included Mark Ingram rushing 72 times, and Gus Edwards actually out-carried Dobbins 144 to 134. Of course, Edwards will be a factor again (if healthy), but the late pick of Tyler Badie and signing of Mike Davis point to the Ravens believing Dobbins and Edwards will be ready for 2022.

Dobbins is also a skilled pass blocker and that will give him the edge in snaps, pushing this toward a potential Browns-like backfield where Dobbins finishes with around 17-18 touches per game and Edwards 14-15. Dobbins averaged 1.02 fantasy points per touch in 2020 and has the upside to repeat that level of success in 2022. You can do the easy math, and all it would take is for Dobbins to see 206-plus touches for him to reach the top 10 and 210-plus points.

2. Travis Etienne, JAX — We didn't get to see Etienne in the NFL after a preseason Lisfranc injury, but if he's back to 100 percent, his talent is undeniable and gives him a chance to be a top-20 running back. This is what we know from his college days: explosive, power to shake tacklers, great acceleration and cuts, more cut-and-go/straight-line type than dance-and-move (his speed can prevent cutbacks and moves).

The Jaguars were solid in run blocking before swapping Andrew Norwell (62.7 PFF run grade, 2021) for Brandon Scherff (73.7) and drafting Luke Fortner. Additionally, Doug Pederson replaces Urban Meyer, and Pederson had Miles Sanders lead his backfield with 179-818-3 rushing and 50-509-3 receiving as a rookie before 164-867-6 and 28-197-0 in 12 games in 2020. Pederson isn't afraid to use a true lead and have Etienne sit in the 250-touch range. With that volume, Etienne's ability and the collection of talent in Jacksonville (yes, I'm serious), a top-15 finish — as Sanders had in 2019 — is attainable.

3. D'Andre Swift, DET — Swift was the other running back already in the 2021 piece, and honestly, he already broke out ... a bit ... but there's room for more! We know how talented Swift is, by both watching him play and his metrics, including a top-10 breakaway percent (30.8, per PFF) on the rushing side and 16th best yards per route run (1.41, per TruMedia) in the passing game. Swift averaged 13.1 and 13.8 FPPG in his first two seasons with 5.22 yards per touch (rushing and receiving). Jamaal Williams continues to be an above-average backup, but Swift has top-10 talent ... if he can stay healthy. That's the only issue in Swift's way, as the Lions' offense is set up to be the best in years and a modest 1.0 FPPG uptick for Swift would push him into the top 10.

4. Cam Akers, LAR — If Akers can return from his Achilles injury in under six months — the norm is 9-12 — what can't he do? Well, Akers might not have the ability to be a bell cow or return to pre-injury form. Before you panic, I said, "might." Akers made a miraculous recovery, but he averaged just 2.4 YPC after his return with his best showing being 13-for-48 (3.7) against the 49ers. Akers did add 11-for-86 receiving (7.8 YPR), but Darrell Henderson has shown his passing-game value, despite having low numbers there as well. The upside for Akers lies in his talent, and if Sean McVay gives him 65 percent or more of the work, an RB1 finish is well within reason. However, Akers has Henderson and now Kyren Williams (rookie) vying for touches in an offense with just 420 rush attempts (39.7 rush percent) last year (T-9th fewest rushes). Buy the upside of Akers but at a reasonable cost given the risk of shared and limited touches compared to other potential RB1s.

5. Kenneth Gainwell, PHI — Okay, let's grab a breakout who isn't in the RB1 — even top 15 upside — conversation. While there is no way Sanders finishes with 163 touches for 912 yards and zero touchdowns, there is no guarantee he gets back to the upside of his first two seasons, particularly with the Eagles losing faith in his passing-game work. After 50 receptions on 63 targets as a rookie and 28 on 52 in 12 games (2020), Sanders had just 34 targets in 2021. He did turn them into 26 receptions, but it was his lowest YPR (6.1) and pass snap percentage (55.2) after 10.2 and 7.0 YPR and 65.6 and 63.4 pass snap percentage. Meanwhile, Gainwell had 69.0 pass snap percentage, 7.7 YPR and 1.39 YPRR (yards per route run) to Sanders' 0.81 mark.

Gainwell isn't only a pass-catching back, as he averaged 4.3 YPC with a low 11.8 percent of his runs going for zero or negative yards, and an Elusive Rating (41.4) alongside the likes of Antonio Gibson, D'Andre Swift, Clyde Edwards-Helaire and Chase Edmonds. Gainwell only had four games with more than six carries, where he had 9/37, 13/27, 12/54 and 12/78, including a rushing touchdown in three of those. Gainwell finished as RB41 last year on 101 touches (1.06 FPPT). Get him 145 touches, and we're already inside last year's top 25, topping Myles Gaskin's 151.1 points with 153.7. ▬▬▬

A deep dive on
Saquon Barkley

By Dan Duggan

Saquon Barkley is convinced the tables are going to turn after three consecutive injury-plagued seasons. And the Giants running back doesn't want anyone jumping on the bandwagon if he rediscovers the form that made him the NFL's offensive rookie of the year in 2018.

"For everyone outside in the world who were fans but may not be fans right now, for you guys (in the media) who are going to write something positive or mostly something negative about me, just make sure you guys stay on that side of the table when things turn around," Barkley said after a disappointing 2021 season.

Barkley's bravado is understandable. His immense physical gifts (former Giants general manager Dave Gettleman famously said the 6-foot, 232-pounder was "touched by the hand of God") made him the No. 2

pick in the 2018 NFL Draft, the highest running back selection since Reggie Bush in 2006.

Barkley lived up to the hype as a rookie, juking, spinning and leaping his way to an NFL-high 2,028 yards from scrimmage and 15 touchdowns. His 91 receptions broke Bush's record for a rookie running back.

And then the injuries hit. Barkley sprained his ankle in Week 3 of his second season, missed the next three games and took many more weeks to get fully healthy. He finished with 52 receptions, 1,441 yards from scrimmage and eight touchdowns in 13 games.

Barkley's third season was a disaster. He had 6 yards on 15 carries in the opener and then tore the ACL and meniscus in his right knee the following week.

It was expected last season that it would take Barkley time to regain the explosiveness that once made him the most feared running back in the NFL. Just as he was starting to show signs of becoming that player again, he sprained his ankle in Week 5. He missed four games and never looked right after he returned. He totaled just 593 rushing yards, which tied for 38th in the league with his backup, Devontae Booker. His average of 3.7 yards per carry ranked 45th in the league.

Barkley said recently that he feels healthier, stronger and faster than in recent years after experiencing an offseason that didn't involve rehab from an injury. That combined with a new offensive system and improved line could have Barkley poised for a bounce-back season.

New head coach Brian Daboll arrives from Buffalo, where he coordinated a pass-heavy offense. The Bills ranked 10th (60.4 percent) in 2021 and fifth (64.7 percent) in 2020 in The Athletic's Mike Sando's Cook Index (early-down passing rate in game's first 28 minutes). Daboll's offense should unlock the receiving skills Barkley displayed as a rookie.

"I think this offense is going to put our playmakers in position to make plays, whether it's post-snap, pre-snap — just giving us looks so we can be good out there and let our talent go and work," said Barkley, who lined up in the backfield, in the slot and out wide during spring practices. "I haven't really moved like this since college."

The Giants hope to have finally upgraded their offensive line with the free-agent signing of right guard Mark Glowinski and the selection of right tackle Evan Neal with the No. 7 pick in this year's draft. Barkley's

production has been stunted by subpar blocking in his first four seasons.

Among 15 running backs picked in the first round between 2010 and 2018, Barkley ranks 13th in yards before contact per rush (1.4), which is generally an indicator of the quality of a back's blocking. In that same group, Barkley ranks second in yards after contact per rush (3.1), which is an indicator of how much he is maximizing his opportunities.

A better offensive line should position Barkley to deploy his playmaking skills like he did in his rookie year. Barkley ranked fourth among running backs in fantasy points per game scoring (18.4) in 2018 before dipping to 37th (8.3 points per game) last season. The 25-year-old has no doubts that he's still capable of his early-career production.

"I was a way more confident player in college and early in my career than I was prior to the last year and then last year," Barkley said. "Now I'm starting to get that back, starting to get that swagger back." ═══

A deep dive on
D'Andre Swift

By Chris Burke

Coaches love to tell their players that "the best ability is availability." The Lions may as well print that on D'Andre Swift's page of the media guide.

During his rookie season in 2020, Swift had just started to hit his stride as a featured piece of the offense when a concussion sidelined him for three weeks. Last year, Swift missed the preseason while nursing a groin injury, then suffered a shoulder injury on Thanksgiving that limited him to two games (and 11 carries) the rest of the way.

Before the latter setback, Swift was on pace for 1,650 yards from scrimmage for the '21 season. He'd finish with 1,069 anyway, despite barely playing from Week 11 on.

Since entering the league, Swift has been a borderline elite three-down back with the ball in his hands. But can he weather a 17-game season? And do it with enough in the tank for the Lions to feed him the ball 20 times per week?

"Just staying healthy will definitely be the challenge," Lions assistant head coach Duce Staley said. "And, you know, injuries happen. One of the things Swift and I had a conversation about is, you've got to be able to play through some of these as a running back. We all know there's a difference between being injured and hurt."

Staley keeps hammering home that mentality because Swift can be such a dynamic weapon for the Lions' offense. That'll be true regardless of exactly how the offense operates under head coach Dan Campbell and newly installed offensive coordinator Ben Johnson.

Campbell hasn't committed to one or the other calling plays yet, but Swift's two biggest outbursts of the 2021 season (33 carries for 130 yards at Pittsburgh; 14 carries for 136 yards and a touchdown at Cleveland) came in the first two games after Campbell took over the offense from former offensive coordinator Anthony Lynn.

Then came the aforementioned shoulder injury, courtesy of a hard tackle by Chicago linebacker Roquan Smith.

Perhaps because of Swift's absence, the Lions skewed further from the run game over the season's second half — with or without starting quarterback Jared Goff in the lineup. From weeks 1 through 8 last season, per the Cook Index, the Lions were the second run-heaviest team in the NFL. In weeks 9 through 18, with Campbell calling plays, they dropped to 12th.

Swift, though, doesn't need carries to be effective. In his 26 games, he has 108 receptions and more than 800 receiving yards. Keep in mind, too, that Goff targeted his backs on 24.8 percent of his passes last season, the third-highest rate among quarterbacks with at least 300 pass attempts.

The Lions are going to get Swift the ball. Swift, at an 8.1 yards-after-the-catch clip last season, will make things happen when they do. The numbers need to improve on the ground — Swift averaged 4.1 yards per carry in 2021, down from 4.6 in '20. They should, provided the Lions can keep their potentially dominant offensive line together.

Last year, even though Detroit's projected starting O-line did not play a single regular-season snap together, Swift gained 1.68 yards before contact per rush, third among backs with at least 150 carries. That's a nod to the work done in front of him.

If that line rolls out there in its entirety, well ...

"Yeah, that crosses my mind at least once a day," Swift said. "Having them all healthy, that'd mean the world."

As for himself?

"I feel like if I'm healthy, the sky's the limit," Swift said. "I feel like Duce is going to take me to that level."

Staley is sure as heck going to try. He just needs Swift on the field, as much as possible, to make that leap happen. ▬▬

A deep dive on
Travis Etienne

By Larry Holder

You could make an argument that missing his entire rookie season was a blessing in disguise for second-year Jaguars running back Travis Etienne given the chaos the franchise endured in 2021.

"Just seeing the results, you definitely are like if there was any year to miss, I missed a great one," Etienne said earlier this offseason. "That is just the human element of it."

Etienne may have been referring to the organization in general. But personally, there had to be a twinge of befuddlement in how then-head coach Urban Meyer would have used Etienne.

The chatter after the Jaguars made the former Clemson running back their second first-round pick in the 2021 NFL Draft was how Etienne could be used more as a wide receiver than a tailback. Then Etienne suffered a Lisfranc injury in the preseason, which derailed his entire rookie campaign.

It appears new Jaguars coach Doug Pederson will push Etienne back — primarily (and sensibly) — to his natural position. It seems wise to use Etienne as a running back considering he rushed for nearly 5,000 yards and 70 touchdowns in his four years at Clemson.

Last season, the Jaguars ranked seventh in yards before contact per carry (1.78) and 13th in Football Outsiders' adjusted line yards, another measure of run blocking.

That's partially why James Robinson's numbers as Jacksonville's primary tailback weren't too bad at all: 767 rushing yards (4.7 yards per carry) and eight rushing touchdowns. Meanwhile, quarterback Trevor Lawrence ranked second on the team in rushing yards last season. There's no doubt the Jaguars could use Etienne at least in a split role with Robinson.

That's not to say, though, that Etienne couldn't be an asset in the passing game. In Lawrence's final two seasons at Clemson — which is as far back as TruMedia college data goes — Etienne ranked fourth on the team in targets and second in receptions.

Jacksonville's receiving production from running backs was nearly absent last season. Just 16 percent of the Jags' passing targets in 2021 went to running backs, the fifth-lowest rate in the NFL. Robinson only tallied 33 receptions for 222 yards and no touchdowns.

"Gosh, it's just exciting to get him out here and get him on the grass this whole offseason and really work with him," Pederson said of Etienne in June. "He's doing a great job handling a lot of information we're throwing at the guys and putting him in different spots. (We're) just seeing what he can do right now."

Could the Jaguars use him in a Deebo Samuel/Alvin Kamara-type role?

"We'll take the success those guys have had no matter who it is, whether it's Travis or any of those guys," Jaguars offensive coordinator Press Taylor said in June. "I think it's kind of going to be a case-by-case basis."

Etienne said he's trying to emulate Samuel this offseason. But Etienne seems more suited to play like Kamara with Jacksonville using Etienne as a running back first and receiver second. Kamara played his best, though, without such a heavy load as a runner.

Kamara rushed the ball a career-high 240 times in only 13 games last season. He was only targeted 67 times in the passing game. The sweet spot for a player like Kamara would be 180 carries and 100 targets as a receiver.

Even after the foot injury, Etienne seems capable of pulling off a Kamara-type distribution. Because of Etienne's potential as a receiver, you'd have to imagine he'll have more fantasy value than Robinson. It will come down to whether the Jaguars are willing to limit Robinson's touches enough to allow Etienne to grow like Kamara.

It also will come down to whether the Jaguars can become a semi-consistent team offensively. But a healthy Etienne should certainly help. ▬▬▬

A deep dive on
Leonard Fournette

By Larry Holder

The days of bell-cow running backs throughout the NFL are largely over. The Buccaneers appear to be turning back the clock, though, with Leonard Fournette.

The Jaguars drafted Fournette with the fourth pick in the 2017 NFL Draft with the assumption he'd become an old-school, 300-carry type back. That theory lasted through his rookie season. Then, Fournette evolved into a receiving threat by the end of his Jacksonville career, and that improved skill set has made him a more viable all-around weapon for Tom Brady.

Plus, it has brought fantasy managers far more value with Fournette last season and likely beyond.

And don't think Brady didn't stick a bug in Fournette's ear this offseason when the former LSU star tested the waters in free agency. The GOAT wanted no part in losing Fournette.

"I was just shopping around, seeing what best fit me. ... He (Brady) called me: 'Man, what's your ass doing up there?'" Fournette said at the Bucs' mandatory minicamp for the first time since signing a three-year, $21 million contract to stay in Tampa. "I was trying to figure some things out. He signed back and it was a no-brainer. Why wouldn't I go back?"

According to TruMedia, Fournette produced his best points-per-game average in PPR leagues last season at 18.26 points. In standard leagues, Fournette produced the second-best season of his career with 13.33 points per game. Even while sharing time with Ronald Jones, Fournette averaged a career-best 4.5 yards per carry with 812 rushing yards on 180 carries and eight rushing touchdowns.

The increased value for Fournette came as a receiver with 69 catches on 84 targets for 454 yards and two touchdowns. Fournette's 69 receptions ranked third in the league among running backs behind only the

Steelers' Najee Harris (74) and the Chargers' Austin Ekeler (70). Fournette also ranked third in receiving targets for a running back behind Harris and Ekeler (94 each). Fournette finished ninth among running backs in target share percentage (via Sports Info Solutions, minimum 30 targets) at 10.4 percent.

The music to fantasy managers' ears, though? Jones is no longer in Tampa Bay. The Bucs' 2018 second-round pick signed with the Chiefs this offseason, making Fournette the clear No. 1 running back option for the Bucs.

Fournette tallied 44.3 percent of the Bucs' red zone carries the past two seasons, while Jones came in close behind at 37.3 percent. You'd have to imagine Fournette gobbling up a sizable percentage of Jones' red zone carries in 2022.

And there's little doubt that the Bucs will continue to be one of the league leaders in red zone drives once again after they tied for fifth in red zone drives last season (68). The Bucs were the second-most pass-heavy team in the red zone (63.5 percent of their red zone plays were passes), but this shouldn't leave Fournette out of the equation, especially given how often Brady turned to him in the passing game in 2021.

Giovani Bernard is the most experienced back behind Fournette. The Bucs also drafted former Arizona State tailback Rachaad White in the third round.

Fournette, 27, admitted he came to minicamp a little too heavy. He's listed at 228 pounds, but he said he came to camp at "240-something." He expects to be down to his listed weight for training camp. And Brady will make sure of that.

"Tom called me (during the spring), and he's like, 'Man, what are you doing?' And I said, 'I'm on the (video) game. Stuff you might not know about ... streaming,'" Fournette said. "He said, 'You're streaming?' And I'm like, 'Yeah, people are watching me play the game.' He said, 'Well, guess what: I need you at 7:30 in the morning.' I said, 'I'll be there, man.'"

A fit, healthy Fournette should sneak into the conversation as a top 10 fantasy running back given the trust factor from Brady and the increased opportunities in every phase. ▬▬

Running back
Injury Updates

By Virginia Zakas, Inside Injuries

Travis Etienne, JAC

The Injury: Left foot surgery to Lisfranc joint (August 2021)

What It Means: Etienne likely suffered a torn ligament in the Lisfranc joint, which sits in the mid-foot where the metatarsal (long bones leading to the toes) and tarsal bones (in the arch) meet. He went on to miss the 2021 season. Six months later, he said he was about 80-85 percent. This might seem like a long recovery, but this is a very serious foot surgery and a tough one for football players to recover from. Etienne is expected to be fully cleared for training camp, which makes sense medically.

Injuries to Look Out For: Arthritis in the Lisfranc joint, foot soreness

Expectations for 2022: Etienne's foot should be healed ahead of the 2022 season, but it will take longer to get his burst back. The Lisfranc joint is important for pushing off, so accelerating and cutting are affected. Expect a slower start to the season, but a strong finish.

Cam Akers, LAR

The Injury: Ruptured right Achilles (July 2021)

What It Means: Akers failed to perform at a high level upon his return late in the 2021 season, averaging just 2.6 yards per carry in the postseason, but we shouldn't hold that against him. He never should have been allowed on the field. It's pretty incredible that he was deemed healthy enough to play football, and that bodes well for him as he hasn't dealt with any setbacks or complications. Akers has had a normal offseason and will be a full-go in 2022. Historically, running backs don't bounce back well from a torn Achilles, so I'm hoping Akers is the exception and continues to prove that this won't define his career.

Injuries to Look Out For: Calf strain, injury to opposite Achilles

Expectations for 2022: Though I don't believe Akers will be back to his pre-injury level yet, he should look much better than he did playing just six months after surgery. The hardest part about returning to play at a high level after a ruptured Achilles tendon is explosiveness. It can take 18 to 24 months for this to return to normal, so Akers won't look like the back we saw in his rookie season right away. I see Akers finishing as a top 20 back, but he might not be ready to be the Rams' workhorse right away.

J.K. Dobbins / Gus Edwards, BAL

The Injury: Torn ACL (2021 preseason)

What It Means: The Ravens had horrendous injury luck to start the 2021 season, with Dobbins going down with a torn left ACL in the preseason followed by Edwards a few weeks later. The ACL (anterior cruciate ligament) runs diagonally through the middle of the knee and is the most important of the four knee ligaments. It is crucial for stability. The recovery from an isolated ACL tear is nine to 12 months, but it takes even longer for athletes to get back to their pre-injury form. Just look at Saquon Barkley last season — he was cleared ahead of the season but didn't look like himself. Compensatory injuries such as a hamstring strain are also common, so temper expectations in the first season back. Dobbins' knee injury also involved damage to the LCL, which is the ligament that runs along the outside of the knee. This will lengthen his overall recovery time and increase his injury risk going forward. Edwards' knee injury was an isolated tear, so his recovery should be a bit more predictable. Both running backs are reportedly making solid progress, but they did not participate in OTAs and might not be fully cleared by training camp. Edwards has a better shot at being available in Week 1.

Injuries to Look Out For: Knee soreness, muscular strains (hamstring, quad, groin)

Expectations for 2022: If cleared, Dobbins will be first in line for touches in the Ravens backfield. This could be a situation where whoever is feeling better will get more carries, so I'm expecting a volatile season for Baltimore's running backs. The best-case scenario is Dobbins and Edwards being healthy enough to play so they can split carries. Of course, this will lead to frustration in fantasy, but it's the best thing for their health.

Elijah Mitchell, SF

The Injury: Clean-up procedure on knee (February 2022)

What It Means: Mitchell battled quite a few injuries last season, missing six total games, but his knee was the most serious. Though he did return after the December knee injury, it led to offseason surgery. This was a fairly minor procedure that was likely to address a small meniscus tear. He should be fully recovered ahead of training camp, but there are some long-term complications that can arise. Mitchell's other injuries include a concussion, finger fracture, shoulder sprain and rib injury.

Injuries to Look Out For: Knee soreness and arthritis

Expectations for 2022: Mitchell has high upside, but durability will continue to be a concern heading into his sophomore season. He was pretty banged up last year, and that will lead to an Elevated Injury Risk in 2022. It's not just his knee that is a concern going forward. ▬▬

Scan here for up-to-date content on TheAthletic.com

The Running Backs

A

Jake Ciely's
2022 WR rankings

It's become cliché with people saying it yearly, but wide receiver is truly DEEP. If you look at players in the 30s, you have several who could finish as a WR1 and not surprise anyone. In fact, just looking at 2021, fewer than 2.0 FPPG separates WR30 (Amon-Ra St. Brown, 11.1 FPPG) to WR12 (Tee Higgins, 13.0 FPPG). This lends more weight to taking running backs early, so while others are trying to sift through the timeshares, backups, rookies and other running backs in the "dead zone" (Rounds 4-7 ... ish), you can hit wide receiver and have terrific depth.

As for rookies, we've been spoiled the past two seasons, especially with Justin Jefferson and Ja'Marr Chase. Don't expect anything like those two in 2022, as we're going to see many more WR3 or lower finishes given 1) landing spots, and 2) overall skill sets. As with running back, make sure you're drafting players with a high ceiling to round out your bench. There are always replacement-level wideouts filling the wire, so take chances on the next St. Brown, Darnell Mooney or Deebo Samuel.

Rank	Player Name	Team	BYE	RUSH YDS	RUSH TDS	TGTS	REC	RECV YDS	RECV TDS	FPS	AUC$
1	Cooper Kupp	LAR	7	16	0	158	121	1602	13	299.5	$58
2	Ja'Marr Chase	CIN	10	46	0	142	92	1574	12	279.8	$52
3	Justin Jefferson	MIN	7	18	0	153	100	1469	9	252.6	$43
4	Deebo Samuel	SF	9	310	5	107	68	1126	6	243.1	$39
5	Stefon Diggs	BUF	7	1	0	157	103	1270	10	239.4	$38
6	Davante Adams	LV	6	0	0	144	104	1299	9	238.6	$38
7	CeeDee Lamb	DAL	9	73	0	138	94	1268	8	230.6	$35
8	Mike Evans	TB	11	3	0	127	80	1112	11	219.2	$32
9	Tyreek Hill	MIA	11	94	0	137	94	1147	8	217.5	$31
10	Tee Higgins	CIN	10	1	0	132	87	1251	8	216.6	$31
11	A.J. Brown	PHI	7	6	0	132	80	1154	9	208.1	$28
12	Keenan Allen	LAC	8	1	0	144	101	1099	7	201.4	$26
13	Diontae Johnson	PIT	9	46	0	158	101	1063	7	200.8	$26
14	Michael Pittman	IND	14	36	0	127	84	1113	7	199.4	$25
15	Amari Cooper	CLE	9	1	0	124	79	1100	8	199.3	$25
16	Mike Williams	LAC	8	0	0	116	73	1093	8	195.2	$24
17	Jaylen Waddle	MIA	11	38	1	131	93	1007	7	194.0	$23
18	Allen Robinson	LAR	7	0	0	118	80	1047	8	190.4	$22

Rank	Player Name	Team	BYE	RUSH YDS	RUSH TDS	TGTS	REC	RECV YDS	RECV TDS	FPS	AUC$
19	DK Metcalf	SEA	11	2	0	136	78	1122	6	189.2	$22
20	DJ Moore	CAR	13	48	0	139	86	1137	5	188.6	$21
21	Brandin Cooks	HOU	6	24	0	134	91	1080	5	188.3	$21
22	Rashod Bateman	BAL	10	14	0	119	77	960	9	187.1	$21
23	JuJu Smith-Schuster	KC	8	4	0	127	85	945	8	184.3	$20
24	Terry McLaurin	WSH	14	9	0	129	77	1072	6	183.4	$20
25	Gabriel Davis	BUF	7	0	0	114	65	1000	8	182.6	$20
26	Tyler Lockett	SEA	11	7	0	123	81	1047	5	176.4	$17
27	Elijah Moore	NYJ	10	48	1	118	70	926	7	175.5	$17
28	Hunter Renfrow	LV	6	10	0	113	86	883	7	175.3	$17
29	DeVonta Smith	PHI	7	0	0	116	70	986	7	175.3	$17
30	Courtland Sutton	DEN	9	1	0	112	68	984	7	172.3	$16
31	Darnell Mooney	CHI	14	30	0	125	73	1054	4	171.0	$16
32	Jerry Jeudy	DEN	9	12	0	114	70	981	6	170.2	$15
33	Amon-Ra St. Brown	DET	6	68	1	118	81	872	5	169.6	$15
34	Drake London	ATL	14	1	0	119	71	962	6	169.5	$15
35	Chris Godwin	TB	11	21	0	108	78	910	6	167.9	$15
36	Marquise Brown	ARI	13	2	0	112	72	950	6	167.6	$15
37	Allen Lazard	GB	14	32	0	98	65	843	8	167.3	$14
38	Christian Kirk	JAX	11	4	0	118	77	946	5	162.5	$13
39	Treylon Burks	TEN	6	18	0	109	67	902	6	159.2	$12
40	Adam Thielen	MIN	7	1	0	105	70	794	7	158.6	$12
41	Russell Gage	TB	11	1	0	110	75	860	6	157.4	$11
42	Michael Gallup	DAL	9	0	0	107	61	816	7	154.0	$10
43	Tyler Boyd	CIN	10	16	0	101	72	850	5	151.7	$9
44	Garrett Wilson	NYJ	10	6	0	108	66	858	5	151.6	$9
45	Michael Thomas	NO	14	0	0	109	70	848	5	150.7	$9
46	Brandon Aiyuk	SF	9	14	0	99	60	841	5	148.4	$8
47	Robert Woods	TEN	6	82	1	94	65	740	4	142.2	$6
48	Jameson Williams	DET	6	1	0	97	57	822	5	138.4	$5

The Wide Receivers

Rank	Player Name	Team	BYE	RUSH YDS	RUSH TDS	TGTS	REC	RECV YDS	RECV TDS	FPS	AUC$
49	Tim Patrick	DEN	9	0	0	87	54	736	6	137.1	$5
50	Marvin Jones	JAX	11	0	0	99	61	724	6	136.1	$4
51	Mecole Hardman	KC	8	57	0	82	57	680	5	135.0	$4
52	Chase Claypool	PIT	9	97	0	102	55	761	3	135.0	$4
53	Chris Olave	NO	14	2	0	90	54	789	4	131.6	$3
54	Kenny Golladay	NYG	9	0	0	98	53	781	4	131.1	$3
55	Alec Pierce	IND	14	4	0	93	58	756	4	130.3	$2
56	DeAndre Hopkins	ARI	13	0	0	84	57	738	5	129.9	$2
57	Van Jefferson	LAR	7	16	0	84	46	703	6	129.6	$2
58	Jarvis Landry	NO	14	19	0	95	60	727	4	128.8	$2
59	George Pickens	PIT	9	0	0	100	59	767	4	128.6	$2
60	Kadarius Toney	NYG	9	34	0	90	59	702	4	127.0	$1
61	Robbie Anderson	CAR	13	28	0	107	55	692	4	126.8	$1
62	Jakobi Meyers	NE	10	3	0	102	69	732	3	125.5	$1
63	Jahan Dotson	WSH	14	1	0	93	56	694	4	123.3	$0
64	Skyy Moore	KC	8	1	0	88	54	637	5	122.1	$0
65	Christian Watson	GB	14	10	0	82	50	680	4	121.1	$0
66	Rondale Moore	ARI	13	86	0	77	56	616	3	120.5	$0
67	John Metchie	HOU	6	0	0	88	58	681	4	118.7	$0
68	Byron Pringle	CHI	14	0	0	84	53	623	4	113.5	$0
69	Curtis Samuel	WSH	14	89	1	80	50	539	3	112.9	$0
70	DeVante Parker	NE	10	0	0	80	49	656	4	111.8	$0
71	Joshua Palmer	LAC	8	4	0	84	45	582	5	108.7	$0
72	Donovan Peoples-Jones	CLE	9	0	0	66	40	642	4	107.5	$0
73	Cedrick Wilson	MIA	11	3	0	72	46	564	4	105.3	$0
74	Marquez Valdes-Scantling	KC	8	5	0	66	36	597	4	104.1	$0
75	K.J. Osborn	MIN	7	3	0	75	43	560	4	102.1	$0
76	Jalen Tolbert	DAL	9	1	0	69	43	547	4	99.3	$0
77	Jamison Crowder	BUF	7	1	0	75	49	534	4	99.2	$0
78	Nick Westbrook-Ikhine	TEN	6	0	0	72	43	546	4	97.1	$0

Rank	Player Name	Team	BYE	RUSH YDS	RUSH TDS	TGTS	REC	RECV YDS	RECV TDS	FPS	AUC$
79	D.J. Chark	DET	6	1	0	82	41	563	3	95.8	$0
80	Kendrick Bourne	NE	10	62	0	51	37	483	3	95.2	$0
81	Sterling Shepard	NYG	9	10	0	77	49	534	2	94.7	$0
82	Devin Duvernay	BAL	10	76	0	65	39	431	4	94.5	$0
83	Nico Collins	HOU	6	0	0	77	44	574	3	94.3	$0
84	Randall Cobb	GB	14	6	0	56	38	449	4	91.1	$0
85	Sammy Watkins	GB	14	5	0	60	39	504	3	90.7	$0
86	Jalen Guyton	LAC	8	42	0	48	33	472	3	85.5	$0
87	Corey Davis	NYJ	10	0	0	64	36	477	3	83.4	$0
88	Terrace Marshall	CAR	13	0	0	81	47	493	2	83.2	$0
89	Zay Jones	JAX	11	2	0	64	38	475	3	82.4	$0
90	David Bell	CLE	9	0	0	49	32	432	3	75.6	$0
91	Wan'Dale Robinson	NYG	9	32	0	53	34	376	2	73.1	$0
92	Velus Jones	CHI	14	9	0	56	34	407	2	72.9	$0
93	A.J. Green	ARI	13	0	0	57	31	405	2	70.7	$0
94	Parris Campbell	IND	14	0	0	55	34	409	2	70.3	$0
95	Olamide Zaccheaus	ATL	14	1	0	60	36	405	2	69.2	$0
96	James Washington	DAL	9	2	0	43	27	374	2	64.7	$0
97	Dee Eskridge	SEA	11	38	0	52	29	342	2	63.9	$0
98	Bryan Edwards	ATL	14	0	0	51	27	359	2	61.4	$0
99	Laquon Treadwell	JAX	11	0	0	43	27	360	2	60.7	$0
100	KJ Hamler	DEN	9	10	0	43	25	340	2	60.5	$0
101	Laviska Shenault	JAX	11	39	0	47	30	315	2	59.8	$0
102	James Proche	BAL	10	0	0	44	27	332	2	59.8	$0
103	Braxton Berrios	NYJ	10	55	1	43	27	277	1	59.2	$0
104	Isaiah McKenzie	BUF	7	62	1	41	24	267	1	58.6	$0
105	Jauan Jennings	SF	9	0	0	44	26	283	2	56.2	$0
106	Calvin Austin	PIT	9	0	0	47	30	325	1	55.6	$0
107	Anthony Schwartz	CLE	9	17	0	40	24	296	2	55.5	$0
108	Tyler Johnson	TB	11	0	0	32	23	275	2	50.8	$0

The Wide Receivers

Rank	Player Name	Team	BYE	RUSH YDS	RUSH TDS	TGTS	REC	RECV YDS	RECV TDS	FPS	AUC$
109	Demarcus Robinson	LV	6	0	0	35	19	249	2	44.8	$0
110	Marquez Callaway	NO	14	7	0	30	18	263	1	43.9	$0
111	Quez Watkins	PHI	7	11	0	32	19	259	1	43.6	$0
112	Chris Conley	HOU	6	0	0	31	19	249	1	41.9	$0
113	Amari Rodgers	GB	14	12	0	28	17	218	2	41.0	$0
114	Tyquan Thornton	NE	10	0	0	27	17	244	1	37.7	$0
115	Josh Reynolds	DET	6	2	0	30	18	214	1	37.3	$0
116	Damiere Byrd	ATL	14	0	0	34	20	222	1	36.3	$0
117	Zach Pascal	PHI	7	0	0	28	16	180	1	34.8	$0
118	Freddie Swain	SEA	11	8	0	25	15	194	1	33.2	$0
119	Jalen Reagor	PHI	7	37	0	26	15	159	1	33.0	$0
120	Rashard Higgins	CAR	13	0	0	29	18	209	0	32.2	$0
121	Darius Slayton	NYG	9	1	0	24	13	188	1	31.8	$0
122	Ashton Dulin	IND	14	28	0	22	13	150	1	31.0	$0
123	Dyami Brown	WSH	14	0	0	25	15	199	1	31.0	$0
124	Auden Tate	ATL	14	0	0	30	16	194	1	30.9	$0
125	Jaylon Moore	BAL	10	0	0	22	14	164	1	30.5	$0
126	Breshad Perriman	TB	11	2	0	19	11	182	1	30.2	$0
127	Nelson Agholor	NE	10	15	0	21	14	143	1	30.1	$0
128	KhaDarel Hodge	ATL	14	0	0	28	15	189	1	29.7	$0
129	Noah Brown	DAL	9	0	0	23	14	164	1	29.4	$0
130	Miles Boykin	PIT	9	0	0	25	15	182	1	28.8	$0
131	Ben Skowronek	LAR	7	0	0	20	13	152	1	28.4	$0
132	Malik Turner	SF	9	0	0	23	13	169	1	28.3	$0
133	Equanimeous St. Brown	CHI	14	0	0	22	12	155	1	27.2	$0
134	Tre'Quan Smith	NO	14	13	0	18	11	133	1	26.2	$0
135	Keelan Cole	LV	6	0	0	18	10	143	1	24.4	$0
136	Ray-Ray McCloud	SF	9	0	0	21	13	146	0	24.2	$0
137	Romeo Doubs	GB	14	0	0	18	11	147	1	24.2	$0
138	Richie James	NYG	9	0	0	18	11	143	1	24.0	$0

Rank	Player Name	Team	BYE	RUSH YDS	RUSH TDS	TGTS	REC	RECV YDS	RECV TDS	FPS	AUC$
139	Olabisi Johnson	MIN	7	0	0	19	12	125	1	23.4	$0
140	Khalil Shakir	BUF	7	8	0	15	11	110	1	22.3	$0
141	Tutu Atwell	LAR	7	0	0	18	10	120	1	22.3	$0
142	Racey McMath	TEN	6	0	0	15	10	130	1	22.2	$0
143	Dez Fitzpatrick	TEN	6	0	0	16	10	122	1	21.6	$0
144	Danny Gray	SF	9	0	0	17	10	117	1	21.4	$0
145	Andy Isabella	ARI	13	0	0	17	11	142	0	21.2	$0
146	Deonte Harty	NO	14	14	0	13	8	122	0	20.1	$0
147	Kyle Philips	TEN	6	0	0	17	9	105	1	19.3	$0
148	Dante Pettis	CHI	14	0	0	20	10	124	0	19.0	$0
149	Antoine Wesley	ARI	13	0	0	14	9	107	1	18.6	$0
150	Greg Ward	PHI	7	0	0	16	10	109	0	18.5	$0
151	Quintez Cephus	DET	6	0	0	14	9	107	1	18.4	$0
152	Cam Sims	WSH	14	0	0	14	9	113	0	18.3	$0
153	Brandon Zylstra	CAR	13	0	0	15	9	108	0	18.2	$0
154	Jakeem Grant	CLE	9	9	0	14	9	93	0	17.6	$0
155	Preston Williams	MIA	11	0	0	15	9	108	0	17.5	$0
156	Ihmir Smith-Marsette	MIN	7	0	0	13	8	98	1	17.3	$0
157	DeAndre Carter	LAC	8	0	0	12	7	98	1	17.1	$0
158	Mike Thomas	CIN	10	0	0	12	8	94	1	16.6	$0
159	Phillip Dorsett	HOU	6	0	0	11	7	98	1	16.5	$0
160	Dazz Newsome	CHI	14	0	0	13	8	96	0	16.1	$0
161	Mack Hollins	LV	6	0	0	10	6	83	1	14.7	$0
162	Denzel Mims	NYJ	10	0	0	12	6	93	0	14.5	$0
163	Simi Fehoko	DAL	9	0	0	12	7	80	0	14.5	$0
164	Jamal Agnew	JAX	11	0	0	12	7	81	0	14.4	$0
165	Trent Sherfield	MIA	11	0	0	11	6	71	1	13.7	$0
166	Kendall Hinton	DEN	9	0	0	10	6	73	0	13.3	$0
167	Josh Gordon	KC	8	0	0	10	6	77	0	13.2	$0
168	Mike Strachan	IND	14	0	0	12	7	77	0	13.0	$0

The Wide Receivers

Rank	Player Name	Team	BYE	RUSH YDS	RUSH TDS	TGTS	REC	RECV YDS	RECV TDS	FPS	AUC$
169	Juwann Winfree	GB	14	0	0	10	6	67	1	12.9	$0
170	Kalif Raymond	DET	6	18	0	9	5	55	0	12.1	$0
171	Jason Moore	LAC	8	0	0	9	6	69	0	11.7	$0
172	Chris Moore	HOU	6	0	0	8	6	62	0	11.6	$0
173	Erik Ezukanma	MIA	11	0	0	9	5	61	0	11.5	$0
174	Jalen Nailor	MIN	7	0	0	8	5	68	0	11.3	$0
175	Marquez Stevenson	BUF	7	0	0	7	5	62	0	11.0	$0
176	Dezmon Patmon	IND	14	0	0	9	5	63	0	10.0	$0
177	Stanley Morgan	CIN	10	0	0	7	4	56	0	9.7	$0
178	Jaelon Darden	TB	11	0	0	8	5	55	0	9.6	$0
179	Penny Hart	SEA	11	0	0	8	5	58	0	9.5	$0
180	Tylan Wallace	BAL	10	0	0	7	4	54	0	9.2	$0
181	Dax Milne	WSH	14	0	0	9	5	52	0	9.1	$0
182	Montrell Washington	DEN	9	0	0	5	3	34	0	6.3	$0
183	Jeff Smith	NYJ	10	0	0	4	2	31	0	5.1	$0
184	Ty Montgomery	NE	10	0	0	3	2	23	0	3.8	$0
185	Makai Polk	BAL	10	0	0	2	1	12	0	2.2	$0

Who are the 2022 NFL fantasy football breakout wide receivers? Gabriel Davis, Rashod Bateman and more

By Jake Ciely

The 2022 fantasy football breakouts series continues. We have the top five breakout wide receivers plus some bonus talk.

Rookies and non-qualifiers

- **Michael Pittman, IND —** Pittman had a breakout 2021 season with an 88/1,082/6 line, more than doubling his receptions and yards from the previous season while going from 6.1 fantasy points per game (FPPG) to 11.3. Matt Ryan is an upgrade from Carson Wentz at quarterback, but maybe not as much as many would expect. Though Ryan threw for more yards (3,968 to 3,563), he had seven fewer touchdowns on 53 more attempts than Wentz. Sure, Ryan's receiving corps was one of the worst in the league, but he has thrown for more than 26 touchdowns just once since 2016, which was his 2018 campaign of 4,924/35 on 608 attempts. With Alec Pierce (drafted) and Parris Campbell (healthy), plus Mo Alie-Cox gaining relevancy, Pittman might see a similar target volume (129) and would need a jump in yards per route (YPR) and touchdowns to reach higher than last year's WR19 finish.

- **Darnell Mooney, CHI —** Mooney checked in as WR24 last season with 81/1,055/4 on 140 targets. Yes, Mooney should have one of the highest target shares for wideouts, but there is a built-in ceiling with a quarterback like Justin Fields. The Bears attempted 542 passes last year, and that was with Fields averaging fewer than 30 attempts per start. The Bears might not attempt 500 passes in all of 2022, which would mean Mooney might barely top last season with something in the neighborhood of

150 targets — if he gets a ridiculous 30 percent target share. Like Pittman, Mooney would need to see a jump in touchdowns, which seems difficult, and/or a boost in catch rate, which also seems dubious with Fields at quarterback.

- **Jaylen Waddle, MIA —** Waddle had a terrific rookie season with a 104/1,015/6 line on 140 targets, which was a 23.4 percent target share. The Dolphins traded for Tyreek Hill, and you don't need me to tell you that Waddle will likely see a drop in share considering tight end Mike Gesicki was his main competition for targets last season. After Gesicki (112), the next highest in targets was DeVante Parker, with 73 in 10 games. Waddle could see some backfield work as teams copy Deebo Samuel's use, but WR17 could be Waddle's ceiling without a Hill injury.

- **Treylon Burks, TEN; Drake London, ATL; Garrett Wilson, NYJ; et al —** Though rookies don't qualify, and we've been spoiled the past two years with Justin Jefferson and Ja'Marr Chase, some interesting youngsters are ready to make an immediate impact. You can see the rookie-only dynasty ranks here, but Burks and London slide into heavy-volume roles as their teams' (likely) No. 1 receivers. Wilson was the best all-around receiver in the class and presents a formidable duo with Elijah Moore. Jameson Williams is one of the best talents and will hopefully be healthy to start the season. Skyy Moore is off to play with Patrick Mahomes, Chris Olave could become the best rookie if Michael Thomas misses more time, Christian Watson is raw but gets to play with Aaron Rodgers, and Pierce fits in nicely with Pittman, as noted above. Don't be surprised if two to four of the rookies are WR3s or better.

Top five breakout wide receivers

1. Gabriel Davis, BUF — Davis' touchdown rate is up with Mike Evans' (18.6 percent for Davis' two seasons, while Evans was 18.9 percent last year). It's a lofty expectation for Davis to carry that rate with a high volume of targets, but Josh Allen and Davis have a Russell Wilson/Tyler Lockett connection. Lockett didn't reach 18 percent — his closest was 17.5 percent in 2018 — but averaged 11.5 percent over the past four seasons, which looks to be Davis' floor. Where is this headed? Well, Cole Beasley and Emmanuel Sanders are gone, vacating 184 targets from 2021, and Jamison Crowder isn't going to absorb all of those, obviously. Davis is the No. 2 and could easily double his 63 targets from last season (62 in his rookie year). Put Davis at

The Wide Receivers

120 targets and now you are looking at something like 67/1,099/8 at a 12 percent touchdown rate. That puts Davis at 191.4 points, or WR20, for 2021, and if you add a slightly better catch and/or touchdown rate, he is suddenly pushing the WR1 tier. It's not hard to see how Davis could take off in 2022.

2. Rashod Bateman, BAL — In Lamar Jackson's best season, Mark Andrews was his top receiver (64/852/10), with Marquise Brown second with a 46/584/7 line, then Hayden Hurst, Willie Snead and a mix of others accounting for the remaining 269/1,226/13. As you can see, Jackson shared the wealth and had a high touchdown rate (8.7 percent). In two of Jackson's better passing games of 2021 (weeks 5 and 9), Brown saw heavy doses of targets (10, 11) but also lower air yards per target (10.0, 7.6). Jackson's ability to hit his target early in the play helps with receivers getting open easily.

Well, good news for Bateman and Jackson, as Bateman has great acceleration and release off the line and through routes. I mentioned last year that Bateman is like a NASCAR driver through traffic, and he had 6.9 yards of cushion as a rookie, ranking 13th best, per Next Gen Stats (Brown was 7.7). As an aside, Devin Duvernay had 7.9, second only to Rondale Moore. Bateman also has nice downfield ability and slides into the No. 1 wideout role, likely forming a top trio of Andrews-Bateman-Duvernay. As we've seen, the top two carry the bulk, and Bateman seeing 130-plus targets would push him to around 80-plus receptions, 1,000-plus yards and a handful of touchdowns, or enough production to reach the WR Top 25.

3. Elijah Moore, NYJ — The excitement over Garrett Wilson seems to have glossed over the fact that Moore is a great talent in his own right. Moore started slow in his rookie campaign, dealing with missed preseason time because of a quad strain. He also missed Week 4 because of a concussion suffered in Week 3. Though Moore missed the final five games because of another quad injury, he was terrific from weeks 8 to 13. How terrific? He was just WR2 overall, behind only Justin Jefferson, and still fifth in FPPG for receivers, behind Jefferson, Deebo Samuel, Cooper Kupp and Robert Woods (two games). Moore had 51 targets, 34 receptions, 459 yards and all five of his touchdowns during that stretch, also ranking fifth in yards per route run (2.59), behind Jefferson, Samuel, Kupp and Kendrick Bourne. Though Moore played with Zach Wilson only in weeks 12 and 13 of that span, he had built chemistry through the early-season struggles.

Moore is smooth and clean in his routes, has suddenness in his stops and disguises route direction to consistently separate and find space. This is largely why he saw success with Mike White and Wilson, and it's why he's ready to take a leap in Year 2. With 120-plus targets, Moore will push for 75 receptions and 1,000 yards, and if you add in six to eight touchdowns, we're talking Top 25 or better.

4. Kadarius Toney, NYG — Josh Allen's enormous leap came in 2020, which included the swapping out of John Brown for Stefon Diggs as his top receiver. As seen with other quarterbacks struggling with accuracy, getting help from receivers with separation ability versus big-body or big-play types helps significantly. Yes, rumors had the Giants shopping Toney this offseason, but it reportedly had more to do with off-field concerns than his ability.

Toney accelerates off the line and boosts it when tracking down a deep ball with short-space elusiveness rivaling running backs. Some see Toney only as a slot receiver, but like Sterling Shepard and Christian Kirk, he's proven stronger in the slot but capable and dangerous outside. Toney spent nearly 60 percent of his rookie season in the slot, but again, that number can be more balanced in 2022. Even if he's primarily the slot weapon for Daniel Jones, Cole Beasley spent 80.4 percent of his time in the slot from 2019 to 2020, and he had stat lines of 106/67/778/6 and 107/82/967/4 in 15 games each season, finishing as WR34 and WR29 (he was in the slot 88.3 percent of the time last season but had a down year in his final Bills season).

5. Courtland Sutton and Jerry Jeudy, DEN — Exit Teddy Bridgewater and Drew Lock, enter Russell Wilson. The end. OK, while you know it's not that simple, let's add a bit of context. For his career, Lock has thrown 14.2 percent of his passes off target (per TruMedia), along with the likes of Brandon Allen, Matt Barkley and Cooper Rush. Meanwhile, Wilson has just a 6.5 percent off-target rate over the past five years, even with a shaky 2021 at 12.5 percent (Bridgewater is pretty solid at 8.7 percent). Sticking with the past five years for Wilson versus Lock's career and Bridgewater's past three years, Wilson averages 9.3 air yards per attempt, while Lock is 8.5 and Bridgewater 8.0. And then there is the 3.93 touchdown-to-interception ratio versus Lock's 1.25 and Bridgewater's 2.57. This just in: Wilson is an enormous upgrade for Sutton and Jeudy. That said, they don't rank higher on this list since Sutton was already WR20 in 2019, and while Jeudy should be in that range, there is a possibility he shares too many targets with Tim Patrick and KJ Hamler to reach 100 targets on the season.

Last year's second chance: CeeDee Lamb, DAL — Lamb was here last year after posting 74/934/5 in his rookie season, good for WR24. Though he improved, Lamb didn't reach the Top 10 as hoped, finishing a mere WR18 with 79/1,102/6. Lamb saw just nine more targets in his second year, and with Amari Cooper in Cleveland, Michael Gallup questionable to start the year and a rookie likely as the team's No. 3 receiver (Jalen Tolbert), Lamb should push for 21 percent or more of the team's targets. The Cowboys threw 647 times last season, and even if they show more balance and drop into the low-600 range, Lamb should push for 130-plus targets, which, with some touchdown improvement, would have him in the 90/1,250/8 range … or inside the Top 10, as we hoped. ▬▬▬

A deep dive on
Hunter Renfrow

By Vic Tafur

Davante Adams said he has been around a lot of talented receivers like new teammate Hunter Renfrow. But none who were at his level so early in their career.

"There's never been a fourth-year (player) with the type of football acumen that he has and his awareness and understanding why he does certain things," Adams said in early June.

And that's why fantasy GMS shouldn't be worried about Renfrow failing to duplicate his breakout 2021 season, one in which he had 103 receptions for 1,038 yards and nine touchdowns. If you're worried about there not being enough footballs to go around with Adams coming over from Green Bay and joining Renfrow and tight end Darren Waller, check your history, people.

New coach Josh McDaniels is bringing over the Patriots offense that has featured such slot stars as Wes Welker and Julian Edelman. And after the Patriots added Randy Moss in 2007, he had 3,765 yards receiving in three seasons while Welker had 3,688.

"He's as everybody advertised him," McDaniels said of Renfrow in March. "He doesn't necessarily look like a Pro Bowl receiver when you see him walk in the door, but he's all that. He's got a great personality, and I am really excited about this opportunity.

"I have been really blessed to be around some really good slot receivers in my time, and I think coaching him is going to be one of those endeavors where you look back on it and go, 'This guy was one of those guys.'"

Renfrow not only is ahead of Welker at this stage of their respective careers — Welker had 96 catches for 1,121 yards and just one receiving touchdown through his first three NFL seasons — but also can do damage when he is not lined up in the slot.

According to Pro Football Focus, Renfrow last season was actually more efficient away from the slot (2.31 yards per route run; 9.3 yards per reception) than in it (1.73 yards per route run; 10.73 yards per reception). The big difference in yards per route run seems mostly due to target frequency: Renfrow saw a target on 30.2 percent of routes away from the slot compared with 20.5 percent in the slot.

Part of that success is due to the total trust that quarterback Derek Carr has in Renfrow. They are very close friends who often play golf when they're not throwing the ball around at the park or at practice. Besides running plays at practice, Carr and Renfrow can often be seen working on what they will do when plays break down and how Renfrow will adjust his route or set up defensive backs.

"I think Hunter and I have spent more time together than any receiver I've ever had on the field and off the field," Carr said last season. "Just the level of communication that we have, it's very high-level. It's one thing for me to go to him or to a receiver and be like, 'Hey, I need you to do it just like this.' And it's another thing for him to say OK and actually see it the same way on the field and do it. And he does it exactly how I need him to do it. … I'm throwing it, and he's making great plays.

"I think he's the best after the catch in the NFL, if not one of the best. I think the first guy always misses and he's super hard to tackle, so you always want to get the ball in his hands."

Among receivers drafted in the fifth round or later since 2000, only three — Tyreek Hill, Marques Colston and Stefon Diggs — have produced more receiving yards in their first three seasons than Renfrow.

Carr had been campaigning for a new contract for Renfrow ever since he got his in April — much louder than he had for Waller, who will cost more — and in June, Renfrow got his two-year, $32 million extension.

That faith was well earned.

Renfrow caught 80.5 percent of his 128 targets last season. The only receiver to receive 100-plus targets and post a better catch rate is Michael Thomas, who did so twice.

So don't be afraid to pay the higher sticker price on Renfrow in fantasy drafts. He has earned your trust. ▬▬

A deep dive on
A.J. Brown

By Bo Wulf

The Eagles hope A.J. Brown is the missing piece.

There are big-picture reasons why the Eagles surrendered the 18th overall pick and a third-round pick to the Titans for the opportunity to make the 25-year-old Brown their highest-paid player (they gave him a four-year, $100 million deal with $57 million guaranteed). For one, it gives them an opportunity to best evaluate whether Jalen Hurts is capable of being the team's long-term quarterback.

But the crux of the Eagles' pursuit of Brown is that, in the short term, they see him as something of a force multiplier for an offense that should now have answers for whatever questions an opposing defense presents. We saw in the second half of the 2021 season that the Eagles, with Hurts at quarterback, can run the ball as well as any team in the league. Now, with three high-level weapons in the passing game, the internal expectation is for the Eagles to have one of the league's most efficient offenses.

In theory, a defense can account for only so much. Shade coverage toward Brown and all of a sudden DeVonta Smith has a one-on-one matchup to exploit. Try to force things over the middle of the field and now Dallas Goedert has room to roam. Try to take away all three and now you're getting the ball run down your throat.

For the Eagles, the upside is obvious. For Brown, there's an interesting possibility on the horizon. He might be better than ever but still see his raw numbers decline.

Think about it this way. Quez Watkins, the Eagles' third-leading receiver in 2021, finished the season with 647 receiving yards. Only once in his three NFL seasons has Brown played alongside a teammate who topped that mark (Corey Davis in 2020). Even if the Eagles turn the dial more toward the pass than they did down the stretch in 2021, Brown will have more competition for targets than he's ever had (at least as a pro). Last year, for instance, the Eagles had five different players lead the team in receiving fantasy points in a game. In Tennessee, Brown was either the Titans' leading receiver or top fantasy producer in eight of his 13 games. After ranking fifth in the league last season in seeing a target on 30.3 percent of his routes, Brown will see that number drop in a more balanced Eagles offense.

Brown might be great. It will just be hard to discern when, which is why Brown told reporters this offseason he expects Smith to be the one "to dominate."

Beyond the attention he commands from the opposing defense, Brown also brings a skill set needed in an offense that struggled to make plays after the catch in 2021.

"He's a bigger guy with a lot of play strength," head coach Nick Sirianni said of the 6-foot-1, 227-pound Brown on the night the team traded for him. "This is one of the stronger receivers in the NFL."

Perhaps no wide receiver other than Deebo Samuel is more feared as an open-field runner than Brown. His 6.16 YAC per reception since entering the league in 2019 ranks fifth. Meanwhile, only 46.5 percent of Hurts' passing yards came via YAC in 2021, the 22nd-highest percentage, according to TruMedia. And lest opposing defenses focus on Brown's ability to get the ball early, they open themselves up to an offense with the potential to make significant strides downfield. Hurts' completion rate on passes downfield ranked ninth in the NFL (Ryan Tannehill ranked 28th), while Smith, Brown and Watkins all ranked in the top 20 in average depth of target.

If it sounds like there's no good answer on how to defend an Eagles offense with Brown in it, well, that's the whole idea. ▬▬

A deep dive on
Michael Pittman Jr.

By Zac Keefer

Four days after it was over, after they had, in the general manager's words, "embarrassed ourselves, embarrassed our owner and embarrassed our city," Michael Pittman Jr. slogged through a workout at the Colts' west-side practice facility while Chris Ballard put to bed an unthinkable loss and late-season collapse.

"We got our ass beat," the GM said in his season-ending news conference, answering for the two January losses that cost the Colts a 97 percent shot at the playoffs.

Pittman, the Colts' leading receiver, should have been readying for a wild-card playoff game that day. Should have been prepping for Cincinnati or Las Vegas or New England or Buffalo. Instead, he was working out inside the team's indoor practice field, stopping to listen to Ballard's comments — the GM addressed reporters some 40 yards away — every few minutes.

He was just four days removed from a standout sophomore season. Pittman delivered on the lofty goal he'd set before the 2021 campaign, doubling his production in every critical receiving category: upping his receptions from 40 to 88, his yards from 503 to 1,082 and his touchdowns from one to six.

Furthermore, he solidified himself as The Guy at wide receiver in Indianapolis, assuming the mantle long held by T.Y. Hilton.

Heading into 2022, he wants more. He wants to be a bona fide, no-questions-asked No. 1 wideout.

"Last year, I said that I was going to double every single category, and I did that," he said. "This year, I'm trying to build on that and become that definite receiver No. 1 that everybody talks about."

Early indications are that Pittman is on track to do that this season. The arrival of new quarterback Matt Ryan should help immensely — the two were in sync during spring practices, and Ryan's quick release should help coach Frank Reich's timing-based offense run more efficiently. Reich has made it clear: Pittman is the top target in the passing game.

But the passing game has to be better in 2022.

Pittman made plays with Carson Wentz, but when the Colts' aerial attack crumbled late last season, Pittman's production dropped. As Wentz's accuracy fell off, the Colts became incredibly run-centric. They stopped throwing down the field.

By season's end, they were the league's most run-heavy team, according to the Cook Index.

Pittman had 55 catches for 729 yards and five scores in the first 10 games. But over the last seven, his yards per catch dropped from 13.3 to 10.7 and he reached the end zone just once, a meaningless late-game touchdown in the Week 18 debacle in Jacksonville.

Despite the collapse of the Colts' passing game, Pittman still finished 17th in fantasy points among receivers, according to standard scoring and PPR, and all but six players ahead of him received more targets than his 129. Two of those players ahead of him, Deebo Samuel and Cordarrelle Patterson, also served as running backs.

Reich does love to spread the ball around, but the Colts gambled a bit this offseason, adding little outside help to the receiver room. They did take a wideout in the second round in Cincinnati's Alec Pierce, but behind Pittman, there is very little proven talent at the position. Returnees Parris Campbell, Dezmon Patmon, Ashton Dulin and Michael Strachan combined for just 28 catches and 237 yards last season.

It was Pittman's show in 2021 and, for the most part, it will be again in 2022.

Bring it on, he says.

"Everybody has their own definition," Pittman Jr. said of becoming a proven No. 1 wideout. "I think I am that. I've just got to go ahead and prove that to other people, with whatever they think it is, whether it's yards, touchdowns, whatever. I'm just trying to make that next jump." ▪▪▪

The Wide Receivers

A deep dive on
Rashod Bateman

By Jeff Zrebiec

Leaning heavily on Ravens wide receivers has not been a great recipe for fantasy football GMs in the Lamar Jackson era.

Marquise Brown had his moments, but there were many weeks over the past three seasons when he was a non-factor in a run-based offense that struggled to create big plays downfield and saw tight end Mark Andrews as its top option through the air and in the red zone.

Will things be any different for Rashod Bateman, who is being touted as a potential breakout candidate in 2022?

It's a fair question, and it's perfectly understandable to be skeptical. However, one look at the Ravens' wide receivers depth chart will give you a reason for optimism. With Brown now with the Arizona Cardinals, somebody has to get the targets that went to him, and Bateman is the most logical option.

Bateman, a first-round pick in 2021 whose rookie year was marred by abdominal surgery that cost him a chunk of training camp and the season's first five games, steps into the team's No. 1 receiver role almost by default. The three receivers behind him on the depth chart are Devin Duvernay, James Proche and Tylan Wallace. They combined for 51 catches on 73 targets for 497 yards and two touchdown receptions last year. Brown, meanwhile, caught 91 of his 146 targets for 1,008 yards and six scores.

Brown didn't want out of Baltimore because he wasn't getting targeted enough in Greg Roman's offense. Only eight wide receivers in the NFL were targeted more than Brown was last year. Brown was more disenchanted by the style of the Ravens offense and the lack of opportunities to make big plays.

In many ways, Bateman is better suited as a wide receiver to make a significant impact for the Ravens than Brown was. At 6-foot-1 and 193 pounds, Bateman has the size and speed combination to win on the outside and the physicality to succeed in the middle of the field. He's able to make contested catches, which the 5-foot-9, 180-pound Brown rarely did, and he also has the determination and power to pick up yards after the catch.

Bateman had an uneven rookie season, finishing with 46 catches on 68 targets for 515 yards and a touchdown. However, there were extenuating circumstances. Bateman missed out on a ton of summer reps when he went down early in training camp with an abdominal injury that required surgery. He returned in time for Week 6, but he wasn't 100 percent and there was plenty of rust to knock off. It was right around the time Bateman started to get comfortable when Jackson then went down with a season-ending bone bruise in his ankle.

Bateman played just six full games with Jackson as his quarterback. According to TruMedia, Jackson ran more routes without Jackson at quarterback (235) than he did with him (174) on the field. With Jackson, Bateman was targeted on 19 percent of his routes and averaged 12.36 yards per reception with an average depth of target of 9.21 yards. Without him, he was targeted on 14.9 percent of his routes and averaged 10.13 yards per catch with an average depth of target of 8.4 yards.

To make up for all the time they missed out on in 2021, Bateman and Jackson worked out together at different points of the offseason. Bateman attended several of Jackson's throwing sessions with his personal quarterbacks coach Adam Dedeaux. Both players are hoping the hours logged in the offseason translate to success in September and beyond.

There are other reasons to be hopeful. The return of J.K. Dobbins and Gus Edwards should force defenses to devote more manpower to stopping the Ravens' running game and open up opportunities outside. The Ravens' pass blocking, which was overrun at times last year, figures to be much improved with the addition of first-round center Tyler Linderbaum and veteran right tackle Morgan Moses, not to mention the potential return of All-Pro left tackle Ronnie Stanley.

The Ravens' decision to not draft a receiver or bid on one of the better free-agent pass catchers was certainly an indication of their belief in Bateman. Fantasy football GMs may struggle to summon the same belief, having been burned by the perceived promise of Ravens receivers before. There are at least reasons, though, to think Bateman's situation could be different. ▬▬▬

A deep dive on
Gabriel Davis

By Joe Buscaglia

The Wide Receivers

By this point, everyone knows what they're getting from quarterback Josh Allen and wide receiver Stefon Diggs. But that duo has never had another boundary receiver as potentially explosive as Gabriel Davis.

Among receivers drafted in 2020, Davis ranks eighth in career fantasy points per game by standard scoring and 11th by PPR scoring. But that hasn't quelled the positivity about his upside. The fantasy community is abuzz about Davis' potential in the Bills' offense, especially after his eight catches for 201 yards and four touchdowns against the Chiefs in the playoffs. But can he live up to the hype — and the quickly rising ADP? Let's examine.

Pros

Davis will walk into the most significant role of his career this fall without much competition and as the unquestioned starter as a boundary receiver. Isaiah McKenzie's first role is as a slot receiver, but he showed he can play on the outside in previous years. McKenzie is likelier to be on the field with Davis than without him. Jamison Crowder is a slot receiver only and a direct Cole Beasley replacement. Khalil Shakir is only a rookie and likely will have some challenges getting on the field early. Davis is also the best blocking wideout they have by a large margin, which should keep him on the field in most formations.

Davis' skills also mesh beautifully with Allen's. His route running has improved and he has become far more deceptive to the defender, helping him turn into much more than just a go-route runner. He has the ability to read zone coverage and strong hands to bring down contested catches. Davis' body control, especially along the sidelines, makes him a constant threat as Allen trusts him implicitly in that area.

Allen is brilliant when improvising, and that's also where Davis shines. One of his top attributes is his ability to work back to the ball and angle himself correctly to encourage a throw, which creates the potential for big plays.

The stats show he's been an impact player, too. Allen averaged 8.89 yards per attempt targeting Davis, more than any other Bills player. The biggest snap and target competition to Davis was Emmanuel Sanders, who is now gone. Sometimes they played together, but when Sanders left the field, Davis' volume increased.

Cons

The biggest potential pitfall for Davis is that the Bills will be working with a rookie play caller this year. New offensive coordinator Ken Dorsey has been coaching in the league for a while now, but this is his first time in that role. There might be some growing pains early.

The Bills could also run the ball more in 2022. Coach Sean McDermott has always wanted that to be a staple of the team, so we could see more two-tight end sets this season than we did with former coordinator Brian Daboll the past two years.

There also has been some unevenness for Davis as a starter. He was held under 50 yards in four of his six high snap-count games at the end of the season.

Lastly, Davis' role is secure, but the Bills still like to rotate their receivers. Last year, Diggs took 86 percent of the snaps, and Davis took almost 85 percent as a starter.

Conclusion

Davis is the most explosive second receiver the Bills have had since pairing Allen with Diggs. He has the talent and opportunity to free up Diggs and make an impact. As a starter, Davis has the potential for spike weeks throughout a season that could carry him to a WR2 or high-end WR3 finish. As long as you are OK with some of the lulls that could accompany the big weeks, he's a fine fantasy asset. Just don't go overboard trying to get him. ▰▰

Scan here
for up-to-date
content on
TheAthletic.com

Wide receiver
Injury Updates

By Virginia Zakas, Inside Injuries

Tee Higgins, CIN

The Injury: Surgery to repair torn labrum in left shoulder (March 2022)

What It Means: Higgins hurt his shoulder in Week 2 but made it through the season without a significant setback. The labrum is a thick piece of tissue that holds the ball-and-socket joint in place. If it is left unrepaired, it leads to instability, increasing the risk of a dislocation and further damage. The recovery is typically around nine months, but it's possible to play before that shoulder is 100 percent healed.

Injuries to Look Out For: Ongoing shoulder instability

Expectations for 2022: The Bengals' Super Bowl run is going to hurt Higgins because he had to delay surgery. Though I'm expecting him to be cleared to play in Week 1, he might not get any playing time in the preseason and won't be feeling back to normal just yet. Higgins can still finish as a WR1, but he's going to have to play through some soreness and weakness in that shoulder to get there.

Odell Beckham Jr., FA

The Injury: Re-rupture of left ACL (February 2022)

What It Means: OBJ initially ruptured his left ACL in October 2020. He missed the first two games of the 2021 season and then slowly improved throughout the rest of the year. Then, in the Super Bowl, Beckham went down, suffering the same injury again. We typically see ACL re-tears within the first nine months post-surgery, but supposedly something wasn't quite right all along. Now he faces a second surgery, which can be more complicated.

Injuries to Look Out For: Knee tendinitis, muscular strain (hamstring, quad, groin)

Expectations for 2022: Though there is a chance Beckham is ready at the start of the season, this seems unrealistic. Don't be surprised if he is placed on the PUP list and misses over a month as he continues his recovery. Not only does the knee need time to fully heal, but the surrounding muscles will experience significant muscle atrophy after surgery. We might see glimpses of the old Beckham in the final months of the season, but my expectations are low. OBJ won't be healthy enough or strong enough to consistently produce in 2022.

Michael Thomas, NO

The Injury: Ankle surgery to repair deltoid ligament + additional damage

What It Means: It's been a long road for Michael Thomas after missing nearly two seasons because of his right ankle injury. Thomas initially suffered the dreaded high ankle sprain in Week 1 of the 2020 season. He returned two months later but then re-injured it late in the season. He was expected to undergo offseason surgery but opted for rehab instead. That didn't work, so Thomas had surgery last June to repair ligament damage and ended up missing the entire season. There was a setback sometime in November as well. The damage to his ankle included a torn deltoid ligament along with other ligament tears, which is very serious.

Injuries to Look Out For: Ongoing problems with right ankle, calf strain

Expectations for 2022: Thomas is no longer a reliable wide receiver. It's been almost a year since his ankle surgery and he still isn't fully recovered. He was not a participant at OTAs and might not be fully cleared for training camp. That's concerning. He was also clearly favoring that ankle in videos that recently surfaced. Thomas is now 29 years old, which is getting up there for a wide receiver with a troublesome injury history. He will enter the season a High Injury Risk. ▬▬

Jake Ciely's
2022 TE rankings

Similar to wide receiver, tight end has a cliché too, and it's been, "This year is finally deeper at tight end." Don't be fooled. Yes, there are often 10-15 tight ends averaging anywhere from low-six to high-eight FPPG. However, the number of tight ends who average 9.0 or more *and* do so with consistent production is still rare. For instance, while Dawson Knox averaged 9.2, he had nine single-digit scores compared to six double-digit games, and seven of those nine didn't even reach 7.0 points.

If you flip ahead to my breakout tight ends at the end of this setion, you'll find quite a few potential Top 10 options for 2022 — at discounted costs. A smart strategy for drafting is that if you miss on the top-6 tight ends, just wait until the final few rounds to take a flyer (or two). Like the running back dead zone, the fail rate of tight ends in the TE7-12 range of ADP is quite high. For example, from TE7-13 last year, Dallas Goedert hit, Noah Fant was okay and the rest disappointed or outright busted. Meanwhile Rob Gronkowski, Zach Ertz (late), Hunter Henry, Pat Freiermuth, Knox and Dalton Schultz ranged from TE14 to undrafted.

Rank	Player Name	Team	BYE	TGTS	REC	RECV YDS	RECV TDS	FPS	AUC$
1	Travis Kelce	KC	8	140	101	1146	9	218.6	$30
2	Mark Andrews	BAL	10	120	79	1013	10	199.7	$24
3	Kyle Pitts	ATL	14	135	83	1215	6	197.8	$23
4	Darren Waller	LV	6	115	75	958	6	169.3	$14
5	George Kittle	SF	9	102	70	891	6	161.5	$11
6	Dalton Schultz	DAL	9	98	73	755	7	155.9	$9
7	Dallas Goedert	PHI	7	96	64	863	5	151.2	$8
8	T.J. Hockenson	DET	6	105	71	709	5	137.7	$4
9	Irv Smith	MIN	7	90	59	656	7	134.5	$3
10	Zach Ertz	ARI	13	97	64	678	5	131.3	$2
11	Cameron Brate	TB	11	93	62	639	6	129.1	$1
12	Dawson Knox	BUF	7	75	47	572	8	126.4	$0
13	David Njoku	CLE	9	76	50	626	6	125.5	$0
14	Pat Freiermuth	PIT	9	97	62	559	6	122.7	$0
15	Cole Kmet	CHI	14	89	58	662	4	121.7	$0
16	Hunter Henry	NE	10	72	47	543	7	119.2	$0
17	Mike Gesicki	MIA	11	92	61	637	3	114.8	$0
18	Brevin Jordan	HOU	6	85	53	550	5	114.0	$0

Rank	Player Name	Team	BYE	TGTS	REC	RECV YDS	RECV TDS	FPS	AUC$
19	Noah Fant	SEA	11	90	59	616	4	113.8	$0
20	Albert Okwuegbunam	DEN	9	71	52	537	5	111.2	$0
21	Robert Tonyan	GB	14	69	48	520	5	109.1	$0
22	Logan Thomas	WSH	14	76	48	518	5	108.4	$0
23	Tyler Higbee	LAR	7	82	55	524	4	105.3	$0
24	Gerald Everett	LAC	8	71	49	519	4	103.6	$0
25	Evan Engram	JAX	11	79	48	535	4	102.9	$0
26	Mo Alie-Cox	IND	14	61	40	507	5	100.7	$0
27	Austin Hooper	TEN	6	73	51	498	4	100.1	$0
28	Hayden Hurst	CIN	10	68	45	486	5	100.1	$0
29	C.J. Uzomah	NYJ	10	67	44	449	3	87.1	$0
30	Dan Arnold	JAX	11	50	31	373	3	69.4	$0
31	Tommy Tremble	CAR	13	61	37	385	2	69.2	$0
32	Adam Trautman	NO	14	47	29	332	3	64.8	$0
33	Ricky Seals-Jones	NYG	9	44	27	300	2	57.5	$0
34	Jonnu Smith	NE	10	42	27	304	2	55.1	$0
35	Geoff Swaim	TEN	6	43	29	234	2	52.7	$0
36	Donald Parham	LAC	8	35	23	229	3	52.3	$0
37	Harrison Bryant	CLE	9	35	22	241	3	51.2	$0
38	Cade Otton	TB	11	37	23	248	2	48.2	$0
39	O.J. Howard	BUF	7	34	22	230	2	46.1	$0
40	Jordan Akins	NYG	9	34	23	240	1	44.1	$0
41	Anthony Firkser	ATL	14	39	25	214	1	40.2	$0
42	Tyler Conklin	NYJ	10	34	21	214	1	39.6	$0
43	Foster Moreau	LV	6	29	19	208	1	39.0	$0
44	Pharaoh Brown	HOU	6	30	20	205	1	38.7	$0
45	John Bates	WSH	14	30	19	224	1	37.9	$0
46	Kylen Granson	IND	14	29	18	186	1	36.5	$0
47	Ian Thomas	CAR	13	32	19	200	1	34.6	$0
48	Will Dissly	SEA	11	29	18	191	1	33.9	$0

The Tight Ends

Rank	Player Name	Team	BYE	TGTS	REC	RECV YDS	RECV TDS	FPS	AUC$
49	Greg Dulcich	DEN	9	26	16	161	1	30.5	$0
50	Trey McBride	ARI	13	24	15	164	1	30.3	$0
51	Nick Boyle	BAL	10	20	13	132	1	27.8	$0
52	James O'Shaughnessy	CHI	14	24	15	156	1	27.1	$0
53	Maxx Williams	ARI	13	21	13	148	1	27.0	$0
54	Brock Wright	DET	6	22	14	137	1	26.6	$0
55	Josiah Deguara	GB	14	20	12	130	1	26.6	$0
56	Daniel Bellinger	NYG	9	21	13	133	1	25.8	$0
57	Drew Sample	CIN	10	19	13	123	1	24.6	$0
58	Hunter Long	MIA	11	18	12	125	1	24.5	$0
59	Jelani Woods	IND	14	18	11	120	1	22.8	$0
60	Marcedes Lewis	GB	14	18	11	107	1	22.0	$0
61	Ryan Griffin	CHI	14	18	11	122	1	22.0	$0
62	Brycen Hopkins	LAR	7	15	9	105	1	19.6	$0
63	Nick Vannett	NO	14	14	8	110	1	18.9	$0
64	Noah Gray	KC	8	15	10	92	1	18.8	$0
65	Tre' McKitty	LAC	8	13	9	93	1	18.0	$0
66	Jacob Harris	LAR	7	13	9	91	1	17.9	$0
67	Tyree Jackson	PHI	7	14	9	85	1	16.9	$0
68	Nick Eubanks	CIN	10	13	8	85	1	16.6	$0
69	Chris Manhertz	JAX	11	13	8	81	1	15.5	$0
70	Zach Gentry	PIT	9	13	8	81	0	14.9	$0
71	Blake Bell	KC	8	12	7	71	1	14.0	$0
72	Charlie Kolar	BAL	10	11	7	74	0	13.8	$0
73	Jeremy Ruckert	NYJ	10	12	7	70	0	13.5	$0
74	Sean McKeon	DAL	9	10	7	69	0	13.1	$0
75	Johnny Mundt	MIN	7	9	6	60	0	11.2	$0
76	Ross Dwelley	SF	9	9	5	56	0	10.8	$0
77	Chigoziem Okonkwo	TEN	6	11	7	65	0	10.8	$0
78	Jacob Hollister	LV	6	9	6	53	0	10.6	$0

Rank	Player Name	Team	BYE	TGTS	REC	RECV YDS	RECV TDS	FPS	AUC$
79	Juwan Johnson	NO	14	8	5	57	0	10.2	$0
80	Grant Calcaterra	PHI	7	9	5	53	0	10.0	$0
81	Jeremy Sprinkle	DAL	9	8	5	50	0	9.5	$0
82	Ben Ellefson	MIN	7	8	5	52	0	9.5	$0
83	Adam Shaheen	MIA	11	7	5	47	0	9.0	$0
84	Charlie Woerner	SF	9	7	4	41	0	8.2	$0
85	Colby Parkinson	SEA	11	7	4	43	0	7.9	$0
86	Jalen Wydermyer	BUF	7	6	4	36	0	7.1	$0
87	Teagan Quitoriano	HOU	6	6	4	39	0	7.1	$0
88	Cole Turner	WSH	14	6	4	39	0	6.8	$0
89	Devin Asiasi	NE	10	5	3	40	0	6.7	$0
90	Eric Tomlinson	DEN	9	5	3	36	0	6.5	$0
91	James Mitchell	DET	6	6	4	32	0	6.1	$0

The Tight Ends

Who are the 2022 NFL fantasy football breakout tight ends? Irv Smith, Albert Okwuegbunam and more

By Jake Ciely

We're wrapping up the 2022 fantasy football breakout series with tight ends. As always, we have the Top 5 breakout picks with some mentions of non-qualifiers and other thoughts.

Rookies and non-qualifiers

• **Kyle Pitts, ATL** — Fantasy football clouded opinions on Pitts, who had one of the greatest seasons for rookie tight ends ... ever. Pitts' 1,026 receiving yards are second to only Mike Ditka (1,076, 1961, in 14 games — again, wow!), and his 68 receptions are No. 3 all-time at the position (Keith Jackson, 81, 1988 and Jeremy Shockey, 74, 2002). Yet, because Pitts had just one touchdown and a seventh-place fantasy finish, many assume Pitts had a disappointing rookie year. Honestly, Pitts could break out on his way to the No. 1 tight end spot, but with Marcus Mariota and Desmond Ridder as his quarterbacks, Pitts likely boosts his production by 20 percent with 5-6 touchdowns. That would move him from TE7 to around TE3, which is a nice jump but a small "breakout" compared to the five below.

• **Dalton Schultz, DAL** — Schultz barely checked in as a TE1 (TE12 overall) in 2020 with 117 points, but made a big leap to TE3 last year, thanks to a 78/808/8 line. Schultz was top 6 in targets, receptions, yards and touchdowns, and with Amari Cooper off to Cleveland, Schultz should be the best No. 3 option for Dak Prescott. James Washington and rookie Jalen Tolbert will compete for the No. 3 receiver role, but Schultz repeating last year's success should be more than attainable, and he deserves to be in the Darren Waller/George Kittle tier.

• **Pat Freiermuth, PIT** — You know I love my boy Air Freier, but he already finished as TE13 in his first season, and now he has either rookie Kenny Pickett or Mitchell Trubisky at quarterback. On top of that, Najee Harris is a great receiving running back, Diontae Johnson is a target hog, and George Pickens could easily unseat Chase Claypool as the No. 2 receiver. Even if Pickens doesn't, Freiermuth is positioned to fight for the No. 3 role/targets, which caps him in the 80-90 range. If Freiermuth gets to 100 targets, there is a chance he reaches the top 10, but that's still only a jump of a few spots.

• **Bad news, rooks** — The tight end draft class wasn't the strongest, we know how infrequently tight ends produce as receivers/in fantasy, and the best rookie (Trey McBride) is buried behind Zach Ertz. Jelani Woods, Greg Dulcich, Cade Otton and others are intriguing for 2023 and beyond, but without injuries ahead of this year's rookies, it's unlikely any reach the top 20, let alone TE1 status.

———————————— A ————————————

Top 5 breakout tight ends

1. Irv Smith, MIN — Smith heads into Year 4 having missed all of last season, and sharing time with Kyle Rudolph during his first two. Smith is a great receiving tight end and matchup problem, showing a bit of his potential with 43/30/365/5 in 2020 with 12.2 YPR (10th overall, sandwiched between George Kittle and Mark Andrews). Smith also averaged 3.1 yards of separation (per NextGenStats), which was the same as DeAndre Hopkins, JuJu Smith-Schuster and Dalton Schultz, and sat just ahead of Travis Kelce, CeeDee Lamb and Brandin Cooks, among others. Smith is great at getting open and will provide Kirk Cousins with a terrific third option ... possibly even pushing Adam Thielen for No. 2 looks. Even in limited time, Smith was also 12th for tight ends with seven end zone targets. Tyler Conklin had 87 targets last year, while No. 3 wideout K.J. Osborn had 82. Smith pushing 90-plus targets is easily attainable, and that would mean a floor of 60/700/5, or around TE11. Smith has all the potential to fly past those marks, reaching 70/850/7, which would have been good enough for TE5, and pushing TE4, last year.

2. Brevin Jordan, HOU — Jordan didn't debut until Week 8, and yet, he had 27 targets in his first seven games, even with just a mere 22.3 snap percentage. Jordan has terrific route work and breaks, often adding yards after the catch (4.95 YAC as a rookie) and can work out of the slot. The Texans need options to step up alongside Brandin Cooks, and while rookie John Metchie can help, he's a rookie. Nico Collins struggled in his rookie year and is more of a downfield threat, and the depth chart behind Jordan is Pharaoh Brown, rookie flyer Teagan Quitoriano and others of little relevance. Get Jordan 70 targets and 50 receptions for around 550 yards and a handful of touchdowns will come with them, putting him in the top 20 tight ends, which looks to be the low end of his ceiling.

3. Albert Okwuegbunam, DEN — You might be wondering why Big O doesn't rank higher, and that's because it's hard to see Okwuegbunam reaching the higher levels, even the TE1 range. Yes, Noah Fant is gone, but Jerry Jeudy missed time last year, Tim Patrick is a great No. 3 receiver, KJ Hamler returns from injury and the Broncos will still be one of the more balanced run-to-pass teams. The Broncos were 11th with a 43.9 percent rush share last year, so even if we're a bit aggressive with the passing increase, we likely check in with around 580 pass attempts on around 1040-1050 plays.

Let's divvy up those targets, starting with Courtland Sutton and Jeudy accounting for about 38 percent combined. The backfield should get around 18 percent, with Patrick, Hamler and the rest of the wideouts around 24 percent. That's 20 percent left over — Fant, Big O and Eric Saubert combined for 27 percent last year. Fant was 17.4 percent himself, so let's say I'm undercutting tight ends a bit and give Okwuegbunam a solid 15 percent of the targets. That gets him 87 for the year, which would put him in the 60-65 reception range, around 650 yards and five or so touchdowns (Fant and Gerald Everett had four each last year). Those numbers put Okwuegbunam in the TE12-14 area, and while that's a great breakout for the TE30 last year, I'm less optimistic given the lean on the backfield and Russell Wilson having one of the best trio of receivers, who could all push Big O to the fourth option ... at best ... possibly lower. Okweugbunam will break out, but don't overpay and take him as high as TE12 in some places and buy all of the risk.

4. Cole Kmet, CHI — Finishing inside the top 12 at tight end in targets, receptions and yards should have you inside the top 12 ... right? Well, not if you're Kmet and finishing with zero — that's right; zero! — touchdowns. Kmet finished TE21 thanks to the lack of scores — just four touchdowns would have put Kmet at TE15. And that's with Kmet not improving his reception rate (64.5 percent), YPR (10.2) or target share (17.7 percent). Yes, the target share is least likely to increase, but with Allen Robinson replaced by Byron Pringle and Velus Jones, Kmet's share looks to be locked in. Jalen Hurts improved from a 52.0 comp percent to 61.3 last year as the Eagles focused the offense around his style. With Matt Nagy no longer limiting Justin Fields —

stylistically — Kmet can continue as one of his top two receiving weapons ... now with more touchdown success.

5. David Njoku, CLE — Like Smith, Njoku is a major threat in the passing game, and with Austin Hooper out of town, the Browns appear ready to "free Njoku." They signed Njoku to a four-year, $54.75 million contract extension, which would suggest their intent on maximizing his value. Odell Beckham and Jarvis Landry are also gone, and the Browns' top 3 receivers should be a mix of Amari Cooper with Donovan Peoples-Jones, rookie David Bell and Njoku. All of the popular receiving metrics are in line with some of the best, similar to Smith, and Njoku has a TE9 finish under his belt already on 88 targets in 2018. Cooper will account for over 20 percent of the team's targets, but Njoku has a strong chance to be the No. 2 target, and perhaps no worse than No. 3. Pencil in Njoku for 80-90 targets, and Njoku should replicate his previous top 10 finish, which makes his breakout ... a breakout in the sense of the last three seasons but not a great breakout, which is why he's last on the list. ▬▬▬

A deep dive on
Cole Kmet

Kevin Fishbain

Fifteen tight ends had at least 80 targets in the 2021 season. Only one didn't score a touchdown.

Cole Kmet.

In May, the Bears tight end detailed two plays he wanted back, both on third down with a chance to score. Those have stuck with him as he entered this offseason focused on becoming a better "hands catcher."

Kmet's only 23 and might be the Bears' second-most-reliable passing target entering 2022 behind Darnell Mooney. He spent time with Justin Fields in Atlanta in February, building a rapport. The other veteran tight ends in the room — James O'Shaughnessy and Ryan Griffin — aren't known for their pass catching. Jimmy Graham is no longer with the team, making Kmet the clear red zone target, even though he did actually lead the team with 12 targets inside the opponent's 20-yard line.

The problem? The Bears rarely got to the red zone, ranking 26th in the NFL in red zone drives. Their passing game was also the worst in the NFL last season. Fields struggled mightily. He was hit a lot, pushing back the Bears into unfavorable spots on the field.

When reflecting on Fields' rookie season, those who believe he can develop into a franchise quarterback often point to the Week 9 game in Pittsburgh. On "Monday Night Football," Fields mounted a comeback in the second half, and Kmet had six catches for 87 yards in the 29-27 loss, including a pair of 20-yard receptions.

That game provided a glimpse into what Fields could be — and what Kmet could bring.

The Bears would also like to see Kmet increase his production in the open field. Of those 15 tight ends with 80 targets last season, Kmet was 13th in average yards after catch — 4.1. Kmet has had trouble maintaining his footing at times, limiting him from showing off his athleticism.

Kmet ran a 4.70 40 at his combine and ranked highly among tight ends in his vertical and broad jumps. His agility wasn't his strong suit, but if he can get the ball in space and go north-south, he should be able to post more chunk plays.

At 6-foot-6, 260 pounds, Kmet has the ideal frame, too, to be that threat up the seam and in the red zone for Fields.

In the past two seasons, however, the production hasn't been there. As a rookie, it took a long time for Kmet to see the field consistently. And then in the second half of last year, Kmet got going. From weeks 9 through 18, he ranked in the top 10 among tight ends in targets (57), receptions (38) and yards (415), but that goose egg in the touchdown category stands out, especially from a fantasy perspective.

What can make this year different for Kmet? For one, the scheme.

"You see how the tight ends are involved in the run scheme, and off of that, the play-action movements and all those types of things can really be advantageous for tight ends," Kmet said. "You see guys around the league in similar offenses, whether it was (Robert) Tonyan a couple years back with Green Bay, or you look at what George (Kittle) has done in San Francisco. You can even look at some things with Minnesota and how they've used tight ends the past five years or so.

You see those things and you can see how tight ends can get really involved in this offense."

In a "rising tide lifts all boats" scenario, a better scheme and improved play from Fields in Year 2 can do wonders for Kmet, who ramped up his production last year but needs to be a consistent red zone threat to be a reliable fantasy player.

It may be tough to project fantasy success from a Bears passing game, but it has nowhere to go but up. ▄▄

A deep dive on
David Njoku

By Zac Jackson

The Cleveland Browns keep waiting for David Njoku's breakout season. They keep paying while they wait, too.

It's rare that a sixth-year player is still considered a potential breakout star, but the Browns believe there are valid reasons Njoku's best is still to come. With an eventual quarterback change to Deshaun Watson and a total remake of the passing game this offseason, the Browns are asking Njoku to take a big step up in playing time and production.

Njoku has been a part-time player in four of his first five seasons. In head coach Kevin Stefanski's tight-end-friendly offense, Njoku logged 47 percent of the snaps in 2020 and 64 percent last year. But the Browns under Stefanski have used Njoku in the red zone and on some quick screens, and the intent there has been to let the 6-foot-4, 246-pound Njoku use his physical gifts to win individual matchups.

He's big and fast enough to be a star. Can he be consistent enough to actually become one? The Browns believe Watson's mobility and arm talent will unlock Njoku's best traits, and the reshaping of the roster should create opportunities for Njoku that haven't existed in the past.

The team's investments in the 2017 first-round pick have been significant. Before the 2021 season, the Browns picked up the fifth-year option on Njoku's rookie contract at a cost of more than $6 million. Ahead of this season, the Browns used the franchise tag — and a guarantee of more than $11 million — to keep Njoku off the market. Then, in late May, they signed him to a long-term deal worth $28 million in guarantees and potentially as much as $55 million over four seasons.

Given that Njoku was targeted just 53 times last season, the Browns continue to pay for his potential rather than his production. These big bets continue to be made on a player who's strong and athletic enough to both become a matchup problem in the middle of the field and chew up valuable yards after the catch. Going back to the drafting of Njoku, the Browns have always seen him as a developmental prospect with raw rare gifts. With these continued investments, it's fair to assume they expect continued development and, eventually, major numbers.

"We certainly want to feature (Njoku)," Stefanski said in June. "(He has) great size, great length in terms of catching the football and being able to go up and pluck contested catches. I think there is an evolution that will continue for David the player. David certainly is deserving of that contract. He earned it.

"He's a big part of what we plan to do. There is no doubt about that. What I am most impressed (about) with David — I would use the word 'evolution' again — is his becoming a complete tight end. There aren't a ton of guys out there who can run, block and catch. He can."

The Browns released Austin Hooper in March, clearing the path for Njoku to become the team's top tight end. The Browns had signed Hooper to what became a bad contract in 2020 in large part because Njoku had not done enough to show he should be in the team's longer-term plans. The team continues to take an optimistic view of Njoku's progress, and fantasy managers should take note.

Njoku's 71-yard touchdown against the Chargers last October came on a screen pass. Njoku stiff-armed a would-be tackler to get himself into space, then showed off his speed on his way to a career-long play and a seven-catch, 149-yard day. He didn't have more than 39 yards in a game the rest of the season.

Njoku has struggled to consistently catch the ball, and that's probably why his snap counts and opportunities have been inconsistent. But the Browns believe in the glimpses, and if you take away the 61 targets Hooper got last season — almost all of them of the short and intermediate variety — there will be chances for Njoku to make more routine catches and set up the potential for big plays later.

In 2019, the offense was a mess, and Njoku suffered a wrist injury early in the season. He eventually opted for surgery and missed three months. He returned for the final month of the season, but he was benched after the coaches felt he didn't fully fight for a ball that ended up getting intercepted by Bengals linebacker Nick Vigil. He finished that season with five catches on 10 targets.

Now, he gets to play in the same offense for a third season and should get the best quarterback play he's had at any point in his career. Regardless of Watson's early-season availability, the Browns will use the play-action game to create chances for Njoku, and the team feels his speed paired with additional experience and opportunity can lead to big things. ▄▄▄

Tight end
Injury Updates

By Virginia Zakas, Inside Injuries

Irv Smith, MIN

The Injury: Surgery to repair torn meniscus

What It Means: The meniscus is a C-shaped piece of cartilage in the knee that acts as a cushion and shock absorber, helping to stabilize the joint. There are two types of procedures to address a torn meniscus. The first is a meniscectomy, aka a trim. The piece of cartilage that is torn is cut out. This leads to a quicker recovery but long term comes with more complications as there is less cushion remaining in the knee. The other option is a repair, where the torn piece is trimmed back together. The recovery is three to six months, but it is the better decision long term as the knee doesn't lose any of that cushion. Based on Smith's timeline, he likely had a repair. Now almost a year removed from surgery, Smith's knee should be fully recovered. He has also had enough time to get full strength back in that leg.

Injuries to Look Out For: Knee soreness

Expectations for 2022: Smith should now be healthy enough to bounce back and have a strong season. He was seen running routes and participating in 11-on-11 drills at OTAs. I'm expecting Smith to be a full-go with no limitations by training camp. He should be in the back-end TE1 conversation. ▄▄▄

A

Jake Ciely's
DST rankings

Rank	Player	BYE	FPS	AUC$
1	Buffalo Bills	7	135.6	$2
2	Pittsburgh Steelers	9	132.8	$2
3	Tampa Bay Buccaneers	11	131.2	$1
4	San Francisco 49ers	9	128.1	$1
5	Los Angeles Chargers	8	127.3	$1
6	Dallas Cowboys	9	126.7	$1
7	Baltimore Ravens	10	125.6	$1
8	Miami Dolphins	11	124.7	$1
9	Indianapolis Colts	14	124.6	$1
10	Arizona Cardinals	13	124.2	$1
11	New Orleans Saints	14	124.0	$1
12	Green Bay Packers	14	123.9	$0
13	Minnesota Vikings	7	122.8	$0
14	Los Angeles Rams	7	122.2	$0
15	Cleveland Browns	9	121.3	$0
16	Denver Broncos	9	120.3	$0

Rank	Player	BYE	FPS	AUC$
17	Kansas City Chiefs	8	119.5	$0
18	Washington Commanders	14	118.8	$0
19	Chicago Bears	14	118.0	$0
20	Cincinnati Bengals	10	117.7	$0
21	New England Patriots	10	115.0	$0
22	Tennessee Titans	6	114.8	$0
23	Carolina Panthers	13	113.1	$0
24	New York Giants	9	107.1	$0
25	Houston Texans	6	106.8	$0
26	Las Vegas Raiders	6	105.7	$0
27	Detroit Lions	6	105.7	$0
28	Philadelphia Eagles	7	104.6	$0
29	New York Jets	10	103.4	$0
30	Seattle Seahawks	11	102.7	$0
31	Atlanta Falcons	14	102.3	$0
32	Jacksonville Jaguars	11	98.5	$0

Fantasy football 2022 IDP rankings: Linebackers Darius Leonard, Roquan Smith get the party started

By Gary Davenport

Before we get to our IDP rankings for the 2022 campaign, here are some tips to keep in mind as you get set to embark on your IDP drafts this summer.

IDP Draft Tips

- Make sure to familiarize yourself with your league's scoring and lineup requirements prior to draft day. Does the scoring favor tackles, or big plays like sacks and interceptions? How do the top IDPs stack up against their counterparts on offense? Are 3-4 rush linebackers lumped in with 4-3 defensive ends as edge-rushers? All that information can help you gauge the value of the IDP positions relative to one another and players on offense.

- In a fairly straightforward IDP setup that starts two defensive linemen, two or three linebackers and a couple defensive backs, the elite defensive players will start trickling off the board in Round 5 or Round 6. A round or two after that, the first big run on IDPs will take place. You don't have to roster one of those elite linebackers or defensive linemen to field a competitive team, but don't get frozen out of that first big run if you pass on the top-end guys.

- Different scoring systems can, of course, impact player values, but in most IDP leagues, linebackers form the backbone of a successful team. You'll want to focus at least two of your first three defensive picks on the position. The other should be used to secure at least one reliable weekly starter on the defensive line — it's easily the shallowest of the three main IDP positions. Wait to draft defensive backs. The position is equal parts deep and unpredictable. There will be upside dart throws available late, and plenty of meat left on the waiver wire if those players don't pan out.

IDP Value Picks

Cameron Heyward – DE, PIT: In two of the last three years, Heyward has eclipsed 80 total tackles and nine sacks on the way to top-five fantasy numbers, but his age (33) leads many IDP managers to undervalue him.

Charles Harris – DE, DET: The former first-round pick had easily the best season his career in 2021, tallying 65 tackles and 7.5 sacks. But with Aidan Hutchinson now in Motown, Harris has landed right back on the IDP milk carton. He's a cheaply available DL2.

Jeremiah Owusu-Koramoah – OLB, CLE: Owusu-Koramoah's rookie season wasn't especially impressive from a statistical perspective, but he's a talented young player and an excellent fit in Joe Woods' defense in Cleveland, which runs nickel sets most of the time.

Alex Anzalone – ILB, DET: Anzalone isn't an especially good NFL player. But he appears slated for a three-down role on a bad Lions defense again in 2022. IDP managers get the same points for tackles made seven yards down the field as they do for one at the line of scrimmage.

Marcus Maye – S, NOS: Maye's 2021 season was an injury-marred mess. But back in 2020 he was a top-25 defensive back, the SS spot in New Orleans has consistently been fantasy-relevant in recent years and Maye is essentially free in most IDP drafts.

George Odum – S, SFO: Odum is a great late-round lottery ticket at defensive back. He has shown he can post numbers when the snaps are there in the past, and he's slated to be San Francisco's starting box safety — a spot that has produced more than one IDP-relevant player. ▬▬

Scan here for up-to-date content on TheAthletic.com

2022 IDP Rankings
Top 100 Overall

Rank	Name / Position / Team
1	Darius Leonard – OLB, IND
2	Roquan Smith – ILB, CHI
3	Bobby Wagner – ILB. LAR
4	Devin White – ILB, TBB
5	Myles Garrett – DE, CLE
6	Jordyn Brooks – ILB, SEA
7	Aaron Donald – DT, LAR
8	De'Vondre Campbell – ILB, GBP
9	Micah Parsons – ILB, DAL
10	Nick Bosa – DE, SFO
11	Blake Martinez – ILB, NYG
12	T.J. Watt – OLB, PIT
13	Jordan Poyer – S, BUF
14	Chase Young – DE, WAS
15	Foyesade Oluokun – ILB, JAX
16	Danielle Hunter – DE, MIN
17	Fred Warner – ILB, SFO
18	Joey Bosa – DE, LAC
19	Derwin James – S, LAC
20	Denzel Perryman – ILB, LVR
21	Chandler Jones – DE, LVR
22	Jeremy Chinn – S, CAR
23	C.J. Mosley – ILB, NYJ
24	Antoine Winfield – S, TBB
25	Cameron Jordan – DE, NOS
26	Logan Wilson – ILB, CIN
27	Kevin Byard – S, TEN
28	Maxx Crosby – DE, LVR
29	Lavonte David – ILB, TBB
30	Cameron Heyward – DE, PIT
31	Budda Baker – S, ARZ
32	Tremaine Edmunds – ILB, BUF
33	Haason Reddick – DE, PHI
34	Cole Holcomb – OLB, WAS
35	Jamal Adams – S, SEA
36	Leonard Williams – DE, NYG
37	DeForest Buckner – DT, IND
38	Eric Kendricks – ILB, MIN
39	Trey Hendrickson – DE, CIN
40	Kyle Dugger – S, NEP
41	Demario Davis – OLB, NOS
42	Harrison Smith – S, MIN
43	Brian Burns – DE, CAR
44	Minkah Fitzpatrick – S, PIT
45	Nick Bolton – ILB, KCC
46	Isaiah Simmons – ILB, ARZ
47	Justin Simmons – S, DEN
48	Robert Quinn – DE, CHI
49	Jeremiah Owusu-Koramoah - OLB, CLE
50	Jessie Bates – S, CIN
51	Montez Sweat – DE, WAS
52	Jerome Baker – ILB, MIA
53	Demarcus Lawrence – DE, DAL
54	Jalen Thompson – S, ARZ
55	Patrick Queen – ILB, BAL
56	Bobby Okereke – OLB, IND
57	Jeffery Simmons – DT, TEN
58	Jayron Kearse – S, DAL
59	David Long – ILB, TEN
60	Chris Jones – DT, KCC
61	Xavier McKinney – S, NYG
62	Josh Allen – DE, JAX
63	Jonathan Allen – DT, WAS
64	Logan Ryan – S, TBB
65	Jamin Davis – ILB, WAS
66	Sam Hubbard – DE, CIN

Rank	Name / Position / Team
67	Johnathan Abram - S, LVR
68	Shaq Thompson - ILB, CAR
69	Vonn Bell - S, CIN
70	Emmanuel Ogbah - DE, MIA
71	Myles Jack - ILB, PIT
72	Quinnen Williams - DT, NYJ
73	Tyrann Mathieu - S, NOS
74	Nakobe Dean - ILB, PHI
75	Zach Cunningham - ILB, TEN
76	Jordan Fuller - S, LAR
77	Kenny Moore - CB, IND
78	Randy Gregory - DE, DEN
79	Kyzir White - OLB, PHI
80	Xavier Woods - S, CAR
81	Devin Lloyd - ILB, JAX
82	Jonathan Greenard - DE, HOU
83	Kamren Curl - S, WAS

Rank	Name / Position / Team
84	Troy Andersen - ILB, ATL
85	Jordan Hicks - ILB, MIN
86	Brandon Graham - DE, PHI
87	Taylor Rapp - S, LAR
88	Zaven Collins - ILB, ARZ
89	Alex Singleton - ILB, DEN
90	Trevon Diggs - CB, DAL
91	Yannick Ngakoue - DE, IND
92	Devin Bush - ILB, PIT
93	Tracy Walker - S, DET
94	Anthony Walker - ILB, CLE
95	Marcus Maye - S, NOS
96	Christian Kirksey - OLB, HOU
97	Marcus Davenport - DE, NOS
98	Deion Jones - ILB, ATL
99	Christian Wilkins - DT, MIA
100	Julian Love - S, NYG

Defenses

2022 IDP Rankings
Top 80 Defensive Linemen

Rank	Name / Position / Team
1	Myles Garrett - DE, CLE
2	Aaron Donald - DT, LAR
3	Nick Bosa - DE, SFO
4	Chase Young - DE, WAS
5	Danielle Hunter - DE, MIN
6	Joey Bosa - DE, LAC
7	Chandler Jones - DE, LVR
8	Cameron Jordan - DE, NOS
9	Maxx Crosby - DE, LVR
10	Cameron Heyward - DE, PIT
11	Haason Reddick - DE, PHI
12	Leonard Williams - DE, NYG
13	DeForest Buckner - DT, IND

Rank	Name / Position / Team
14	Trey Hendrickson - DE, CIN
15	Brian Burns - DE, CAR
16	Robert Quinn - DE, CHI
17	Montez Sweat - DE, WAS
18	Demarcus Lawrence - DE, DAL
19	Jeffery Simmons - DT, TEN
20	Chris Jones - DT, KCC
21	Josh Allen - DE, JAX
22	Jonathan Allen - DT, WAS
23	Sam Hubbard - DE, CIN
24	Emmanuel Ogbah - DE, MIA
25	Quinnen Williams - DT, NYJ
26	Randy Gregory - DE, DEN

Rank	Name / Position / Team	Rank	Name / Position / Team
27	Jonathan Greenard - DE, HOU	54	Jordan Davis - DT, PHI
28	Brandon Graham - DE, PHI	55	Akiem Hicks - DT, TBB
29	Yannick Ngakoue - DE, IND	56	Ed Oliver - DT, BUF
30	Marcus Davenport - DE, NOS	57	Fletcher Cox - DT, PHI
31	Christian Wilkins - DT, MIA	58	Dorance Armstrong - DE, DAL
32	Gregory Rousseau - DE, BUF	59	Javon Kinlaw - DT, SFO
33	Carl Lawson - DE, NYJ	60	Romeo Okwara - DE, DET
34	Aidan Hutchinson - DE, DET	61	Derrick Brown - DT, CAR
35	Jermaine Johnson - DE, NYJ	62	D.J. Reader - DT, CIN
36	Kwity Paye - DE, IND	63	John Franklin-Myers - DE, NYJ
37	Charles Harris - DE, DET	64	Shelby Harris - DE, SEA
38	Josh Sweat - DE, PHI	65	Dexter Lawrence - DT, NYG
39	Travon Walker - DT, JAX	66	Sam Williams - DE, DAL
40	Javon Hargrave - DT, PHI	67	Dayo Odeyingbo - DE, IND
41	Jadeveon Clowney - DE, CLE	68	Christian Barmore - DT, NEP
42	George Karlaftis - DE, KCC	69	Chase Winovich - DE, CLE
43	Zach Allen - DE, ARZ	70	A.J. Epenesa - DE, BUF
44	Grady Jarrett - DT, ATL	71	Payton Turner - DE, NOS
45	Arik Armstead - DE, SFO	72	D.J. Wonnum - DE, MIN
46	Frank Clark - DE, KCC	73	Drake Jackson - DE, SFO
47	Da'Ron Payne - DT, WAS	74	Dante Fowler - DE, DAL
48	Boye Mafe - DE, SEA	75	Kerry Hyder - DE, SFO
49	J.J. Watt - DE, ARZ	76	Vita Vea - DT, TBB
50	Carlos Basham - DE, BUF	77	Kenny Clark - DT, GBP
51	Dre'Mont Jones - DE, DEN	78	Dee Ford - DE, SFO
52	Calais Campbell - DE, BAL	79	Greg Gaines - DT, LAR
53	Denico Autry - DE, TEN	80	Payton Turner - DE, NOS

2022 IDP Rankings
Top 50 Linebackers

Rank	Name / Position / Team
1	Darius Leonard - OLB, IND
2	Roquan Smith - ILB, CHI
3	Bobby Wagner - ILB, LAR
4	Devin White - ILB, TBB
5	Jordyn Brooks - ILB, SEA
6	De'Vondre Campbell - ILB, GBP
7	Micah Parsons - ILB, DAL
8	Blake Martinez - ILB, NYG
9	T.J. Watt - OLB, PIT
10	Foyesade Oluokun - ILB, JAX
11	Fred Warner - ILB, SFO
12	Denzel Perryman - ILB, LVR
13	C.J. Mosley - ILB, NYJ
14	Logan Wilson - ILB, CIN
15	Lavonte David - ILB, TBB
16	Tremaine Edmunds - ILB, BUF
17	Cole Holcomb - OLB, WAS
18	Eric Kendricks - ILB, MIN
19	Demario Davis - OLB, NOS
20	Nick Bolton - ILB, KCC
21	Isaiah Simmons - ILB, ARZ
22	J. Owusu-Koramoah - OLB, CLE
23	Jerome Baker - ILB, MIA
24	Patrick Queen - ILB, BAL
25	Bobby Okereke - OLB, IND

Rank	Name / Position / Team
26	David Long - ILB, TEN
27	Jamin Davis - ILB, WAS
28	Shaq Thompson - ILB, CAR
29	Myles Jack - ILB, PIT
30	Nakobe Dean - ILB, PHI
31	Zach Cunningham - ILB, TEN
32	Kyzir White - OLB, PHI
33	Devin Lloyd - ILB, JAX
34	Zaven Collins - ILB, ARZ
35	Troy Andersen - ILB, ATL
36	Jordan Hicks - ILB, MIN
37	Alex Singleton - ILB, DEN
38	Devin Bush - ILB, PIT
39	Anthony Walker - ILB, CLE
40	Christian Kirksey - OLB, HOU
41	Deion Jones - ILB, ATL
42	Khalil Mack - OLB, LAC
43	Quay Walker - ILB, GBP
44	Alex Anzalone - ILB, DET
45	Kamu Grugier-Hill - ILB, HOU
46	Shaquil Barrett - OLB, TBB
47	Jayon Brown - ILB, LVR
48	Dre Greenlaw - OLB, SFO
49	Matt Milano - OLB, BUF
50	Quincy Williams - ILB, NYJ

Defenses

2022 IDP Rankings
Top 50 Defensive Backs

Rank	Name / Position / Team	Rank	Name / Position / Team
1	Jordan Poyer - S, BUF	26	Tracy Walker - S, DET
2	Derwin James - S, LAC	27	Marcus Maye - S, NOS
3	Jeremy Chinn - S, CAR	28	Julian Love - S, NYG
4	Antoine Winfield - S, TBB	29	J.C. Jackson - CB, LAC
5	Kevin Byard - S, TEN	30	Jordan Whitehead - S, NYJ
6	Budda Baker - S, ARZ	31	Quandre Diggs - S, SEA
7	Jamal Adams - S, SEA	32	Kyle Hamilton - S, BAL
8	Kyle Dugger - S, NEP	33	Marlon Humphrey - CB, BAL
9	Harrison Smith - S, MIN	34	Adrian Amos - S, GBP
10	Minkah Fitzpatrick - S, PIT	35	Justin Reid - S, KCC
11	Justin Simmons - S, DEN	36	Adrian Phillips - S, NEP
12	Jessie Bates - S, CIN	37	Micah Hyde - S, BUF
13	Jalen Thompson - S, ARZ	38	Jalen Ramsey - CB, LAR
14	Jayron Kearse - S, DAL	39	Kendall Fuller - CB, WAS
15	Xavier McKinney - S, NYG	40	JaQuan Brisker - S, CHI
16	Logan Ryan - S, TBB	41	Brandon Jones - S, MIA
17	Johnathan Abram - S, LVR	42	L'Jarius Sneed - CB, KC
18	Vonn Bell - S, CIN	43	Jalen Pitre - S, HOU
19	Tyrann Mathieu - S, NOS	44	John Johnson - S, CLE
20	Jordan Fuller - S, LAR	45	Darnell Savage - S, GBP
21	Kenny Moore - CB, IND	46	Xavien Howard - CB, MIA
22	Xavier Woods - S, CAR	47	Rasul Douglas - CB, GBP
23	Kamren Curl - S, WAS	48	Eddie Jackson - S, CHI
24	Taylor Rapp - S, LAR	49	Ashtyn Davis - S, NYJ
25	Trevon Diggs - CB, DAL	50	Chuck Clark - S, BAL

NFL offensive line grades: The units that help, hinder the most for 2022 fantasy football

By KC Joyner

Offensive lines are the unsung heroes of fantasy football. Those "big hog mollies" (as Keith Jackson used to call them) don't occupy roster spots on fantasy teams, but every player on a fantasy roster owes a great portion of his success to how well his team's offensive line does its job.

Since these blockers are key to fantasy success, it pays to know which offensive lines will help you win leagues and which are more likely to hinder your pursuit of championships.

We're here to assist in that effort by grading every NFL offensive line's expected 2022 performance. We start by gauging the 2021 performance of all offensive lines in 10 key advanced metrics. This system places weights on each of those metrics based on their expected impact on fantasy football performance.

That baseline level is adjusted with weighted grades for offensive line personnel stability and offensive line personnel upgrades made via free agency and the NFL Draft. The personnel stability element is key, as previous studies I performed in this area showed that having the same players on an offensive line in consecutive seasons has a notable positive impact on offensive line performance.

All these factors were combined and turned into 1-100 grades. Each team has an overall offensive line grade, a run-blocking grade and a pass-blocking grade. For quick-reference ease, we have listed the 1-100 grades for each team and assigned a grading tier of 1-7, with 1 being the best and 7 being the worst.

When looking at the overall grades, keep in mind that the pass-blocking grades account for a slightly larger percentage of the overall grades than the run-blocking grades do.

It's also worth noting a few rules of thumb when using these grades to assist with fantasy draft selections.

- Pay most of your attention to the grades at the top and bottom of each category, as those are the blocking groups that will have the largest impact on your fantasy picks.

- Beyond the outliers, these grades are best utilized as draft day tiebreakers, but only when there is a difference of 20 or more points in a grade.

- Know the limitation of this element. For example, superb run-blocking grades can help vault an RB3 into the RB2 tier, but it can't move an RB3 into the RB1 tier.

Now that the preliminaries are out of the way, let's look at which offensive lines are the most likely to help your fantasy team in 2022.

Tampa Bay Buccaneers

Tampa Bay's 100 pass-blocking score was key to the Buccaneers posting a 100 overall score, but don't sell their run blocking short, as they also weighed in with a 71 run score. One key to that latter grade is the addition of run-blocking specialist Shaq Mason, who was acquired from New England in an offseason trade. That could help vault Leonard Fournette above his mid-tier RB2 average draft position (ADP) level.

Los Angeles Chargers

The Chargers spent a lot of personnel capital rebuilding their offensive line last season and added more this year by drafting Zion Johnson, who was the highest-rated guard in The Athletic's Dane Brugler's 2022 NFL Draft Guide. Johnson's varied talents will mesh perfectly with a Los Angeles blocking wall that rates well across the board. This group can help justify Austin Ekeler as an upper-tier RB1 in fantasy drafts.

Philadelphia Eagles

Jeff Stoutland is arguably the best offensive line coach in the league and specializes in run blocking. His skills are a major reason the Eagles have been the best run-blocking team in the league for the past two years despite having battled many offensive line injuries. Fantasy managers might want to consider upgrading Miles Sanders, Boston Scott and Kenneth Gainwell because of this high percentage of run blocking.

Kansas City Chiefs

For those wondering why the Chiefs might be moving more toward a run-centric offense, look no further than Kansas City's 97 grade in run blocking. This isn't a new trait, as the Chiefs also leaned on the ground game a lot in the latter half of their 2019 Super Bowl campaign. This trend seems to be overlooked in the preseason ADPs of Clyde Edwards-Helaire and Ronald Jones, so either could be a value pick.

New England Patriots

The Patriots took a lot of grief for drafting Cole Strange in the first round this year, but it's tough to criticize a club that has a 77 overall grade and a Tier 2 ranking in pass blocking. It might be tough to translate this trait into fantasy value for Patriots players given Bill Belichick's preference for using a running-back-by-committee approach, but it might give Mac Jones a lot of help on his quest for QB2 status.

Arizona Cardinals

The Kliff Kingsbury offense is much more run-centric than generally thought, as the Cardinals rank 10th in rush attempts over the three years in which Kingsbury has been Arizona's head coach. A Tier 2 ranking in run blocking and the addition of guard Will Hernandez, who played for Arizona's offensive line coach in college and thus could have a bounce-back season, should help cement James Conner's RB2 status.

Here are the offensive lines that are most likely to hinder your fantasy team in 2022:

Houston Texans

The Texans had by far the worst grades in this review, as they were the only team with a run-blocking grade lower than 15 and an overall grade lower than 21. Houston's pass blocking isn't much better, as it rates as a Tier 7. The Texans will get some help from first-round pick Kenyon Green, but this group still rates as a potential train wreck for fantasy value, so be cautious when considering any Houston player on draft day.

Chicago Bears

The Bears have a solid Tier 3 ranking in run blocking, which is a relief for David Montgomery's fantasy managers, but their pass blocking is atrocious; Chicago's pass-blocking grade of 2 is next to last in the league. The addition of Lucas Patrick from the Packers will offer some assistance, but this blocking wall is still likely to be a burden that negatively impacts the fantasy values of Justin Fields, Darnell Mooney and Cole Kmet.

Atlanta Falcons

Atlanta's passing game used to be a go-to for fantasy managers when Matt Ryan and Julio Jones were with the club, but the Falcons' aerial attack is likely to be a platoon to avoid given that Atlanta has the lowest pass-blocking grade in this analysis. That won't drop Kyle Pitts out of the TE1 tier given the lack of quality depth at that position, but it does add risk to Drake London's fantasy prospects.

Tennessee Titans

The Titans have the makings of a solid passing game with Ryan Tannehill, Robert Woods, Treylon Burks and Austin Hooper, but that quartet might not receive much assistance from Tennessee's blocking wall that has a pass-blocking grade of 4. This trait won't make those four undraftable by any means, but it does make them volatile enough to aim for the low side of their ADP values.

New York Jets

The Jets' overall grade of 25 ranks them tied for 28th in that category, but there is a silver lining here for fantasy managers, as New York posted a 48 run-blocking grade. Combine that with the addition of former 49ers guard Laken Tomlinson in free agency and it should validate Breece Hall and Michael Carter as solid fantasy selections relative to their ADPs. That positive trend doesn't take hold in the passing game, as the Jets have a pass-blocking grade of 3, so downgrade Zach Wilson, Elijah Moore, Corey Davis and rookie Garrett Wilson.

Scan here for up-to-date content on TheAthletic.com

A

IS IT TIME TO BAN KICKERS FROM FANTASY FOOTBALL?

BY JAKE CIELY AND ALEX MILLER

MY NAME'S JAKE CIELY AND I'VE BEEN CHAMPIONING #BANKICKERS FOR MY ENTIRE CAREER.

THIS ALL STARTED BACK IN 2007, WHEN ROB BIRONAS SCORED 29 FANTASY POINTS THANKS TO... 8 FIELD GOALS AND 2 EXTRA POINTS.

Bironas Fantasy Points : 29

IF YOU TAKE THE TOP 12 KICKERS BASED ON ADP EACH YEAR, THE AVERAGE FINISH IS AROUND 10 SPOTS LOWER.

#2 ADP

#12 FINISH

AND PREDICTING KICKER PERFORMANCE IS GENERALLY A FOOL'S ERRAND.

THE #BANKICKERS GAZETTE

1.6 point difference from average point totals for kickers on the extremes

EXTRA! EXTRA!

GIVEN THE FRUSTRATION AND VARIANCE, KICKERS ARE SIMPLY NOT ENJOYABLE.

HOW ABOUT THAT WEATHER?

WHO WANTS TO TALK ABOUT POLITICS?

UGH. FANTASY KICKERS.

SO JOIN ME IN THE #BANKICKERS MOVEMENT. TOGETHER, WE'LL RESTORE SANITY AND SKILL TO FANTASY FOOTBALL!

X. Mock Draft, Strategy and Analysis

The Athletic 2022 fantasy football mock draft: A surprise at No. 1, zero-RB, zero-WR strategies and more

By The Athletic Fantasy Football Staff

ADP lists are a great resource for helping fantasy football managers understand where players are expected to fall in a typical fantasy draft. Quite often, though, the fantasy drafts that you'll end up participating in won't go according to ADP plan, as individual biases/infatuations can end up drastically skewing the expected results. That's where mock drafts come in. No two drafts are alike, but a look at a mock draft can highlight just how much things can stray from the norm. With that in mind, here is a look at the results of an abbreviated (eight-round) mock draft conducted by The Athletic fantasy football crew in mid-June.

The participants were, in pick order: Renee Miller, Nando Di Fino, Arif Hasan (NFL writer, Vikings), Zac Jackson (NFL writer, Browns), Michael Beller, Jake Ciely, Andrew DeWitt, Jeff Haverlack, Gene Clemons, Brandon Funston, Brendan Roberts, Michael Salfino.

The setup was a half-PPR scoring format, with each team picking eight players, consisting of a QB, two RBs, three WRs, a TE and a flex player (RB/WR/TE).

After the draft, we asked each participant a question specific to their draft.

Question for Renee Miller: Considering you are our resident expert in bias awareness, it shouldn't come as a surprise that you went against the overwhelming industry precedent of taking Jonathan Taylor No. 1 overall, opting for Najee Harris instead. Can you explain your thought process for arriving at the conclusion that Najee warrants the top overall pick?

As I see it, there are at least five running backs who can make a case to be the first overall pick, and Taylor is certainly one of them. It's incredibly hard to repeat as the top fantasy back, so I shook things up a bit and took Harris first. With pluses and minuses for each of the top backs, from health concerns to QB/offensive or time-share concerns, Harris comes out looking like the highest-floor guy to me. Even if his snap count dips a bit from last season, he is still one of the best receiving threats out of the backfield in the league, and improved QB play for Pittsburgh should open the field up to Harris more so than in 2021.

Question for Nando Di Fino: You were the last team to draft a QB, and you opted for Trevor Lawrence over Aaron Rodgers, Kirk Cousins and Derek Carr, to name a few. Was holding out for the last QB more about the typical fungibility of the back half of the QB1 class, or was it more about believing in a major step forward for Lawrence in Year 2?

In this question alone, there are four QBs who I'd be fine either starting on a week-to-week basis or at least giving a shot to do that early and then just picking up a replacement off the wire if things go awry (bonus analysis — I'd rank Rodgers a distant fourth in this group). I think Lawrence and the Jags as a whole are going to emerge as a very talented team that just needed to get away from the dysfunction of Urban Meyer. For whatever reason, Lawrence didn't run much last year,

RD	MILLER	DI FINO	HASAN	JACKSON	BELLER	CIELY
1	Najee Harris (RB1)	Jonathan Taylor (RB2)	C. McCaffrey (RB3)	Nick Chubb (RB4)	Cooper Kupp (WR1)	Derrick Henry (RB5)
2	Kyle Pitts (TE3)	Tyreek Hill (WR9)	Mark Andrews (TE2)	Mike Evans (WR8)	Deebo Samuel (WR7)	Saquon Barkley (RB11)
3	Josh Allen (QB2)	A.J. Brown (WR10)	Aaron Jones (RB12)	L Fournette (RB13)	Keenan Allen (WR11)	Tee Higgins (WR12)
4	Elijah Mitchell (RB22)	Michael Pittman (WR17)	Josh Jacobs (RB21)	Patrick Mahomes (QB4)	Darren Waller (TE5)	Diontae Johnson (WR16)
5	Terry McLaurin (WR18)	Antonio Gibson (RB23)	Justin Herbert (QB5)	DK Metcalf (WR19)	Jalen Hurts (QB6)	Travis Etienne (RB24)
6	Darnell Mooney (WR29)	Dallas Goedert (TE8)	Michael Thomas (WR28)	Miles Sanders (RB28)	Damien Harris (RB27)	Rashod Bateman (WR27)
7	A-Ra St. Brown (WR30)	Chase Edmonds (RB29)	DeVonta Smith (WR31)	J Smith-Schuster (WR32)	C Edwards-Helaire (RB30)	Zach Ertz (TE9)
8	Hunter Renfrow (WR38)	Trevor Lawrence (QB12)	DeAndre Hopkins (WR37)	Hunter Henry (TE12)	Melvin Gordon (RB34)	Tom Brady (QB11)

RD	DEWITT	HAVERLACK	CLEMONS	FUNSTON	ROBERTS	SALFINO
1	Justin Jefferson (WR2)	Ja'Marr Chase (WR3)	Davante Adams (WR4)	Joe Mixon (RB6)	Dalvin Cook (RB7)	Austin Ekeler (RB8)
2	Alvin Kamara (RB10)	D'Andre Swift (RB9)	Lamar Jackson (QB1)	CeeDee Lamb (WR6)	Stefon Diggs (WR5)	Travis Kelce (TE1)
3	George Kittle (TE4)	James Conner (RB14)	D Montgomery (RB15)	Javonte Williams (RB16)	Ezekiel Elliott (RB17)	Mike Williams (WR13)
4	Kyler Murray (QB3)	Cam Akers (RB20)	J.K. Dobbins (RB19)	D.J. Moore (WR15)	Jaylen Waddle (WR14)	Breece Hall (RB18)
5	Jerry Jeudy (WR20)	Amari Cooper (WR21)	T.J. Hockenson (TE6)	Dalton Schultz (TE7)	Joe Burrow (QB7)	Courtland Sutton (WR22)
6	AJ Dillon (RB26)	Allen Robinson (WR26)	Chris Godwin (WR25)	Ken Walker (RB25)	Brandin Cooks (WR24)	Marquise Brown (WR23)
7	Elijah Moore (WR33)	Matthew Stafford (QB8)	C Patterson (RB31)	Gabriel Davis (WR34)	Devin Singletary (RB32)	Allen Lazard (WR35)
8	Tony Pollard (RB33)	Dawson Knox (TE11)	Adam Thielen (WR36)	Dak Prescott (QB10)	Pat Freiermuth (TE10)	Russell Wilson (QB9)

and he has the capability to get 4-5 points on rushing yards alone any given week (which is the equivalent of 100-125 passing yards). So I was fully comfortable waiting and targeting Lawrence, and if he was swiped from my grasp, I would've just happily moved on to Carr ... and then Cousins ...

Question for Arif Hasan: You went with essentially a zero-WR draft, not taking your first wideout (Michael Thomas) until Round 6. Was that intentional, and how do you feel about your WR position in the aftermath?

I actually was intending to follow a more standard strategy, waiting on flex and QB until late, but felt the options available to me there were good ahead of what looked like some cliffs in value at those positions. But I am generally pretty comfortable waiting on receiver, and this year in particular there seemed to be more value in the draft later on than there typically is. While that could just be me holding on to past production too much (two of my picks have historically been strong performers, but there are reasons to believe they won't replicate that), I still think the middle of the receiver group seems to be flatter than normal, and I wanted to take advantage of that.

Question for Zac Jackson: You cover the Cleveland Browns, so it's notable that you invested in Nick Chubb with the No. 4 pick. With the potential for a lot of changes for the Browns offense in terms of personnel and philosophy, what leads you to be so bullish about Chubb?

I believe Chubb is steady among a bunch of transition and a bunch of questions. And I also believe that he's much more than a steady runner. He's a home-run threat, and regardless of Deshaun Watson's status, I think Chubb is sitting on a monster season. If the Browns have to play half (or more than half) of the season without Watson, they'll be a run-first offense in the third year of the same system that plays to Chubb's strengths and has one of the league's better offensive lines. Even if Watson plays, the Browns will give him a better run game and offensive line than he ever previously had. Chubb's numbers were down last year because the pass offense cratered and the Browns didn't need him at the end of the year. They need him this year, and he's sitting on a big season.

Question for Michael Beller: You ended up being the lone zero-RB representative, eschewing RBs for the first five rounds. How do you think your strategy turned out, and would you have done anything differently given the benefit of hindsight?

I'm happy with how the team turned out, and I wouldn't do anything differently. I didn't set out to go zero-RB, but there was a WR at the top of my board in each of the first three rounds when the draft rolled around to me. Kyle Pitts or Josh Allen would've fallen to me in the third round in a perfect world, but them's the breaks. I like this squad.

Question for Jake Ciely: Among RBs with at least 10 games played in 2021, Saquan Barkley, whom you selected as RB10, finished outside the top 25 in half-PPR per-game scoring. Why should Barkley be considered among the top 10 at the position in 2022 drafts?

We knew Barkley would have a slow start last year with nearly every medical expert suggesting October was when we'd see the "real" Barkley. The good news is Barkley looked like himself before then with near-Barkley explosiveness and cuts in Week 3, and even more so in Week 4, when everyone exclaimed, "He's back!"

The Athletic Giants writer Dan Duggan mentioned Barkley lacked that "second gear" explosiveness after the return from a freak ankle sprain (he stepped on a defender's foot in Week 5). There was a glimmer of hope for 2022 when Barkley ripped off 102 yards on 21 carries against the Bears in Week 17, and that was without Daniel Jones at quarterback. That glimmer became a ray of hope with the addition of Alabama rookie Evan Neal to the offensive line and the arrival of Brian Daboll. Talent has never been the question. If Barkley is back to 100 percent and the offense is halfway respectable, he's one of two or three running backs with the upside to challenge Jonathan Taylor as the top running back. People will regret letting Barkley slide to the second round.

Question for Andrew DeWitt: You took Kyler Murray as the No. 3 QB off the board, ahead of the likes of Patrick Mahomes and Justin Herbert. Can you give us your glass-half-full spin on Murray's fantasy prospects for 2022?

I'm sensing a big shift back toward valuing quarterbacks, and I think we'll see even more of that this year. I used to be the guy who never took a quarterback early. When looking at teams that won the 2021 fantasy championships, they mostly had a stud quarterback who consistently put up points. Having a quarterback who consistently runs for 50-70 yards per game and can rush for touchdowns is a cheat code.

Murray severely sprained his ankle in Week 8 last year, missed three games and still finished as the No. 11 QB. He didn't run much after injuring that ankle, and I'm just gambling that Murray's injury history is a bit of bad luck and he can stay healthy this year. Plus, the addition of Hollywood Brown gives him another dangerous weapon.

Question for Jeff Haverlack: You invested in two Rams skill position players — Cam Akers, Allen Robinson — with something to prove in 2022. Were they players you were specifically targeting heading into the draft, and what are your expectations for them this season?

Not only that, but I also selected Matthew Stafford at quarterback. In redraft leagues, I'm not against stacking players from a top offense, not only because it allows me to participate in the offensive production from a high-scoring team but also because it stacks the bye weeks. One of my redraft pet peeves is being down a top player, sometimes two, across several weeks. If I have the opportunity to load many of my players into a single bye week, it lessens the long-term pain and allows me to focus on a replacement roster for just one or two bye weeks. Sure, it can make for a very challenging single week when those players are on their bye, but I've been surprisingly successful in piecing together a competitive roster for that week in the past. Robinson and Akers represented value selections and were my WR3 and RB3, respectively. While I didn't target them specifically, I couldn't pass up the opportunity to stack those players in that offense both as third options within their position. In all drafts, I'm somewhat known as a garbage man. I'm not opposed to picking up others' trash — especially when it's valuable.

Question for Gene Clemons: Josh Allen has been the top fantasy QB each of the past two seasons, but you opted to take Lamar Jackson as the top signal caller off the board. With Jackson coming off an injury-marred 2021 and with his top WR target (Marquise Brown) now in Arizona, explain your reasoning for his being the top fantasy QB in 2022?

Jackson's season seemed destined for trouble as he watched a record number of teammates miss the season or a significant amount of time because of injury before succumbing himself. With everything the Ravens and Jackson went through last season, he was still a top-10 fantasy quarterback, on track for over 4,000 passing and 1,100 rushing yards. He has built up his body this offseason, many offensive weapons will return, and the offensive line has been improved. It might be a sequel to 2019, when Jackson went full God Mode to a unanimous MVP.

Question for Brandon Funston: You had as balanced and straightforward a draft path as anyone in this mock.

Which pick gave you the most pause before you made your decision?

My Round 6 pick (Ken Walker) gave me the most pause. I was vacillating between Walker and WR Allen Robinson. Ultimately, I decided on Walker because there were a few more WRs on my target list for the following pick (Robinson, Amon-Ra St. Brown, Rashad Bateman, Darnell Mooney, Gabriel Davis) than there were RBs who I would have been happy with (Walker, Damien Harris, AJ Dillon, Miles Sanders). As it turned out, those RBs went quickly, while the WRs spread out just enough for me to get one of my guys at WR (Davis) when my next pick came around.

Question for Brendan Roberts: You had a balanced and fairly true-to-ADP draft. That said, which of your picks were you least confident in making, and why?

Ezekiel Elliott in Round 3. After a mini-run of RBs during the round, I knew I needed to take my second back, and I felt he was the most reliable (i.e., not a wild-card pick) back to fill that role. But it's not lost on me that his yards-per-game average has fallen each of the past three years after heavy usage his first three years in the league, and his backup, Tony Pollard, figures to get more work. He's a highly motivated lead back in an explosive offense, but there's a certain level of angst that comes with selecting a back who has been in obvious decline in recent years to be a fantasy starter.

Question for Michael Salfino: You took Mike Williams as the No. 13 WR off the board, well above his back-end top-20 ADP at the position. Is this a case of taking "your guy" at the turn because you have such a long time to wait for another crack at him? And with the benefit of hindsight, would you have done anything differently if given the chance?

I'm a believer in QB-centric WR rankings. So I like Mike Williams more than the market. This game is about imagining tomorrow's headlines. Can I see Mike Williams leading the NFL in touchdown catches, riding the Justin Herbert wave and posting a 1,000-plus-yard season like Mike Evans in his prime? I definitely can see that; it would not surprise me one bit. The team just gave him a monster contract, so obviously it thinks highly of him, and that's good enough for me at the Round 3-4 turn. ■■■■

Fantasy football's first tier: A refresher on why the top picks this year are so good

By Gene Clemons

With the 2022 season on the horizon, I thought it would be helpful for fantasy general managers to brush away some cobwebs and remember why the elite are worthy of the top picks. Skill, opportunity, athleticism and even new additions at quarterback should help these top-tier players keep their gold status.

Hand it off and throw it to him!

Christian McCaffrey, RB, Carolina Panthers: Everyone has seen what McCaffrey can do at the height of his powers: 1,000 yards rushing and 1,000 receiving. Although Carolina still has issues at quarterback, McCaffrey did not need stellar QB play to go 1K/1K, so there's no reason to believe struggles at the position could stop him from doing it again. He will get plenty of carries, and the targets will still be there. Expect McCaffrey to get somewhere between 20 and 25 touches per game. Never forget that in his seven-game sample last season, he averaged 4.5 yards per rush and 9.3 yards per reception. If he would have played a full season, he would have recorded another 2,000-yard-plus campaign.

Austin Ekeler, RB, Los Angeles Chargers: Ekeler is "McCaffrey Lite," but he finally played a full season as a starter, and the results were undeniable. He was just shy of 1,000 yards rushing and added 70 receptions with over 600 yards receiving. Two years ago, those numbers were flipped; he had over 500 yards rushing and 92 receptions with close to 1,000 yards receiving. And last year he added 20 touchdowns. He is a points per reception (PPR) gold mine and plays in an offense tailor-made for his skill set. Is he the best runner in the league? No. Is he the best receiver? No. But Ekeler is good at both, and because of the weapons around him, he gets to operate in relative space.

Alvin Kamara, RB, New Orleans Saints: With a healthy Jameis Winston under center last season, Kamara was RB5 and well on his way to a repeat performance of 2020, when he ran for 900-plus yards, hauled in 83 receptions for over 700 yards and scored 21 touchdowns. Without Winston, though, the entire offense was disjointed, the quarterback position was unsettled, and Kamara's receiving numbers and touchdowns suffered. The positive takeaway is Kamara looked strong while carrying the football 240 times (the highest total of his career). Even with the additions the Saints made at receiver, look for Kamara's receiving numbers to climb back toward his career pace. More competent quarterback play — and more weapons on the perimeter — means there is less attention on the box, which will likely open things up further for Kamara.

Who cares about the catches?

Jonathan Taylor, RB, Indianapolis Colts: Who needs receptions when you're carrying the ball 332 times for 1,800 yards and 18 touchdowns? Those numbers alone would have Taylor as the top PPR running back coming into the season, but just for fun, add 40 receptions for 360 yards and two additional touchdowns and you'll see why he is the clear RB1. That's what you call avoiding a sophomore slump.

So, what does he do in Year 3? Honestly, whatever he wants! The Colts have quality receivers on the outside, good tight end production and the best offensive line in the NFL. With the addition of Matt Ryan, defenses will need to pick their poison. Focusing all your attention on stopping Taylor could produce record days through the air for the Colts. There's nothing to suggest Taylor is going to fall off anytime soon, especially when he's getting 20 carries and three targets a game.

Derrick Henry, RB, Tennessee Titans: If you want to know why Derrick Henry is a top-tier running back, it's this simple: He rushed for almost 1,000 yards and 10 touchdowns in eight games last season. Then, after sustaining an injury that would have ended the season of most players in the league, he was able to return in the playoffs. Simply put, he's an alien (or maybe a cyborg). Who needs receptions and receiving yards when you are knocking on the door of 2,000 yards rushing every season? Even if you don't want to say he's the best running back in football, it's hard to argue that he hasn't been the most dominant back in the game over the past four years. Why would any fantasy GM doubt his ability to be ready to carry the load once again? The injury gave him the rest he needed after a four-year span culminating in more than 1,000 carries. The reset means many more defenders will be making business decisions before deciding to tackle Henry.

Always on target!

Cooper Kupp, WR, Los Angeles Rams: No other receiver has experienced a season like Kupp did in 2021 — and there's a good chance we have seen the best season Kupp has to offer. It is extremely difficult to duplicate 145 receptions, 1,947 yards and 16 touchdowns when many of those numbers are predicated on factors beyond his control. But if you're a fantasy GM, getting your hands on Kupp can still be the difference between winning and losing your league. Why? Targets! In his past three seasons as a starter for the Rams, Kupp has been targeted 449 times. And he's hauled in 331 of those chances. That means he catches 73.7 percent of the balls thrown in his direction. So even when the regression occurs, it will still net him 150-170 targets, which will translate to well over 100 receptions and a fantasy impact that will still be extremely high. All of that production and nobody will tell you Kupp is the most athletic — or even the most versatile. What they will tell you is he is surgical in his route running, and when you give him the opportunity, he makes you look like a genius for calling his number.

Justin Jefferson, WR, Minnesota Vikings: Jefferson is part of the influx of ultra-skilled and -athletic receivers who have taken the league by storm. After 88 catches on 125 targets for 1,400 yards and seven touchdowns in his rookie season, he followed it up with 108 catches on 167 targets for 1,616 yards and 10 touchdowns in 2021. He's tall, he has long arms and he is fast, but he can also operate inside confined spaces. He has so many ways to catch the ball that all a quarterback needs to do is get it within the catch radius and there's a good chance it will be plucked by Jefferson. It also helps him to remain free from the attention of multiple defenders because they have to worry about Adam Thielen on the other side, Irv Smith Jr. at tight end and, of course, Dalvin Cook at running back.

Big, big target!

Travis Kelce, TE, Kansas City Chiefs: Kelce was finally usurped as TE1 in 2021 after a three-season reign as the best fantasy tight end in the NFL. Does that mean it is time to punt on him? Absolutely not! It's not like Kelce did not command respect last season. His performance would have made him a top-10 receiver in the league. With Tyreek Hill taking his talents to South Beach, 20 percent of the offense's targets are free to be dished out by the best quarterback in the NFL. Something tells me the Patrick Mahomes-to-Kelce combination will be lighting up scoreboards in 2022. If Kelce was targeted 134 times last season, how many targets will he see now that Hill is no longer there? ▬▬▬

The No. 1 pick is overrated, according to five years of ADP and end-of-season data

By Michael Salfino

This is another draft season where people are thrilled to get the first pick so they can grab a running back who scored 20 TDs last year — and they're despondent if they pick late. But do draft results back up the notion that the first slot is such a difference-maker? Are the PPR points per game from that slot so much better than the averages of the other slots?

No, they are not. In fact, the first slot would not even be my pick if I had first choice of any slot. Keep in mind we're looking at just points per game to mute the impact of injuries, which tend to be random.

Looking back on five years of ADP data courtesy of FantasyData, the first round is regression alley. Granted, we should expect this, as we're drafting the players typically who were dominant scorers the year before. Still, even if we know full well they're going to score less, the odds are good they'll score more than we can expect from the rest of the field.

If we chart the picks at each slot the last five years, we see that the first four slots average 19.5 PPR points per game the season the players are drafted; the middle four 17.7; and the last four 17.5. Interestingly, the No. 6 slot the past five years has averaged 21.7 points in the period — the highest of any position. So you can make a decent case that historically, at least in the past five years, the sixth slot is most desirable. Here are those slot averages from 2014-2019:

First round fantasy PPG, last 5 years

PICK	PPR PPG
1	21.3
2	16
3	20
4	20.8
5	17.3
6	21.7
7	15.1
8	16.7
9	16.8
10	19.3
11	18.8
12	15.2

The sixth pick is the only one that has outperformed prior year points — in other words, the player taken sixth scored 18.5 PPR PPG the year before versus 21.7 "this" year. The fourth and 11th slots have broken even. The 10th is break even, basically, and every pick in that slot the past five drafts has generally been a WR (there's a lesson here).

Position-wise, the vast majority of first-round picks have been RBs. They are down about 9 percent in points per game. Wide receivers are not much better, down 8.3 percent.

The worst pick by far the past two years, measured by the points per game you draft versus what you get (aka the biggest bust position), has been No. 2 — down 31 percent on average.

Of course, regression must be expected, looking at the data. We're probably not getting the type of return on a per-game basis that the player we drafted just delivered the season prior. The thing that makes you a first-round pick, especially one in the upper reaches of the round, also sets you up for a fall. Gravity, as the song says, always wins.

This year, I like being in the middle of the draft (Nos. 5, 6, 7). There's not much expected regression (19.4 to 18.2), and you also have a crack at a running back who has a chance to be the No. 1 RB or the top wide receiver in the draft — if you feel that Ja'Marr Chase is basically in the same bucket as Cooper Kupp (which is reasonable). ▬▬▬

Do not draft: Kyle Pitts, DK Metcalf and more fantasy football players to avoid

By Dominick Petrillo

Every year there are players we stay away from in fantasy football. Whether it be for fear of injury or the player being on a bad team, there are reasons for all of these decisions.

Of course, not all of these decisions work out for us. Sometimes a player we think will bust ends up busting out instead. But I am still taking a stand. Unless the ADP of the players I've listed here drop, they will not find a place on my fantasy teams this season.

Amari Cooper, WR, CLE — We know Cooper has skills. You aren't picked in the first round of the NFL draft without having talent. The reason Dallas traded him for a bag of balls is to clear money to sign others ... like Michael Gallup. This was made easier for the Cowboys to swallow as Cooper was coming off his worst season — 68 receptions, 865 receiving yards, eight TDs. With young star CeeDee Lamb under control for at least four more seasons and Gallup, although coming off a major knee injury, still cheaper than Cooper, it made sense for the Browns to go after him. By doing so, they have paired him up with new quarterback Deshaun Watson to start another rebuild of the Cleveland offense.

But how long will Watson sit if he does get suspended? This is the key factor in not wanting to pay the top 20 WR price for Cooper. If Watson does miss a large chunk of time, Cleveland will count on Jacoby Brissett to lead the offense, and he's proven to be less than inspiring. This will mean the team relies even more on the run game of Nick Chubb and Kareem Hunt. The team rushed on 46 percent of offensive plays in 2021, and with Brissett behind center, this could climb above the 50 percent threshold. If this happens, and if the Browns lean more heavily on newly high-paid TE David Njoku, there is not much meat left on the bone for Cooper to thrive.

Cooper, pending a shocking trade or signing, is the WR1 for the Browns. But with the uncertainty at the QB position, what is this really worth in 2022? Not a pick in the first four rounds.

J.K. Dobbins, RB, BAL — With Dobbins and Gus Edwards both missing the 2021, season, the Ravens went from a run-first team in 2020 (55 percent run), to a pass-first team in 2021 (43.6 percent run). With both players back, and hopefully healthy, the Ravens should get back to their bread and butter. But this also means more rush work for Lamar Jackson, who also took a step back in rush production in 2021 while concentrating on the pass game due to the injuries in the backfield.

As a rookie in 2020, Dobbins had what was seen to be a good rookie season. In 15 games, he compiled 805 rush yards and nine TDs on 134 rushes. But a lot has changed since then. LT Ronnie Stanley has been injured again and LT Orlando Brown Jr. was dealt to Kansas City. Although Marquise Brown has been the WR1 for Baltimore and is now in Arizona, TE Mark Andrews has also taken a leap forward in production for the team.

With Edwards, Dobbins and Stanley all coming back from major injury, the run game will look a bit different than it did in 2020, the last time all three were on the field together. And this is the hesitation I feel in taking Dobbins in the beginning of Round 3 of drafts. He might get there. But it will take a while for him to get there. By the time he does, you could have gotten him from his disgruntled manager, while drafting someone else in the third round.

Ezekiel Elliott, RB, DAL — The past two seasons for Elliott have been the two worst of his career. After having a career-low 244 carries and 979 yards in 15 games in 2020, Elliott finished with 237 carries and 1,002 rush yards in 17 games in 2021.

While an iron man to start his career, nagging injuries have also begun to catch up with Elliott. As a result, the team has started to transition to more of a committee with Elliott and Tony Pollard, who is seemingly more explosive at this stage.

While Elliott only averaged 4.2 YPC in 2021, Pollard was able to average 5.5 on 130 carries. His career average of 5.1 YPC is also a full half yard higher than the career mark of Elliott.

With Dallas no longer having the top offensive line in the NFL, it will be incumbent on the running back behind it to be elusive. This more fits the mold of Pollard. Elliott will be there. His bloated contract makes it a certainty. But Pollard could see more work. At RB14 and with an ADP at the end of the second round, this is just a bit too high for my liking, especially considering the other options at this point of the draft.

Travis Kelce, TE, KC — Kelce has been the best tight end in the NFL since the career fade of Rob Gronkowski. There have been contenders in recent years in George Kittle, Andrews, and Darren Waller, but Kelce has been able to hold them all at bay. This might just be the year where things change a bit.

While Kelce is still great, at 32, he is on the older end of the spectrum when it comes to elite playmakers. To add to this, Tyreek Hill was traded to Miami. This means teams will be able to focus more on Kelce than in previous years. Even with JuJu Smith-Schuster and Marquez Valdes-Scantling joining the fray, Kelce will still be the first option for Patrick Mahomes. And unlike previous seasons, he will also get the coverage commensurate with this level of attention.

In studies done researching lost targets, those targets have been shown to not go to other receivers. In most cases, the beneficiaries of lost targets are running backs. So, while Clyde Edwards-Helaire may be in line for more work and finally a breakout season, Kelce might be in line for his standard season. While his 2021 numbers of 92 receptions, 1,125 yards and nine TDs are great, they might be just a bit too high for what he will get in 2022. Taking this at the beginning of the second round, where his ADP projects, is too rich for my blood. I would rather pass on him for a similar production level further down in drafts. This way I can focus early on the RB and WR positions.

DK Metcalf, WR, SEA — With Russell Wilson in Seattle, Metcalf had an elite down-field thrower to pair with his elite down-field abilities. With the wildly inconsistent Drew Lock (or Geno Smith) trying to get him the ball, things do not look good. And this is coming from a blind guy.

The Seahawks, for the first time in many years, are a bad team. The Seahawks have tried to fix the offensive line by adding Charles Cross in the NFL Draft. But the rest of the team has gotten significantly worse since the final game of 2021. With the limited route-running repertoire of Metcalf, expect Tyler Lockett to be the main threat in this offense. Metcalf finished as the fantasy WR11 last season. In 2022, he will be lucky to finish top 20.

Darnell Mooney, WR, CHI — Mooney has skillful hands and great speed. Speed to burn in fact. But he has never been the No. 1 in an offense. This is not the offense you want to have to attempt such a feat.

Allen Robinson has departed to the Rams, and Jimmy Graham has just ... well, disappeared. Cole Kmet will need to make a large leap forward and David

Mock Draft, Strategy and Analysis

Montgomery will also be counted on to finish as a top 5 running back like he did in 2020 (RB4). Outside of Mooney, Kmet and Montgomery, there's not much left for inexperienced QB Justin Fields to work with. In his second season, Fields will also have a new head coach, new offensive coordinator and new offensive scheme to learn. All while trying to get comfortable with a new set of players.

The dearth of surrounding talent to go with all these changes will affect Fields. But it will also affect Mooney, who will find it a challenge to get open downfield for the big play for which he is known.

This is a tough situation all around in Chicago. From quarterback to offensive line to wide receiver, the 2022 season is going to be a learning process. Let someone else get angry while they try to figure it out.

Kyle Pitts, TE, ATL — The highest-drafted tight end ever, Pitts was anything but a tight end during his rookie season. With Julio Jones traded to Tennessee and Calvin Ridley missing games for personal reasons, Pitts spent much of his time as a wide receiver, something that, at 6-foot-6 and 245 pounds, he was uniquely qualified to handle. Although he only managed one TD, his 68 receptions and 1,026 yards both ranked among the top 3 for a rookie TE in NFL history.

In Year 2, things could be far different. He will once again be the No. 1 target for the Atlanta offense, one which is no longer run by former MVP Matt Ryan. After a failed attempt to lure Deshaun Watson, the team was forced to trade Ryan to Indianapolis. With this move, it left the Falcons in desperate need of a replacement. They ended up settling for Marcus Mariota. Although his best seasons came in Tennessee with Arthur Smith as his offensive coordinator, he no longer has a similarly talented rest to lean on.

Pitts will be counted on to do far more in 2022 than he was as a rookie. With not only Ridley missing the season but Russell Gage now in Tampa Bay, Pitts is the clear top option. Cordarrelle Patterson was a remarkable story in 2021, but until he can prove himself for more than one season, expectations must be tempered that he can repeat.

During his Pro Bowl rookie season, Pitts was on the field for 74 percent of the Falcons' offensive snaps. This is a lofty number for a tight end in today's NFL. Even the best tight end in the NFL, Kelce, was only on the field for 77 percent of snaps after being on the field for 81 percent in 2020. This means the on-field activity for Pitts will need to increase without an increase in snap count. On top of this, after appearing on the field in 774 snaps in 2021, Pitts is likely to be on the field less in 2022 just based on the talent on the Falcons. There will be more three-and-out possessions and less sustained drives behind Mariota. With all of these factors in play, Pitts makes a dangerous selection in Round 4 of a fantasy draft. Similar to my take on Kelce, I would rather take a high-end wide receiver or RB2 in this spot. ▬▬

The offseason's 5 biggest moves: What do they mean for fantasy football?

By Gene Clemons

One player being traded in the offseason can cause a ripple effect. For instance, Tyreek Hill's being traded to Miami has all types of questions attached to it. Who will gobble up those targets? Will Travis Kelce be the same without Hill? How will it affect Patrick Mahomes? Will Hill cut into the targets for Jaylen Waddle and Mike Gesicki? And will this make Tua Tagovailoa a viable fantasy option?

The league is full of moves like these, and identifying the most significant transactions — and how far their ripples go — can give you a leg up in your leagues.

Matt Ryan traded to the Colts

The Falcons tried to land Deshaun Watson in a trade and failed. What they succeeded in doing, however, was alienating their future ring of honor quarterback, Matt Ryan. He was quickly shipped to the Colts, a team looking for better quarterback play after the Carson Wentz experiment flopped. Although Ryan is the most immobile quarterback the team has had since Peyton Manning, he is probably also the most accurate and poised in the pocket. If he can play to his standard, it can open even bigger running lanes and check-down opportunities for Jonathan Taylor and Nyheim Hines — and turn Michael Pittman Jr. into a legit WR1. The move hurts the value of Falcons tight end Kyle Pitts but could help the backfield, because a quarterback like new Falcons acquisition Marcus Mariota is a plus in the run game, which gives Atlanta a chance to play 11-on-11 as Mariota keeps opposing defenses honest.

Allen Robinson joins the Rams

The Rams have no interest in being a one-year wonder. They have made that crystal clear based on the T-shirts they rocked that said "F those picks!" So they signed Robinson, who had been floundering under bad management, suspect coaching and uninspiring quarterback play in Chicago. Now Robinson gets to fill the role occupied by Robert Woods and Odell Beckham Jr.

The targets are going to be there for Robinson opposite (or next to) Cooper Kupp, who will undoubtedly get the lion's share of the attention. It elevates Robinson's ceiling in fantasy but it also keeps Kupp's value high, as defenses are unable to key in on him without allowing Robinson to have a record day. Matthew Stafford should continue to put up top-tier numbers with Robinson, who will represent the new blood necessary to keep a team that has reached the pinnacle motivated to make a second run.

Russell Wilson traded to the Broncos

For the record, there's no earthly understanding of why you would want to get rid of a player the caliber of Wilson in his prime for ... DRAFT PICKS! But what do we know? We're just consumers who watch teams with no legit franchise quarterback flounder, hoping to "Forrest Gump" into a franchise guy like the Seahawks did with Wilson years ago. It was a decent haul for Seattle, but this changes everything for the Broncos, who have an abundance of weapons — weapons that have not been properly unlocked over the past couple of years because of conservative play calling and suspect quarterbacking.

Wilson brings in a legitimate run element, which means defenses have to account for him. That's great news for Javonte Williams and Melvin Gordon, who will both probably continue to be fantasy plays on a weekly basis. It also means that Courtland Sutton, Tim Patrick and Jerry Jeudy all have plus value with Wilson delivering the ball. Wilson remains as a viable weekly play with so many weapons at his disposal and being coached by Nathaniel Hackett, an offensive-minded head coach who understands how to "Let Russ Cook," having come from a staff that managed Aaron Rodgers.

Davante Adams traded to the Raiders

Adams got paid this offseason, but it also means he is going to learn what life is like without Aaron Rodgers. In steps Derek Carr, who has become one of the more level-headed and consistent quarterbacks in the NFL despite years of having to overcome the negative stigma of his brother's NFL failures.

Adams will upgrade the receiving corps of the Raiders, who have really been without a dynamic playmaker outside. His arrival is great for tight end Darren Waller, because the defense can't condense on him. And slot machine Hunter Renfrow, who gets to have the focus taken away from him, should also see an uptick in production. Obviously, Carr gets a boost because this is the best receiver he has ever been able to play with (all respect to Antonio Brown, but he wanted no part of the Raiders). Even ex-Chiefs receiver Demarcus Robinson should see a boost from the arrival of Adams.

For the Packers, it means Allen Lazard, rookie Christian Watson and tight end Robert Tonyan get a boost from the massive number of targets that are now available. Can free-agent receiver Sammy Watkins be a legitimate option for the Packers? We shall soon find out!

Tom Brady retires, then unretires

When Tom Brady retired, the fantasy future of the Buccaneers was up in the air. What would happen to the value of Mike Evans and Chris Godwin? Luckily for Buccaneers fans, the organization, and fantasy football players, Brady went home and soon decided he could let the kids get another year of life under their belt before dad was unleashed on them. Now with Brady officially back, Evans and Godwin are both big fantasy producers, and former Atlanta Falcon wideout Russell Gage may even be fantasy-relevant. Tight end Cam Brate will be the biggest beneficiary of Rob Gronkowski's retirement (and remember that O.J. Howard signed with Buffalo in free agency). ▬▬

Who will be 2022's biggest fantasy surprises? This year's Deebo Samuel, Matthew Stafford and more

By Brandon Howard

The 2022 NFL football season is near, and it's time to begin identifying players who are capable of fantasy success that mirrors that of last year's top performers. Last season we saw Deebo Samuel break out as a "wide back," sixth-round rookie running back Elijah Mitchell rush for nearly 1,000 yards, 13-year veteran Matthew Stafford win a Super Bowl with his new team and second-year quarterback Joe Burrow make a Super Bowl appearance.

Following coaching changes, free agency and the 2022 NFL Draft, some players will certainly be in position to duplicate the individual production of the above-mentioned players. They might not experience the team success of Stafford and Burrow, but their numbers will definitely help your fantasy team post points in abundance this season.

This year's Deebo Samuel is ... Curtis Samuel

Before signing with Washington during the 2021 offseason, Curtis Samuel had just posted his best season in the NFL. He racked up 851 yards on 77 receptions while adding 200 yards and two touchdowns on 41 carries. Last year he dealt with a groin injury that limited him to five games in which he caught six balls for 27 yards, but he vows that will not happen to him again. By all accounts, Samuel is feeling great, and he looks every bit as fast as he did during his time with the Buckeyes.

Speaking of his time at Ohio State, multiple Buckeyes coaches and graduate assistants told me upon his arrival on campus that he was their best running back recruit since Maurice Clarett. Though OSU used him in more of a Percy Harvin role, he was a gifted ball carrier. Samuel had 97 carries for 771 yards and 74 receptions

for 865 yards in his final season with the Buckeyes. He has shown flashes of being the same back who put up big numbers on the ground at OSU during his time in the NFL, but he has yet to put it all together. Entering his fifth season at just 25 years old, look for Samuel to have his best year yet.

With the likes of Terry McLaurin and Jahan Dotson on the outside, the Washington Commanders will likely use a ton of 11 personnel with Samuel holding down the slot. If the opposing defenses are in their money packages (dime, nickel personnel), it wouldn't shock me to see the Commanders motion Samuel into the backfield to line up with Antonio Gibson in split-back or in a broken I formation.

As far as his success at wide receiver, it will be important to see just how healthy and consistent quarterback Carson Wentz can be during the season.

This year's Elijah Mitchell is ... Isaiah Spiller

Isaiah Spiller might not be the size-speed prospect Mitchell was, but he was my No. 1 back in this year's draft. Much like Mitchell, Spiller landed on a team that looks to be well on its way to becoming a perennial power. The Los Angeles Chargers offense features a variety of dynamic threats: budding star quarterback Justin Herbert, wide receivers Keenan Allen and Mike Williams, and the versatile Austin Ekeler in the backfield. Though Ekeler put up 911 yards on the ground and 647 yards receiving in 2021, the Chargers still felt the need to address the running back position in the draft.

With pick No. 123 this year, the Chargers selected Spiller out of Texas A&M. Though he doesn't possess Mitchell's breakaway speed, he can be every bit as productive. Spiller has a knack for knowing when to be patient and when to explode through the hole. He's also every bit as good as Najee Harris when it comes to setting up blocks. He has excellent vision and enough quickness and burst to capitalize on what he sees. Despite hauling in just 25 catches last season, Spiller is a natural pass catcher and a dependable checkdown option. Ekeler might have put up excellent numbers last season, but in a way, his stats can be viewed as empty calories. In tight games, the Chargers were unable to engage in their four-minute offense to close out games.

When teams forced them to run against heavier fronts, the Chargers relied heavily on Herbert's arm to finish games, which isn't a sustainable practice for any QB and/or offense. The Chargers brass knew they needed to do a better job of closing out games to make the playoffs, and that's why Spiller was brought in. Expect him to be the Chargers' go-to guy in the waning moments of games this season. It appears he was drafted to be the Chargers' closer, and I'm positive he'll look like a world-beater in the fourth quarter if deployed in such fashion.

This year's Matthew Stafford is … Russell Wilson

Russell Wilson is the latest high-profile quarterback to leave the team he was drafted by to become the face of another franchise. This offseason the Broncos surrendered their 2022 first-, second-, fourth- and fifth-round picks, along with their 2023 first- and second-round picks, to acquire Wilson. They also parted with tight end Noah Fant, quarterback Drew Lock and defensive end Shelby Harris to become the highest bidder in the Wilson sweepstakes.

Wilson comes to Denver with more postseason experience than Stafford had, and his winning ways are guaranteed to rub off on his young receiving corps. With Courtland Sutton's size and speed, Jerry Jeudy's route running and shiftiness after the catch and K.J. Hamler reportedly back to full speed after hip and knee injuries, Wilson will have little trouble moving the ball down the field. With Wilson at the helm, the Broncos will rely heavily on the scramble drill. Wilson is one of the best QBs in the NFL when it comes to post-snap recognition and secondary reaction skills.

Few secondaries will be able to keep up with the Broncos' top three receivers once Wilson begins buying time and scrambling outside the pocket. Additionally, Denver has two good running backs in Melvin Gordon and Javonte Williams. Rushing lanes will be wider for them this season, as defenses will have to keep the backside closed at all times to account for the Broncos' newly acquired, dual-threat quarterback. Whether it's on the ground or through the air, the Broncos offense is poised to put up big numbers in 2022.

This year's Joe Burrow is … Trey Lance

Burrow played a major part in getting the Cincinnati Bengals to the Super Bowl last season. Though there isn't a second-year quarterback who is capable of duplicating Burrow's Super Bowl run, Trey Lance is the lone quarterback heading into his second season who is set up for long-term success. He has protection up front, a run game and plenty of talent on the flanks. If he wins the starting job over Jimmy Garoppolo, his running ability is going to make the 49ers offense that much more dynamic.

Though he endured his fair share of struggles as a rookie, it's important to remember Lance played essentially one season at North Dakota State. It was known among NFL scouts that it would take Lance some time to assimilate to the NFL. Still, he has the requisite tools to become a top-10 QB. Lance has a cannon for an arm, retains information and is a tremendous athlete. Despite his raw ability, he'll need to improve in several areas if he hopes to get the 49ers back into the playoffs in 2022.

Lance will need to do a better job of eliminating sacks and pressures this season. He can accomplish this by making better pre-snap reads/adjustments and refraining from dropping his eyes and staring at the rush. Much like Tua Tagovailoa, he'll also need to learn what an open wide receiver looks like in the NFL, compared with college. Last but certainly not least, Lance is somewhat reckless as a runner. He'll need to learn how to take prudent risks while protecting himself when he takes off and runs. ▰▰▰

Brandon Howard's scouting report: 3 under-25-year-olds primed for a breakout in 2022

By Brandon Howard

It's never easy to project what will become of some of the younger players in the league. Numerous variables could catapult them to stardom — or prevent them from reaching their apex. Whether it be offensive philosophy, a lack of supporting talent, quality depth at their position or unsuitable usage, it seems there are plenty of reasons for a young NFL player to fail. However, several things are working in the best interests of high-round players that increase their chances of having success.

Now more than ever, coaches are implementing college schemes into their offense and acknowledging they work at the pro level. This enables coaches to ease young players into the league by asking them to execute concepts they're already familiar with. In addition to familiarity with offensive philosophy, front offices are finding success by pairing their quarterback with the same weapons they had on the flanks during their collegiate years.

From a historical perspective, some teams have done a better job developing talent than others, but that doesn't mean perennial cellar dwellers can't find a way to prep their young players for success in 2022. Some of the teams and players I believe are ready for a breakout season just may surprise you.

Jalen Hurts, QB, Philadelphia Eagles

Since taking over for Carson Wentz, Jalen Hurts has been subject to criticism that does not reflect his play. I wish I knew what it would take to convince Eagles fans to cut the young man some slack. In his first full season as Philadelphia's starting quarterback, Hurts led the Eagles to a 9-8 record. He also made his first playoff appearance in 2021 at just 23 years old, making him the youngest quarterback in Eagles franchise history to start a playoff game. Instead of lauding him for accomplishing such a feat so early in his career, fans and media took every opportunity during the Eagles' 31-15 wild-card loss to Tom Brady and the Tampa Bay Buccaneers to highlight his shortcomings.

Never mind the fact Hurts was essentially a rookie in 2021, as last season was his first full campaign as an NFL starting quarterback. While we're at it, let's summarily dismiss the fact that outside of his former Alabama teammate Devonta Smith, his receivers were not very detailed in their route running. Multiple times on vertical routes, they were unable to hold the red line, which left Hurts very little space to drop the ball in between the sideline and the numbers. After seeing marginal growth from their receiving corps, the Eagles traded their first- and third-round picks in the 2022 NFL Draft to acquire A.J. Brown. Brown is as physical as they come, and I think it's safe to surmise he'll rarely, if ever, be bumped off the red line.

In addition to acquiring a top-notch talent on the flanks, Hurts, who completed 61.3 percent of his passes last season, has worked to improve upon his accuracy during the offseason. He's emphasized tying his feet to his eyes, which facilitates better lower-body mechanics and subsequently — improved accuracy. Lastly, Hurts is finally working in the same system for two consecutive seasons for the first time since high school. For that reason, I fully expect Hurts to prove to his critics and Eagles fans that he is the long-term answer at quarterback while enjoying the best season of his young NFL career.

D'Andre Swift, RB, Detroit Lions

Despite the fact D'Andre Swift failed to go over 1,000 yards rushing in 2021, he was able to rack up over 1,000 yards of total offense. Swift rushed for 617 yards and five touchdowns while hauling in 62 receptions for 452 yards and two touchdowns, and it could've been more but he had a few things working against him. For starters, Jamaal Williams is not a better running back than Swift and should never come close to having more carries than Swift.

Unfortunately, Williams finished 2021 with 153 carries compared with Swift's 151. A big part of the reason Williams has taken on the role of leader in Detroit is that his personality mirrors Lions head coach Dan Campbell. However, fantasy GMs should not allow Williams' favor within the organization to deter them from incorporating Swift into their lineup. Covering the Dolphins, I had the pleasure of watching and admiring Campbell's talent evaluation prowess from afar. He loves guys who play violently (like Williams), but he's not nearly as opposed to playing the guy who has a little more flair and pizazz to their game as I originally thought. As smart as Campbell is, I firmly believe he'll eventually conclude that Swift needs more touches.

Last season the Lions' offensive line was ostensibly one of their strongest units — at least until injuries set in. Left tackle Taylor Decker suffered a spiral fracture to his finger, which cost him the first eight games of the season. Decker's injury forced rookie Penei Sewell to move to left tackle while Decker was out. Center Frank Ragnow was lost for the season after Week 4 due to turf toe, and left guard Jonah Jackson and right guard Halapoulivaati Vaitai missed a total of three games combined. With that said, it's hard for an offensive line to jell when multiple guys are playing out of position. With Taylor Decker (LT), Jonah Jackson (LG), Frank Ragnow (C), Halapoulivaati Vaitai (RG) and Penei Sewell (RT) all back in the fold, expect this unit to become one of the best in the league and open massive holes for Swift in 2022.

Rashod Bateman, WR, Baltimore Ravens

After Marquise Brown was traded to the Arizona Cardinals, Rashod Bateman will now step into the WR1 role for the Baltimore Ravens. Baltimore selected Bateman with the 27th pick in the 2021 NFL Draft, but he spent a large portion of his rookie season recovering from a groin injury. Though he played 12 games, he did not have a ton of time to develop chemistry with quarterback Lamar Jackson. Despite Bateman and Jackson's limited time together, Bateman managed to put up a solid rookie season. He finished the season

Mock Draft, Strategy and Analysis

with 515 yards and one touchdown on 46 receptions and he'll likely do a lot more damage in Year 2.

At 6-foot-1, 193 pounds, Bateman is an underrated athlete. His college film shows he's plenty fast given the way he ate up cushion when Big 10 cornerbacks played off of him. Nonetheless, there are plenty of talent evaluators who scout the helmet and not the player. And to be honest, when's the last time we had a burner wide receiver out of Minnesota? That's why it was a shock to scouts and coaches in attendance when he was timed as fast as 4.39 in the 40-yard dash during the Gophers' pro day. Bateman's speed is a big plus, but he's also an exceptional route runner who does a tremendous job of essentially turning into a running back once he gets his hands on the football. My favorite part about his game is that he's capable of playing all three wide receiver positions. He lined up outside and inside for the Gophers and had success no matter where he was on the field.

I look forward to the Ravens using him all over the field but especially in the slot or reduced splits that allow him to run option routes in the middle of the field, where Lamar Jackson has a great deal of success. Bateman will get his fair share of work on the outside, but when lined up in the slot or in a reduced split, defenses will have to pick their poison. Will they pay closer attention to Mark Andrews down the seam or will they carry Bateman down the field in hopes of preventing the big play? This is a shell game that could pay big dividends for Bateman this season as he continues to build upon the chemistry he began building with Jackson during offseason workouts. ▄▄▄

Deep sleepers: Six under-the-radar picks who could pay big dividends

By Brandon Marianne Lee

So often we see these sleeper articles and it's the same people. It makes you wonder if there really are sleepers anymore.

We all have the same access to the numbers, so the guys with great metrics can't be true sleepers. For those of you who want numbers only, this article isn't for you. To find real gems, you need to explore context and look at factors that could change the numbers in the future. I'm going to get a little contrarian and actually go deep to get our creativity flowing. That's how you win. Be bold. Be different.

Seattle Quarterback (TBD)

Yep, I support you taking a chance on Geno Smith or Drew Lock. Why? Because they still have DK Metcalf and Tyler Lockett. They still have a strong run game that has to be defended, regardless of matchup, because you know Pete Carroll is all about pounding the rock. And both Smith and Lock have the ability to move, so there will be some extra fantasy points to bring up the fantasy floor. Neither has played consistent football recently, so there are no numbers, just circumstances. That's scary, so few will take a chance on either of these players. You can grab them at the very end of your draft or plug them in as a DFS bargain.

I especially love picking up Smith at the end of SuperFlex league drafts. As the preseason goes on, if it looks like Lock is coming up, switch them out. For now, Carroll is leaning toward Geno. And by the way, Smith's last start was Week 8 of last year. He scored 22.6 fantasy points in four-point touchdown pass scoring leagues, with two touchdowns via the air and one on the ground against the Jaguars. Points will happen (especially in juicy matchups).

Chase Edmonds, Miami, RB

Chase Edmonds is the highest-ranked player on this list, but he's a starter still going outside of the top 32 running backs off the board. Let's start with the other running backs in Miami. First, Raheem Mostert is still healing and hopes to be ready for Week 1. He will likely have a role, but he's 30, he's never started more than eight games in a season and the last time he scored 10 or more fantasy points in a game was in Week 12 of 2020 (10.3 PPR points). Myles Gaskin has never been consistent. Only once has he rushed for more than 50 yards in back-to-back games in his three years with Miami. And Sony Michel is a guy who flashes, causing the fantasy community to get all hot and bothered, but then he quickly fades away.

Edmonds is getting paid at least double the amount of every other back on this team (his cap number is $5.5 million and Gaskin is second at $2.56 million). Edmonds has durability issues, but he's an experienced pass-catching back (who averaged 4.4 targets per game last year — 10th among RBs), and if they rotate in the other three backs on early downs to keep Edmonds in tiptop shape, he'll end up being a perfect seventh/eighth-round pick.

Brian Robinson, Washington, RB

Shared backfields are a huge part of the game, so instead of only focusing on the stud backups, open your mind to the less flashy part of a running back duo. Last year, Antonio Gibson struggled with a pesky shin injury. He also had a toe injury toward the end of the year, the same injury type that kept him out for two games as a rookie. In his two years in the league, despite missing time, Gibson has the seventh-most carries. He's also tied for the most lost fumbles in that time. Playing through injuries and fumbles often go hand-in-hand, so that's not a judgment, rather a telltale sign that we should listen when coach Ron Rivera says he's looking to use Gibson and rookie Brian Robinson as a one-two-punch like his original "running back by committee," DeAngelo Williams and Jonathan Stewart.

In 2011, Williams carried the ball 155 times and Stewart logged 142 carries. Back when those two were splitting carries, the bell-cow running back was the norm, but now so many teams divvy up run duties that we don't even blink an eye at that type of usage. The big difference, and why I'm loving Robinson this year, is that Gibson's ADP puts him in the fifth round and Robinson goes in the 15th round. So ... who would you rather? Note: We have a J.D. McKissic pass-catching wrench to keep in mind, but that's what is going to keep Robinson's ADP low. Consider that a gift.

Van Jefferson, Los Angeles Rams, WR

You can get a true sleeper from a Super Bowl-winning team? I guess so.

The Rams still want Van Jefferson, a former second-round pick, to be a large part of their future. His father was a player and a coach. Jefferson is known for his work ethic. Again, we're looking for things that go beyond numbers. But, hey, let's also talk about numbers. He broke his foot so he couldn't do the 40 at the combine, but at the Senior Bowl, he clocked a suburb max speed of 21.05 mph. Last year, he caught 50 balls on 81 targets for 802 yards and six touchdowns while playing in 80 percent of the team's snaps. The Rams used three-wide receiver sets on a league-high 86 percent of their snaps. It's very easy to imagine a world in which Jefferson becomes a 1,000-yard and/or 10-touchdown player. And you can get him in Round 16. Outrageous.

Braxton Berrios, New York Jets, WR

A fun piece of trivia: Who was the 11th highest-scoring wide receiver from week 15 to 17 last year in PPR formats? I know you know, but this proves the Braxton Berrios invisible man routine is wild. Friends, the Jets let Jamison Crowder walk, and Crowder was the leading fantasy wideout for the team for two years running. All through camp, there's been talk about Berrios and his leadership and his connection with Zach Wilson. The Athletic Jets beat writer, Connor Hughes, labels Berrios "clearly still Wilson's safety blanket." And he's free! He is typically undrafted at this point, with an Underdog ADP at the 17th round. The Jets' outside receivers are young, and while teeming with potential, they will need to develop. If you're like me thinking, "Hmmm ... isn't it a little late for a breakout?" Well, he's only 26 with very little mileage. He has so much more potential than his ADP, especially in PPR formats.

Cole Kmet, Chicago, TE

Breakout candidate Cole Kmet basically has it all. It's his third season and he's only 23 years old, the fourth-youngest starting tight end in the league (only Kyle Pitts, Tommy Tremble and Brevin Jordan are younger). He has the easiest schedule for his position. The touchdown-stealing veteran, Jimmy Graham, is no longer with the team. Despite being on the field for 83 percent of the team's snaps last year, as opposed to Graham's 27 percent, Kmet scored zero touchdowns. That will change. The "under the radar" element here is that waiting on a tight end is a strategy I would suggest this year. Get two later tight ends with upside and one will hit, or you can play the matchups each week.

There is a lot of uncertainty at the top of this position whether it's age (Travis Kelce), quarterback concerns (Kyle Pitts) or usage questions after the team's offseason moves (Darren Waller). Instead, I would use your top picks for the other positions and keep your eye out for the Kmet-type plays and target them later. His current Underdog ADP puts him in the 12th round. So even if he doesn't pop, who cares? You usually drop the players you take in Rounds 12-plus for your waiver picks. Shoot your shot. ▬▬▬

Mock Draft, Strategy and Analysis

A

XI. Expert Roundtables

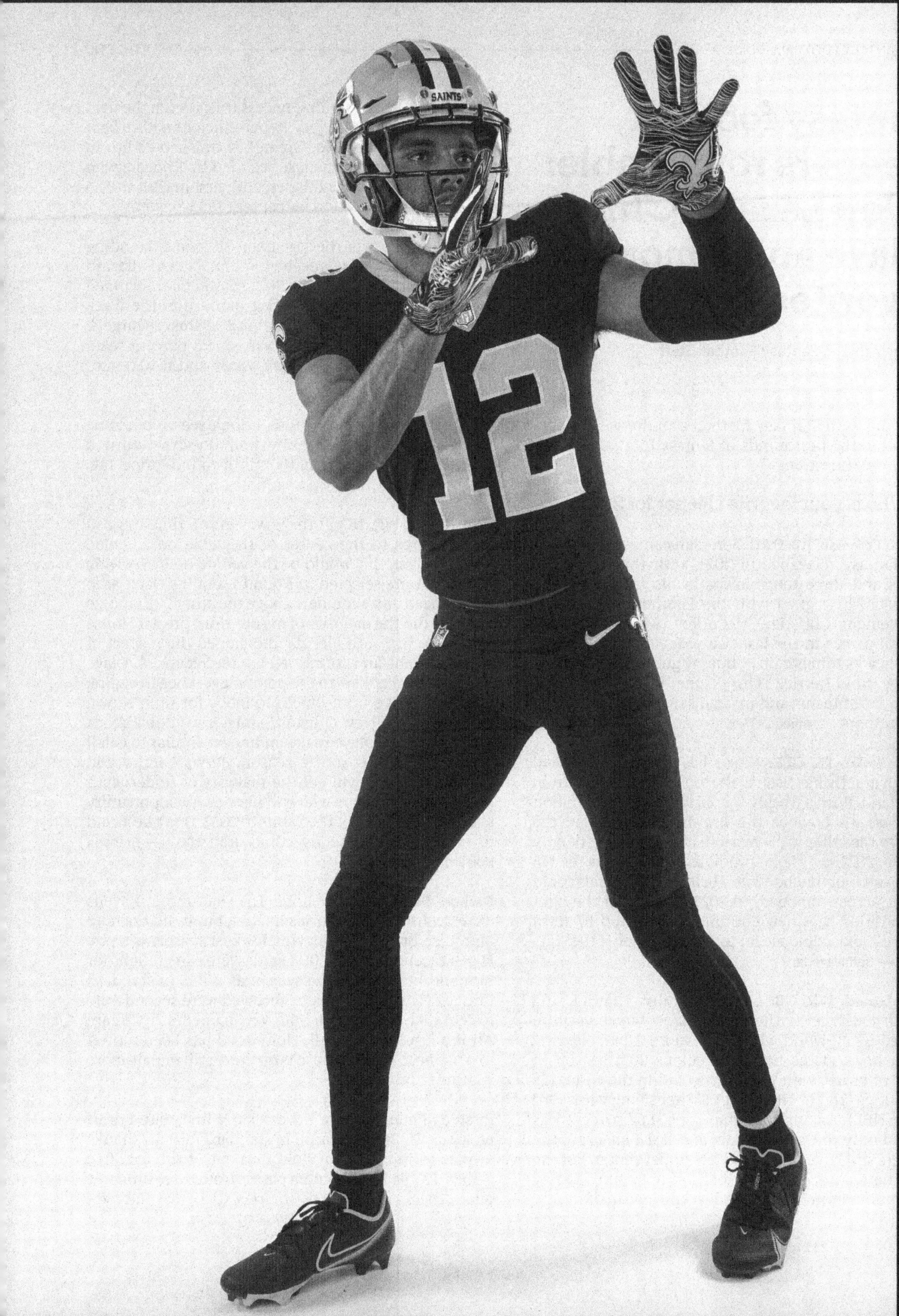

Fantasy football sleepers roundtable: Allen Lazard, Chris Olave and 8 more favorites

By The Athletic Fantasy Football Staff

Welcome to the fantasy football roundtable — where we gather the best minds in fantasy football and ask one simple question:

Q: Who is your favorite sleeper for 2022?

D'Onta Foreman, RB, CAR: Foreman came roaring back into fantasy relevance in 2021, with three 100-yard games and three touchdowns in his last six. In the offseason, he signed with the Panthers, to backup/complement Christian McCaffrey, who has played 10 total games in the last two years. Chuba Hubbard complicates things a little, but my guess is Foreman — a 26-year-old Derrick Henry clone — could've signed with a lot of teams and instead saw opportunity with the Panthers. — Nando Di Fino

David Njoku, TE, CLE: Njoku has been left for dead though quietly has risen to the top of the depth chart in Cleveland. With a freshly signed four-year, $56 million contract, it's obvious the Browns have handed the reins to the athletic 25-year-old in a tight end friendly system. 2021 saw Njoku produce 36 receptions for 475 yards and four touchdowns. I believe those totals could double across the board in 2022. Every year the tight end position sees new entrants into the top 10 and I believe Njoku could vie for top 5 production if the stars align. — Jeff Haverlack

Allen Lazard, WR, GB: Listen carefully. That sucking sound you hear is the galaxy-sized target vacuum created by all-world wideout Davante Adams leaving Green Bay. Adams had a ridiculous 2021 season in terms of usage, with 169 targets (2nd in the NFL), 123 receptions (2nd in NFL) and 1,553 receiving yards (3rd in the NFL). Adams' team target of 31.63 percent was second only to Cooper Kupp, and last I checked, the Packers still have Aaron Rodgers under center. For the AR12 detractors, I'm sorry, but I'm not compelled by the arguments he's turned to dust and long in the tooth.

Though the Packers didn't necessarily stretch the field vertically in 2021, Rodgers' hyper-efficient nature kept the offense on the field. Green Bay finished eighth in passing yards per game last year, led by Rodgers who was first in QB DVOA (27.8 percent), first in QBR (105.9) and third in completion percentage (68.9 percent).

My 2022 sleeper is the last man (or lizard) standing in the Packers wide receiver room, Lazard. Lazard battled injuries early in the 2021 season but reclaimed a prominent role in the passing game after the Week 13 bye as the clear No. 2 WR behind Adams: 28 targets, 21 receptions, 290 receiving yards, 15.8 percent team targets, 24.4 percent team air yards and a 10.0 yard ADoT.

Going off the board as WR45, I don't see an outcome where Lazard stays healthy and doesn't return a windfall profit at his early ninth-round price tag. — John Laghezza

Chris Olave, WR, NO: If there was ever a time to push all the chips to the center of the table on a rookie wide receiver, this would be the year to do it. Six wide receivers were selected in Round 1, but it's Olave who stands head and shoulders above the other 2022 rookie WRs. He did the majority of his pre-draft prep at House of Athlete in South Florida and gained the respect of many current and former NFL wide receivers. Olave impressed onlookers to the point players began calling their respective front offices to lobby for him. Now a member of the New Orleans Saints, it wouldn't shock me at all to see Olave make an impact similar to Odell Beckam Jr. in his rookie season. Jarvis Landry and Michael Thomas will get the majority of underneath targets, but it's Olave who will have every opportunity to stretch the field for the Saints in 2022. Don't be afraid to take this rookie early come draft day. — Brandon Howard

Rashod Bateman, WR, BAL: The Baltimore Ravens were decimated by injuries in 2021, but it did not stop Marquise Brown from having his best season as a pro. His 91 receptions and 1,008 yards were career highs for him and he finished the season as WR25 in standard formats. The 146 targets he received were second only to Mark Andrews (153), who was named a first-team All-Pro last season. Well, Hollywood has been moved to Arizona, but all of those targets are still in Baltimore waiting to be claimed.

In steps Bateman! The Ravens' 2021 first-round draft pick was WR80 last season in standard formats thanks in part to injuries that held him out of the first five games. He also had to catch passes from three different quarterbacks because of injuries to Lamar Jackson and Tyler Huntley. Bateman was still able to finish the season with 46 receptions and 515 yards. This year, there's a 23 percent target share out there for someone to claim and it is clear based on the Ravens' draft that he will be given every opportunity to fill it. As a bigger, stronger receiver than Brown, Bateman will be able to haul in some of the passes that Brown was unable to. I am very bullish on Bateman this year as everyone in the Ravens organization — including Jackson (who is looking for a new massive contract) — will be anxious to put a disappointing 2021 in the rear view mirror. — **Gene Clemons**

Miles Sanders, RB, PHI: Go ahead, laugh at Sanders. Keep using him as a punchline. Put me in the jokes while you're at it. While you're snickering at a zero-touchdown season that isn't possibly repeatable, Miles and I will rest confidently on the fact he returned from a midseason ankle injury to run for 454 yards on 74 carries (6.14 YPC) over his final five regular-season games. As you haughtily declare 2022 "Kenneth Gainwell SZN!!!," Miles and I will quietly note that neither he nor Boston Scott covered themselves in glory last year. Jalen Hurts' game-breaking ability as a runner clearly limits Sanders' upside. There's no way around that. Still, there's an easy path to 170 carries and 50 targets in an ascending offense. Sanders is the archetype of a post-hype sleeper. — **Michael Beller**

Irv Smith Jr., TE, MIN: Irv Smith Jr. is expected to pick up where he left off both mentally and physically before a knee injury derailed his 2021 season. Nearly every time he's been given a real opportunity on the field, he's impressed, living up to the (then-) rookie hype. Unfortunately, those opportunities have been few and are now far between, which leads to his depressed 2022 ADP, which has him around the 19th TE going off boards. The Vikings were an above-average passing offense in 2021, despite the lack of a reliable third pass catcher, and new head coach Kevin O'Connell is expected to improve on those numbers. Smith's ability to play that third-receiver role — with smart route running, good hands and speed — is not in doubt, so assuming he stays healthy through the summer, I'll be thrilled to wait on Smith to fill this tricky roster slot. — **Renee Miller**

JuJu Smith-Schuster, WR, KC: Can a sleeper have a rookie WR21 finish, plus two other finishes of WR18 and WR9, on his resume? Well, it would seem no, but in fact, it's a strong yes. People are more fascinated with a rookie and a receiver who has never reached 700 yards or higher than WR50 in his three years. Those receivers are Skyy Moore and Mecole Hardman, and the underrated wideout in Kansas City is former stud Smith-Schuster.

While the concern over Smith-Schuster succeeding as a team's No. 1 seem warranted after some struggles, Travis Kelce is the true "one" in Kansas City. On top of that, the Chiefs adjusted the offense to a more spread-out and intermediate-field game plan, seeing better results than heaving it downfield to Tyreek Hill multiple times and not being able to rely on anyone after Kelce and Hill. Smith-Schuster fits the new offense better, along with Hardman replacing Hill, but used more as a mixed-in deep-threat (Marquez Valdes-Scantling as well), and Moore profiling as a great complement to JJSS and Kelce. No, I don't expect Smith-Schuster to reach 25 percent or more of the target share, but he doesn't need that volume to finish as a top 25 receiver, and he's a fantasy afterthought now. JJSS can easily reach 80-plus receptions, 900-plus yards and 7-plus touchdowns on his way to that top 25 status. — **Jake Ciely**

Tim Patrick, WR, DEN: Everyone knows that the Broncos got a huge upgrade with the Russell Wilson trade. Anyone who loves fantasy loves Courtland Sutton and Jerry Jeudy and the only thing they love more is to debate who will have the better season. And yet, I would be zero percent surprised if Patrick scores more fantasy points than either of them — considering that is exactly what happened last year ... and the year before.

To get them, you need to pick Sutton or Jeudy in the 5th-ish round. Patrick ... how does the 13th round sound to you? Honestly, I feel like I'm the "I feel like I'm taking crazy pills" gif right now. Over the offseason, the Broncos rewarded Patrick with a three-year, $34.5 million contract. He's consistently been a red zone threat (for the few times the Broncos could get to the red zone in the pre-Wilson era). He puts up more yards after the catch than both Sutton and Jeudy. And don't get me wrong, I am not down on Sutton and Jeudy, I just don't know how we can all get the player just as likely to succeed — in the 13th round. At minimum, he's not "eight rounds later in the draft less likely to succeed." — **Brandon Marianne Lee**

Tyler Allgeier, RB, ATL: Not only did the Falcons use one of their precious draft selections on Allgeier, a bruising back from BYU, but they also released Mike Davis after a forgettable season in 2021 — his first after coming in from the Panthers.

The Falcons found a gem in Cordarrelle Patterson, but they need receivers. Last year, Patterson caught 52 passes for 548 yards and five touchdowns — to me, this means he can be moved back out to receiver, which is where help is badly needed in Atlanta with Calvin Ridley suspended and Russell Gage in Tampa Bay. This will leave Allgeier as the main back behind Marcus Mariota (I understand there are Damien Williams fans out there, but hear me out). Bad offense or not, the Atlanta Falcons will score. When they do get down low, the big, bruising Allgeier will be a key cog in getting into the end zone. And you can get him with the last pick of your fantasy drafts. Sign me up. — Dominick Petrillo ▰▰▰

Breakout fantasy player from each team

By The Athletic NFL Writers

Arizona Cardinals

Rondale Moore: The second-year wide receiver was underused as a rookie last year, but the Cardinals have much bigger plans for him this season as a slot receiver after the departure of Christian Kirk. He could be an especially important piece of Arizona's offense through the first six weeks of the season while DeAndre Hopkins serves his suspension. Moore is different from Hopkins, but quarterback Kyler Murray will have to find someone else to depend on, and the speedy and versatile Moore is a good option here, along with newly acquired receiver Marquise Brown. — Lindsay Jones

Atlanta Falcons

Tyler Allgeier: The rookie fifth-round running back might end up being the most anonymous player on this list, but he's going to get some work. Starting running back Cordarrelle Patterson lost effectiveness as the season went on last year, and head coach Arthur Smith is determined to re-establish some semblance of the running game he had as offensive coordinator in Tennessee two seasons ago. Allgeier was third in the NCAA in yards (1,606) and carries (276) last season. He's a Smith-style back. — Josh Kendall

Baltimore Ravens

Rashod Bateman: The Ravens traded Marquise Brown and didn't draft a wide receiver or target any of the top available pass catchers in free agency. That's partly because they believe Bateman, a first-round pick last year, is ready to assume the No. 1 wide receiver role. Bateman flashed as a rookie with 46 receptions despite missing five games and much of training camp and playing sparingly with Lamar Jackson. With little competition for targets beyond Mark Andrews, and Jackson back healthy, Bateman figures to get plenty of opportunities. — Jeff Zrebiec

Buffalo Bills

Gabriel Davis: No other Buffalo skill player comes close to Davis for breakout honors. The Bills moved on from Emmanuel Sanders and Cole Beasley, clearing the runway for Davis to be close to an every-snap starter for the first time in his career. Davis flashed starting potential when Sanders missed time in 2021 and then exploded with a four-touchdown game against the Chiefs in the playoffs. The third-year player is in a high-powered passing attack in which defenses focus on star wideout Stefon Diggs, and he has a great rapport with quarterback Josh Allen. Davis has every opportunity to have an outstanding season. — Joe Buscaglia

Carolina Panthers

Tommy Tremble: The second-year tight end looked to be just scratching the surface of his potential as a rookie, when he became the youngest tight end in NFL history to score a rushing touchdown. Tremble also had one receiving touchdown among his 20 catches (for 180 yards). The Panthers re-signed fifth-year tight end Ian Thomas mostly for his blocking ability. It's the athletic Tremble, a third-round pick from Notre Dame, who stands to benefit most from the arrival of Ben McAdoo, whose New York offenses heavily featured the tight end. — Joseph Person

Chicago Bears

Justin Fields: Think about what Mitch Trubisky did in 2018. He threw for 3,223 yards and 24 touchdowns, but he also ran for 421 yards and three more scores. He had a 95.4 passer rating and a 71.0 QBR. It went downhill after that with former coach Matt Nagy, but for one season, things clicked. Trubisky started for a playoff team but also became an option for fantasy teams. Fields is learning a new offense in his second season with offensive coordinator Luke Getsy, but he should be expected to deliver something similar to Trubisky's second year, albeit for a worse team. Bears coach Matt Eberflus has commended Fields and his development throughout the offseason program. — Adam Jahns

Cincinnati Bengals

Tee Higgins: Higgins has already broken out in a sense, but set against the overwhelming amount of discussion about Ja'Marr Chase, he still flies under the radar. Plus, keep in mind defenses will pay more attention to Chase in his second season. Look at the second half of last year when defenses shifted their attention and Higgins took off. From Week 8 on (including the playoffs), Higgins was eighth in the NFL in yards per route run and fantasy points per game, both ahead of Chase. Joe Burrow loves going the other way when coverage rolls to Chase. Now spread those results over an entire season. — Paul Dehner Jr.

Cleveland Browns

David Njoku: If you go down this list, you likely won't find many sixth-year players on it. But the Browns keep betting on Njoku, and with the departure of Austin Hooper and an eventual quarterback change to Deshaun Watson, the team believes Njoku will finally create big plays more regularly. Njoku will be 26 this summer, and he was always a developmental prospect whose maturation was probably stunted by constant coaching and scheme changes. With Watson in and Njoku poised for more chances, the Browns believe we'll finally see Njoku become a reliable pass catcher and a major matchup issue in the middle of the field. — Zac Jackson

Dallas Cowboys

Tony Pollard: Cowboys fans will say they've heard this before, but with the loss of wide receivers Amari Cooper and Cedrick Wilson, Pollard will benefit with more opportunities in the passing game. He was being used more in the slot during the team's OTAs this spring. He has proved he can be counted on as a runner and a receiver. And in each of Pollard's three seasons, his rushing attempts, targets, catches and total yards have increased. Even with a healthy Ezekiel Elliott, Pollard will have plenty of opportunities to make his biggest impact during the final year of his rookie contract. — Jon Machota

Denver Broncos

Jerry Jeudy: The first two seasons haven't exactly gone as planned for the wide receiver who was selected by Denver with the 15th pick in the 2020 NFL Draft. Oh, there have been flashes, like his five-catch, 140-yard performance against the Raiders during the final game of his rookie season. But Jeudy has struggled to create consistent momentum, whether because of drops, quarterback inefficiency or injuries. With Russell Wilson now in place at quarterback, there should be no more barriers to Jeudy reaching his considerable potential. — Nick Kosmider

Detroit Lions

D.J. Chark: It wouldn't be a "breakout" so much as a bounce back, but don't forget about Chark as he moves from Jacksonville to Detroit. The Lions believe quarterback Jared Goff can be effective pushing the ball downfield — his best showings in L.A. came with burner Brandin Cooks in the lineup — and Chark can challenge defenses deep. However, Detroit's coaching staff also believes there is more nuance to Chark's skill set than the Jaguars let him display. Chark will get chances from the slot and in catch-and-run spots. He's not that far removed from a 1,000-yard season. — Chris Burke

Green Bay Packers

Christian Watson: The door is wide open for an unheralded wide receiver to take the reins atop Green Bay's depth chart without Davante Adams and Marquez Valdes-Scantling, and I'd put my money on Watson to break out in his rookie season. Of his 180 career touches at North Dakota State, 57 went for at least 20 yards. The second-round pick can be the big-play threat the Packers badly need, and if he grasps the playbook, he should be in line for a steady workload this season. — Matt Schneidman

Houston Texans

Nico Collins: Despite missing three games as a rookie last season, Collins, a third-round pick, finished second on the team in targets (60), receptions (33) and receiving yards (446). Though that might speak more to the roster's lack of receiving talent than anything else, Collins is in line to be the No. 2 receiver opposite Brandin Cooks again this year, ideally catching passes from an improved Davis Mills. The Texans drafted receiver John Metchie III in the second round this year, but he's still working his way back from an ACL tear he suffered in the SEC championship game, which could limit his immediate impact. — Aaron Reiss

Indianapolis Colts

Nyheim Hines: Though it's a little bold — on a roster that includes Jonathan Taylor — to pick a running back to break out, there's a lot of optimism building that fifth-year running back Nyheim Hines will once again be a spark for the Colts offense this season. Coach Frank Reich has pledged to get him more touches — he had 56 fewer in 2021 than 2020, a product of Taylor's

Expert Roundtables

eruption and Carson Wentz's decision-making. Even with Taylor expected to get a heavy load this season, Reich has made it clear he's going to get the ball more to Hines, who is excellent at creating chunk plays out of nothing. "If I was a fantasy owner," Reich said this spring, "I think I'd pick Nyheim this year." New quarterback Matt Ryan, who has a quicker release and sees the middle of the field better than Wentz, should help get Hines much more involved. — Zak Keefer

Jacksonville Jaguars

Travis Etienne: Etienne missed his entire rookie season due to injury, but he could be back to his Clemson heyday with a healthy return in an upgraded Jaguars offense. How he'll split duties with James Robinson remains to be seen, but Etienne can be involved in the passing game as well as a playmaker in the ground game. Make sure he's fully healthy in training camp, but there's real upside to him. — Greg Auman

Kansas City Chiefs

Marquez Valdes-Scantling: As he enters his prime, Valdes-Scantling could record close to 1,000 receiving yards in the Chiefs' revamped offense for a few reasons. Along with Mecole Hardman, Valdes-Scantling should be one of Patrick Mahomes' top deep threats. As opposing defenses focus on limiting Travis Kelce's production, Valdes-Scantling could thrive in one-on-one matchups, especially if Mahomes creates advantageous opportunities by scrambling out of the pocket. Valdes-Scantling has been the Chiefs' best receiver in their offseason program. — Nate Taylor

Las Vegas Raiders

Derek Carr: Carr has thrown only 30 or more touchdown passes once in his career, but there's a good chance that will change this season. He has an elite group of perimeter pass catchers this year led by Davante Adams, Darren Waller and Hunter Renfrow, he has a skilled receiving back in Kenyan Drake, and he will have Josh McDaniels dialing up plays. The offensive line is a concern, but Carr will put up big numbers if it can hold up. — Tashan Reed

Los Angeles Chargers

Josh Palmer: The Chargers drafted Palmer in the third round in 2021, and he showed a lot of promise in his rookie season when he got opportunities. Palmer is a clean route runner. He has good hands. He can play outside and in the slot, and he is big and physical at the catch point and after the catch. His trust in and chemistry with Justin Herbert grew down the home stretch last season — the result of spending many days running routes and catching balls from the star quarterback after practice. Palmer had at least five targets in four of his last five games. With a full year to groom his game, Palmer has a chance to carve out an even more sizable role in the Chargers offense in 2022. — Daniel Popper

Los Angeles Rams

Allen Robinson: Is it weird to name a player of Robinson's high-profile status? Yes, but hear me out. The sentiment from Rams players and coaches is that Robinson has only scratched the surface of his abilities, particularly with respect to his versatility. The Rams are going to line him up all over the field, similar to Cooper Kupp. Unlike Kupp, though, Robinson will also be a high-point and contested-catch threat whom quarterback Matthew Stafford loves — and the Rams haven't had. — Jourdan Rodrigue

Miami Dolphins

Mike Gesicki: The tight end was a fantasy disappointment last season, grabbing only two touchdowns in an otherwise productive year. New Dolphins coach Mike McDaniel comes from a 49ers offense in which tight ends can put up huge numbers, and despite the additions made in the backfield and at receiver, he'll logically be a much greater end zone factor than he was last season. He should be able to challenge if not surpass his career high of six touchdowns. — Greg Auman

Minnesota Vikings

Irv Smith: I'm sure fantasy football writers are done with attempting to hype up Smith, but after not seeing the field in 2021, it's clear Smith has underperformed. But if he was finally going to make good on his expectations last year, an injury that ended his season is no reason to think he can't hit his goals in 2022. With a more pass-friendly coaching staff and a scheme that intends to send him downfield more often, he has the ability to exceed even the numbers he was supposed to hit in 2021. — Arif Hasan

New England Patriots

Rhamondre Stevenson: The 24-year-old running back has impressed everyone in Foxboro this spring, and he should get increased opportunities to mix in with Damien Harris. Stevenson is a battering ram who has aspirations of becoming a three-down back. I'm not sure I'd expect him to overtake Harris or significantly eat into James White's snaps on passing downs, but

Stevenson should be even more impressive in his second season. — Jeff Howe

New Orleans Saints

Chris Olave: Perhaps the first-round pick is an obvious choice, but Olave is going to get every opportunity to get the ball this season. The Saints are coming off a year in which the wide receivers room struggled to make an impact. And even though Michael Thomas is expected to be back this season, he's still rehabbing the ankle injury that has kept him off the field for the majority of the last two years. That will give Olave a lot of reps as the Saints go into training camp. It would be surprising if Olave didn't get off to a solid start considering the opportunity available. — Kat Terrell

New York Giants

Kadarius Toney: This seems like an obvious answer on the surface. Toney had a monster two-game stretch early in his rookie season (16 catches for 267 yards) and is electric with the ball in his hands. If he stays healthy, his ceiling is extremely high. The problem is Toney totaled only 23 catches for 153 yards outside of that two-game explosion. A wide variety of injuries limited him to 10 games, and he has missed most of the spring due to knee surgery. So questions linger about Toney, but his upside makes him a strong breakout candidate. — Dan Duggan

New York Jets

Elijah Moore: The second-round pick was the story of offseason workouts and training camp last year as he seemed to make big play after big play. He had a slow start to 2021 (likely due to Zach Wilson's struggles) but really turned it on before suffering a season-ending quad injury. He caught 34 passes for 459 yards and five touchdowns from weeks 7 through 12. Moore is back and healthy this year. An improved Wilson and a talent-infused receiving corps (Garrett Wilson was drafted in the first round) should help him break out this season. — Connor Hughes

Philadelphia Eagles

Dallas Goedert: Last year was supposed to be Goedert's breakout season, but the Eagles didn't trade Zach Ertz until October and shifted to a run-heavy offense during the backstretch of the season. Goedert is the unquestioned top tight end in 2022 and is poised to build on his 56-catch, 830-yard campaign last season. Goedert's target share could be complicated by the presence of A.J. Brown and DeVonta Smith, although the Eagles are expected to pass the ball more and gave Goedert a four-year, $57 million contract with the belief he could be one of the NFL's elite tight ends. Goedert ranked fifth among tight ends in yards last season even though he ranked 17th in targets. If his targets jump from 76 to the 90-100 range, the Eagles and your fantasy team will benefit. — Zach Berman

Pittsburgh Steelers

Pat Freiermuth: Some might suggest Freiermuth's rookie campaign was his breakout season with 60 receptions on only 79 targets and seven touchdowns in fewer than 60 percent of the offensive snaps. But with Eric Ebron gone and the Steelers likely to attack the middle of the field more with likely starting quarterback Mitch Trubisky, Freiermuth's numbers could skyrocket him into one of the top six tight ends in the league by the end of the year. Freiermuth became a red zone target for the Steelers last year with his athletic ability and good hands. He scored six touchdowns in a seven-game span, and Matt Canada's motion offense should allow him to rack up some easy catch-and-run opportunities. — Mark Kaboly

San Francisco 49ers

Brandon Aiyuk: It's hard to characterize someone with 50-plus catches in each of his first two seasons as a breakout player, but Aiyuk seems like a good candidate to move to the next level. He came on strong at the end of 2021, averaging 71.3 receiving yards per game over the last eight weeks, including a 94-yard outing in Trey Lance's Week 17 start. He has been healthy this offseason, has trained with Lance and, unlike counterpart Deebo Samuel, has been part of the 49ers' offseason program every step of the way. It's no stretch to say he could lead the team in receiving in 2022. — Matt Barrows

Seattle Seahawks

Kenneth Walker III: Walker might end up as the most productive running back on Seattle's roster when it's all said and done. The rookie second-round pick was a big play waiting to happen at Michigan State, leading the nation last fall with over 1,000 yards after contact. The 41st pick in the draft is already the de facto RB2 behind Rashaad Penny because of Chris Carson's neck injury. Because Penny has an extensive injury history, it's expected Walker will earn some starts and make the most of those opportunities in Seattle's run-first offense. — Michael-Shawn Dugar

Expert Roundtables

Tampa Bay Buccaneers

Rachaad White: A running back and third-round pick from Arizona State, White is in a good position to challenge for the No. 2 role behind starter Leonard Fournette. He's an excellent pass catcher, so if he can prove himself in pass protection, he can chip into Gio Bernard's role on third downs and Ke'Shawn Vaughn's role as the top backup to spell Fournette when he needs a drive off. Look for more of an offensive balance between the run and pass. — Greg Auman

Tennessee Titans

Nick Westbrook-Ikhine: He has already exceeded expectations for an undrafted free agent out of Indiana in 2020 who struggled to catch the ball in his first training camp. The 2021 season qualifies as a breakout: 38 catches for 476 yards and four touchdowns. But he's here because he continues to get better and because the Titans' reliance on him is about to increase significantly. That's what happens when A.J. Brown is traded and Julio Jones is cut. Robert Woods is ahead of schedule in his ACL rehab and will be good. First-round pick Treylon Burks? Hard to say. It's been a shaky start for him. It has been an eye-popping spring, however, for Westbrook-Ikhine, who has Ryan Tannehill's full trust. — Joe Rexrode

Washington Commanders

Logan Thomas: Yes, it's odd going with a 30-year-old tight end coming off an ACL tear rather than, say, a first-round wide receiver selection in Jahan Dotson. To boot, it's unclear whether Thomas will be available for Week 1. The thinking is Carson Wentz throws to the tight end position more than any quarterback this side of Lamar Jackson and thrives when looking for big targets. The 6-foot-6 Thomas is the only Washington pass catcher with size, and he could be overlooked in fantasy drafts. The impressive Dotson is the easier call, but the Commanders have a deep bunch of wide receiver and running back types, while Thomas, who caught 72 passes in 2020, is the only tight end with more than one year of experience. Projecting 70-plus receptions might be tough, and we'll have to gauge the knee recovery/rust, but Thomas is a unique option for his tight end-friendly quarterback. — Ben Standig ▬▬▬

Fantasy football league winners roundtable: Tony Pollard, Lamar Jackson lead the pack

By The Athletic Staff

Welcome to the fantasy football roundtable — where we gather the best minds in fantasy football and make one simple demand:

Q: Name the player you will draft this season who will be your team MVP and win you a title.

Michael Pittman Jr., WR, IND: I watched a lot of Colts games last year because I had Michael Pittman Jr. everywhere. And he looked good. The problem was that passes thrown to him just kind of floated in the air way too long or were off-target. Enter Matt Ryan. The former Falcons quarterback will make Pittman a stud as his primary target in Indianapolis. I can see Pittman going in the third or fourth round and producing first-round numbers, forcing discussions in December of whether Pittman will be a first-rounder in 2023. He is a stud; he just needed a QB to get him the ball properly. — Nando Di Fino

CeeDee Lamb, WR, DAL: I'm all-in on CeeDee Lamb in 2022. With the physicality, speed and now WR1 role due to the departure of Amari Cooper, the third-year receiver will be the apple of QB Dak Prescott's eye, and greater chemistry and production should follow. Lamb produced 79 receptions, 1,102 yards and six touchdowns in 2021, all of which should rise as the team's top wideout option. I expect the Boys' run game will return to top form, which should help keep all arrows pointed straight up for Lamb. — Jeff Haverlack

Lamar Jackson, QB, BAL: Lamar Jackson is arguably the most disrespected player in the NFL. People seem to go out of their way to tell you all the things they feel he cannot do. And they conveniently gloss over all the things that make him the most difficult matchup in football. When Jackson is at the height of his powers, he is QB1 and RB1 combined. People act like 2019 never happened. They talk as if he was not the top performer in all of fantasy sports, and they fail to discuss his weekly decimation of defenses. In nine of the 15 games he played that season, he scored over 25 points in standard formats; six of those games were over 30 points, and three of those six were over 35 points. In 2020 he was still a top 10 performer. In 2021, despite dealing with multiple injuries and playing in only 12 games (some while still nursing ailments), he was QB14. This offseason there has been a lot of conversation about paying Jackson, as his contemporaries have received massive contracts. It will all be fuel for the 25-year-old former MVP. I would not be surprised to see a 2019-type performance from Jackson this year, and fantasy football GMs will reap the benefits and ride him all the way to a championship. — Gene Clemons

Courtland Sutton/Jerry Jeudy, WR, DEN: DK Metcalf averaged 1.63 fantasy points per target in 46 career games with Russell Wilson as his quarterback. Tyler Lockett put up 1.78 fantasy points per target in 108 games with Wilson. For the sake of comparison, Cooper Kupp averaged 1.91 fantasy points per target last season, Davante Adams was at 1.67 and Justin Jefferson finished with 1.65. The question to ask isn't will a Broncos receiver finish as a WR1 this season but which Broncos receiver will finish as a WR1 this season? If I can have only one, I want it to be Courtland Sutton, but I'll be doing what I can to leave every draft this summer with him or Jerry Jeudy. — Michael Beller

Najee Harris, RB, PIT: We could debate all summer about whether you can win or lose your league with your first-round pick. So much comes down to injury luck, but on the premise that you cannot lose your league with your first-round pick, and therefore put yourself in a better position to win, I'm drafting Najee Harris whenever I have the chance (often up to pick eight). He's the youngest of the first-round running backs, he plays for a team that boasts a run-heavy game plan and he led all running backs in receptions last season (74 on 94 targets, tied with Austin Ekeler for the league lead) with zero fumbles. One concern in 2021 was that the Steelers had one of the least effective passing offenses in the league, which led to few red zone attempts for Harris (30, ranked 25th in the league). If that goes up even a little, he has a chance to be the best fantasy skill player this season. But even if he isn't No. 1, Harris has an outstanding chance of being a player you can set and forget for 20 fantasy points per game. — Renee Miller

Jalen Hurts, QB, PHI: Gene Clemons is rightfully in on LJax, so I'll go elsewhere with a quarterback who is eerily similar in my preseason thoughts to where Jackson was in 2019. I've referenced this often when talking about trusting projections, and in 2019, Jackson was my QB2 before I adjusted him down, believing my projections were aggressive. As you know, they were wrong, more because Jackson was the QB1 by 80 points. This isn't a brag, as I've seen some adjusted projections be spot on and some miss where I should have trusted them. Well, we're back to wondering about trusting them because Jalen Hurts checks in as the QB2, about 30 points behind Josh Allen and 10 ahead of Justin Herbert.

Many would likely be surprised that Hurts had a 61.3 completion percentage last season given the narrative that — just like Jackson — he "can't throw." Let's not forget Hurts had a rookie in DeVonta Smith as his top receiver, Jalen Reagor busting and losing his spot to Quez Watkins, and Dallas Goedert dealing with injuries. Hurts now has A.J. Brown as his top option, pushing each talent down for greater depth, plus a second season in an offense designed for Hurts' style. Oh, and Hurts doesn't need to throw for 4,500 yards and/or 30 touchdowns to reach QB2, as he should run for (about) 800/8 again, possibly more. Hurts will be my 2022 quarterback in every league possible. — Jake Ciely

Josh Allen, QB, BUF: League winner is such an interesting term. To me, it has to be more than just a big return on your draft position. I think about a player who can finish first overall, but also one who can be acquired. Is Kupp a league winner? He can certainly finish first overall, but unless you draw a top draft slot, he isn't an option. So my league winner for 2022 is the only player in the NFL to outscore Kupp in 2021. He happens to be available in the third round, and I haven't been able to pass on him, personally, inside the top 36.

Last season, Josh Allen was in the top six among all QBs in dropbacks, attempts, completions, passing yards, passing TDs and sack rate. If that's not enough, he's at the helm of the betting favorite to win the Super Bowl while simultaneously offering a second skill set. Allen's contributions on the ground are a second player's worth of stats to pair with that QB1 passing production. Allen rushed for 763 yards and six TDs on 122 attempts (which outperformed Saquon Barkley, Darrell Henderson, Miles Sanders and Clyde Edwards-Helaire in terms of rushing), and it resonates throughout his team's stat sheet. The ability to improvise and get first downs is the main reason the Buffalo Bills were top-five in points scored and drive success rate in 2021. After the way last season ended, I expect him to play like a man possessed from the first kickoff this fall. — John Laghezza

Michael Thomas, WR, NO: Mine is either a league winner or a bust. And for where he's going, it's worth the risk/doesn't even matter if he busts. Michael Thomas is going in the sixth round of fantasy drafts. In my personal best-ball and dynasty leagues, which is anecdotal, he's going even later. This man was considered one of the future greats and was the WR1 of the 2019 season. No one was better than him. Let's get the risk out of the way — it's is his ankle. Two years to mend an ankle is scary, so that's baked into his average draft position (ADP). He could get hurt again; he could also not play. That's a bust. OK, I get that. I'm not, however, going to get on board with the argument that he can't excel with Jameis Winston because he needs volume and Winston's not Drew Brees.

In 2020, Thomas logged over 100 yards in two of his four games with Taysom Hill. Also, before last season, Winston was a volume guy. In 2019, he averaged 39.13 pass attempts per game, and in 2021 only three quarterbacks averaged more: Tom Brady, Patrick Mahomes and Herbert. Sure, New Orleans has a new head coach, Dennis Allen, who is a defensive mind, but it has the same offensive coordinator, Pete Carmichael, who's been around since the 2009 Super Bowl. Sean Payton did the play calling, so some people are worried, but the mindset remains, so we probably won't see anything drastic. Will Jarvis Landry or Chris Olave take away some of his looks? Sure. But somehow Thomas was able to put up huge numbers when everyone knew he was going to get the ball. The threat of someone else getting the look instead might help rather than hurt. And either way, Thomas goes off the board so late that the upside on his fantasy draft capital is tremendous. — Brandon Marianne Lee

Tony Pollard, RB, DAL: Tony Pollard, like other backs on different teams, is in a backseat role to another perceived starter. But in Pollard's case, he might, at this point, be more talented than the starter. Just think of what we were missing with Ekeler sitting behind Melvin Gordon. The same sentiment can be said about Pollard playing behind Ezekiel Elliott. Elliott was great. But with his bloated contract, the Dallas Cowboys need to decide what to do with him after this season. To do so, they need to discover Pollard's true ability in the offense.

Pollard is currently going off the draft board as the first pick of the eighth round. This puts him as the RB34 for fantasy, which is far below what I see as his floor for 2022. And this is the true definition of a league winner — someone you can get below their floor.

While playing on only 35 percent of the snaps in 2021, Pollard caught 39 passes in the offense. With Amari Cooper now in Cleveland, this will be a key reason he is able to see more of the field. By getting on the field more, Pollard will find more targets and more rushes out of the backfield. If this were a hot takes article, I'd suggest Pollard will finish with a higher fantasy running back ranking than Elliott. But since it is not a hot take article (it's not, right?), I will say he'll finish higher than his RB34 price. Much higher. — Dominick Petrillo ▬▬▬

Inside Info: Our NFL writers answer one fantasy question for each team

By The Athletic NFL Staff

Week 1 of the NFL season is not until Sept. 8, but it's never too soon to start thinking about your fantasy football draft.

With training camp and the preseason still to come, we thought it would be a good time to check in with each NFL team on one fantasy question of great importance heading into 2022.

Arizona Cardinals

Kyler Murray seems less enthusiastic about running with each passing season, his annual December fade has hurt fantasy managers when they need him most and this offseason has been rife with drama surrounding Murray's desire for a new contract. Should fantasy managers be worried about taking Murray as a top-eight quarterback for 2022?

My concern about Murray would be less about scheme and more about his injury risk and how much we've seen his performance drop when he's dealing with nagging injuries. That said, few quarterbacks provide the type of scoring potential Murray does as one of the best deep-ball passers and running threats in the NFL. So if you're willing to take the risk he might have a dip at some point in the season, he still has a very high upside. — Lindsay Jones

Atlanta Falcons

A rookie has finished as a top-15 fantasy receiver in each of the past three seasons. Drake London is the top rookie receiver selected in the 2022 NFL Draft. Given Atlanta's obvious need at the position, how far-fetched is it that he keeps that streak of rookie top-15 finishes alive?

Not at all — if only because of opportunity. London walks into the best room in the league for a player looking for targets. I mean, somebody other than Kyle Pitts has to catch some passes, and Olamide Zaccheaus (31 catches) is the only wide receiver on the team who had more than one catch for the Falcons last year. Atlanta has loaded up on free-agent wide receivers, but none should challenge London at the top of the pecking order. — **Josh Kendall**

Baltimore Ravens

With Marquise Brown traded to Arizona, how do you see the wide receiver targets and performance breaking down?

It always feels fruitless to predict a big fantasy season from a Ravens wide receiver, and this year is no different with tight end Mark Andrews still around and a run-oriented team expected to be healthier in the backfield. A 2021 first-round pick, Rashod Bateman figures to get the most wide receiver targets. The Ravens believe he's ready to break out. Baltimore will likely add a veteran receiver at some point, but as of now, Devin Duvernay and James Proche are in line for increased opportunities. Proche has gotten limited playing time in his first two seasons. He's a reliable slot target with good hands. — **Jeff Zrebiec**

Buffalo Bills

Gabriel Davis became a star in the playoffs — specifically in the game against Kansas City. His regular season, however, was just OK. Which Davis should we expect in 2022?

The reality is somewhere in the middle. While it's unrealistic to think Davis can have that type of impact every week, he'll have far more opportunities than he ever has before. The Bills took things slowly with Davis over his first two years. He only played out of necessity in 2020, then once he turned a corner last year, he took over as WR2 by the end of the year. He'll be a full-time starter for the first time in 2022 and is likely to bust loose as the best running mate Stefon Diggs has had since coming to Buffalo. — **Joe Buscaglia**

Carolina Panthers

Christian McCaffrey has missed significant time because of injury in each of the past two seasons. Will Carolina continue to feed him his usual 20-plus touches per game, or will backups D'Onta Foreman and Chuba Hubbard be more heavily involved in the backfield mix this season?

The Panthers plan to change their practice approach with McCaffrey, taking a lot of the reps off him during the week in the hope that the lightened workload will help him get through the season. Like last year, McCaffrey isn't expected to play any of the preseason games, either. The Panthers have other options, including the recently acquired Foreman, a big back who filled in admirably for Derrick Henry last year in Tennessee. But Matt Rhule — who starts the season on the hot seat — has made it clear McCaffrey will continue to get his touches early and often. — **Joseph Person**

Chicago Bears

With Chicago evaluating Justin Fields' ability to be the team's long-term answer at quarterback, what changes do you expect the new coaching staff to implement to help Fields best accentuate his dual-threat talents?

Luke Getsy's offense will be a bit of a mystery until the regular season, but based on where he's been, we can expect some RPOs, an outside-zone run scheme and a vertical passing game, all things that should complement Fields' skill set. That could lead to more rushing yards and an increase in big-play opportunities through the air, but Fields is working with a limited group at receiver and along the offensive line. There will be a lot of pressure on the scheme and Fields' own improvement to generate more production. — **Kevin Fishbain**

Cincinnati Bengals

Is Hayden Hurst a deep sleeper we should be paying attention to in our drafts?

Yes. His signing flew under the radar of the offensive line improvements, but the Bengals think it could end up being one of the most impactful moves of the offseason. Hurst offers a higher ceiling in the pass game than C.J. Uzomah, and the solid numbers Uzomah put up last year should be considered the base of expectations (49 receptions, 493 yards, five touchdowns). Hurst was overshadowed by Mark Andrews and Kyle Pitts in Baltimore and Atlanta, but he arrived remarkably motivated, still a first-round-pick caliber of athlete and only 28. He'll be the starter and see constant single coverage. — Paul Dehner Jr.

Cleveland Browns

This offense is almost completely rebuilt from 2021. But Donovan Peoples-Jones remains. Is he poised to break out this season or will rookie David Bell step in?

Peoples-Jones is going to get the first crack as the starter on the outside opposite Amari Cooper. The Browns will have a role for Bell, too, and that role may grow as the rookie becomes more comfortable. But Peoples-Jones should be poised for a leap in his third season. He's rangy, he's talented and the internal belief is he'll have more opportunities with Deshaun Watson at quarterback. Peoples-Jones has had a few big moments over the past two years. With improved consistency and an eventual quarterback upgrade, he's a high-upside fantasy sleeper. — Zac Jackson

Dallas Cowboys

With Ezekiel Elliott showing high-mileage wear and tear down the stretch of 2021 and Amari Cooper's nearly seven targets per game dealt to Cleveland, are we going to see a sharp rise in Tony Pollard's touches, both as a rusher and in the passing game?

I'm not sure if it will be a sharp rise, but it is expected to increase. Pollard played through a torn plantar fascia during the final five games of the regular season and the playoff loss to the 49ers. If he can stay healthy, the opportunities will be there. The Cowboys didn't make any huge offseason additions in terms of offensive playmakers. They replaced Cooper and Cedrick Wilson by signing veteran James Washington to a one-year deal and drafting Jalen Tolbert in the third round. Opposing defenses will be focused on Elliott, CeeDee Lamb and Dalton Schultz, so Pollard's versatility should make him one of offensive coordinator Kellen Moore's most productive weapons. — Jon Machota

Denver Broncos

With most of the offense returning, whose style best fits Russell Wilson's among the receivers?

K.J. Hamler. That's not to suggest the 2020 second-round pick out of Penn State, who is making his way back from ACL and hip injuries suffered last September, will be Denver's leading receiver, but he could end up becoming a favored deep target for a quarterback who loves to air it out more than anyone in the league. In three games played last season, Hamler averaged 20.1 air yards per target. For context, among receivers

with at least 50 targets in 2021, Cleveland's Donovan Peoples-Jones led the league at 15.43 yards per target. If Hamler is fully recovered from his injury — his progress has been encouraging at every turn — expect some deep-ball fireworks in 2022. — Nick Kosmider

Detroit Lions

Rookie Amon-Ra St. Brown was a fantasy revelation over the final six weeks of the 2021 regular season, averaging 8.5 catches, 103.5 yards from scrimmage and 1.0 touchdown per game. How much will new additions Jameson Williams and D.J. Chark, not to mention the return of T.J. Hockenson, who missed the final five games with a thumb injury, limit St. Brown's potential to pick up where he left off?

The targets (and, thus, the overall stats) might dip a bit. Over the final six weeks of last season, St. Brown saw a whopping 67 targets, more than any NFL receiver other than Justin Jefferson (69). But the rapport St. Brown developed with Jared Goff is very real, so the second-year receiver will remain the preferred option in short and intermediate passing windows. Goff isn't the biggest risk taker in football, either. He's going to default to the safe throw over the potentially heroic one, which means he'll find St. Brown often as the pocket breaks down. — Chris Burke

Green Bay Packers

With Davante Adams now in Las Vegas, Green Bay doesn't have an obvious go-to option in the passing game. Who is most likely to lead this team in receptions when the dust settles?

Allen Lazard may not lead the team in receiving yards or touchdown catches, but he's a good bet to lead the way in catches given his sturdy hands and how much trust he has built with Aaron Rodgers over the past three seasons. Rodgers expressed confidence in Lazard becoming WR1 for the Packers this spring. Lazard isn't much of a deep threat, but he's reliable in the short and intermediate passing game, which will lead to plenty of opportunities on third downs and deep in the red zone. — Matt Schneidman

Houston Texans

Will Marlon Mack be a stud in this Pep Hamilton offense, or is rookie Dameon Pierce the favorite to lead?

For a few years in a row now, it's been hard to know what the Texans are thinking when it comes to running backs. Though the team has begun getting younger now that it has accrued more draft capital,

Houston's free-agent signings, including 33-year-old Jerry Hughes and 34-year-old Mario Addison, show the Texans still believe having veterans in the rotation is important, even if Houston won't contend this year. Given how drastically the Texans need to improve their running game, coach Lovie Smith might lean on Mack to start the year before giving way to Pierce. — Aaron Reiss

Indianapolis Colts

This receiving corps seems like it could be full of sleeper candidates. Is there anyone you like a little deeper on the depth chart to have a fantasy impact in 2022?

It's always a tricky proposition picking a wide receiver in Frank Reich's offense, because the Colts head coach and play caller has stated time and again his intention to spread the ball around. Now, Michael Pittman Jr. is a solid bet for another 1,000-yard season, but beyond him? It's a bunch of question marks. New quarterback Matt Ryan will help — his quicker release will allow Reich's timing-based offense to run more efficiently, plus he sees the middle of the field better than his predecessor, Carson Wentz. Speedster Ashton Dulin is a name to keep an eye on; Reich will dial up some deep shots to him this year. Parris Campbell has looked strong this spring, but the injury question will loom over him until he stays healthy for a full season. Michael Strachan and Dezmon Patmon should fight for the remaining balls, but all told, the group behind Pittman is unproven, and any fantasy impact figures to be inconsistent. — Zak Keefer

Jacksonville Jaguars

With Doug Pederson in charge, do we have a sense of the receiver pecking order? And will Travis Etienne see the bulk of the backfield touches, or will it be a committee?

The money given to Christian Kirk suggests he'll have the highest share of targets, but he's never been in that role before so we don't know how he will handle that. Marvin Jones is the most proven of the group, and Zay Jones seems little more than a late-round gamble. Etienne has the potential to outperform all of them if he can become the primary back. Expect a ton more production from Trevor Lawrence, but it's still not clear who benefits most from that. — Greg Auman

Kansas City Chiefs

With Tyreek Hill gone, is there any reason to believe that Josh Gordon, with a full offseason and time to learn this offense, could be a fantasy factor?

Gordon should be a more viable option for Patrick Mahomes this upcoming season for the reasons you mention. The Chiefs want to have a more balanced passing attack, but Gordon will need to have an impressive start in September to earn an increased role. When training camp starts, Gordon could be behind Mecole Hardman, Marquez Valdes-Scantling, JuJu Smith-Schuster and rookie Skyy Moore on the depth chart. The best way Gordon can be a factor is by being a reliable, tall target for Mahomes inside the red zone as opposing defenses focus on Travis Kelce. — Nate Taylor

Las Vegas Raiders

Hunter Renfrow broke out with a 1,000-yard season in 2021. Will Davante Adams' presence make it easier for him to repeat that?

My first thought was no, given that Darren Waller will also get a lot of targets, but when I looked back at Randy Moss' three years in New England, Wes Welker had more than 1,000 yards receiving each of those seasons. And then you factor in that quarterback Derek Carr is one of Renfrow's best friends and has a keen sense of what option route Renfrow will run and how deep. Carr also mentioned Renfrow before Waller when he was talking about who needs a new contract next, and that recently came to pass for Renfrow. Adams, Waller and Renfrow will be open as soon as the ball is snapped, as they all have great separation skills at the line of scrimmage, and Renfrow will be the safety checkdown if Carr is rushed in the pocket. Fantasy players who target Renfrow will benefit from Carr getting rid of the ball quickly. — Vic Tafur

Los Angeles Chargers

With almost the entire offense returning, should we expect anything new from the Chargers in 2022, fantasy-wise?

Yes, two things. First, the Chargers replaced Jared Cook with Gerald Everett at the top of their tight end depth chart, and they hope Everett will provide a more explosive yards-after-catch dynamic at the position. They plan to get the ball in Everett's hands in a variety of ways, from screens to flat routes to jet sweeps, and he could be poised for a career season. Second, the Chargers drafted running back Isaiah Spiller in the fourth round, and the rookie has a clear path to claiming the RB2 spot behind Austin Ekeler. That battle will be decided in training camp, with Joshua Kelley and Larry Rountree also in the mix. If Spiller can claim that role, the days of trying to guess the Ekeler handcuff could finally be over. — Daniel Popper

Los Angeles Rams

Cam Akers was a feel-good story in the Rams' run to a Super Bowl title last season, returning from a preseason torn Achilles injury in Week 18 and leading the backfield in touches in the postseason. But he posted a paltry 2.4 yards per carry and 2.31 yards after contact per attempt along the way. Will he be able to live up to his top-20 RB fantasy draft value in 2022?

I have no reason to believe Akers won't be back on track in 2022. It's actually a bit unfair to contextualize his 2021 stats, considering what he came back from (with zero live onboarding time). He told me in minicamp that he's "100 percent," and I also expect Akers to be worked into the passing game at an even higher volume than he was previously. — Jourdan Rodrigue

Miami Dolphins

This backfield looks like it'll be pretty great in real life, but it could cause fantasy players headaches. Will a lead back emerge? Or will we see a tough-to-predict rotation?

Mike McDaniel has a history of using multiple backs to great overall success but not necessarily to the delight of individual fantasy GMs. His Dolphins backfield looks much the same way — Chase Edmonds will catch a ton of passes and probably has the best scoring potential, Sony Michel can do everything and Raheem Mostert has shown glimpses of huge fantasy showings when he's healthy. So take a late-round flier on one, sure, but none of them is a sure enough bet to draft high, even in PPR formats. — Greg Auman

Minnesota Vikings

The Vikings were one of the most run-heavy offenses in the NFL under the previous coaching regime. How might the offense differ under new head coach Kevin O'Connell? And which primary skill-position player(s) will be most affected?

O'Connell has all but said he's going to be throwing the ball more, and we should see attempt totals from Kirk Cousins closer to his Washington numbers (598 per 17 games) than he has had in the past three years in Minnesota (550 per 17 games), which lines up with

Matthew Stafford in Los Angeles (601) and Jared Goff in Detroit (629). We should see some gains for Justin Jefferson and Adam Thielen, but the biggest boost could be for third receiver K.J. Osborn, who could become a high-end flex player and smart bye-week fill-in. — Arif Hasan

New England Patriots

The Patriots had a boring offseason in fantasy terms. So who among the returnees should we expect to take the biggest leap in 2022?

Running back Rhamondre Stevenson has impressed everyone in Foxboro this spring, and he should get increased opportunities to mix in with Damien Harris. Stevenson is a battering ram who has aspirations of becoming a three-down back. I'm not sure I'd expect him to overtake Harris or significantly eat away at James White's snaps on passing downs, but Stevenson should be even more impressive in his second season. — Jeff Howe

New Orleans Saints

After one of the greatest four-season runs by a wide receiver to start an NFL career, an ankle issue has derailed Michael Thomas' past two seasons. With Drew Brees and Sean Payton out of the picture, is it still within reason to hope that Thomas can return to his past All-Pro form?

The Saints' 2021 season showed how much they still need Michael Thomas, and that hasn't changed even with the additions of Chris Olave and Jarvis Landry. If Thomas is healthy, he'll get a high volume of catches. Health still remains the question, however, as Thomas continues to rehab his ankle and didn't participate in OTAs. The good news is that he has already spent part of the offseason working with the rookie Olave, and if he remains on track for training camp, it's a positive sign that the old Thomas could return. He'll certainly get the opportunities and won't lack for catches if he's on the field. — Katherine Terrell

New York Giants

What is the most plausible outcome in Brian Daboll's first season as the Giants head coach: Daniel Jones silences his doubters and takes a major step forward in his development, Saquon Barkley delivers a season reminiscent of his electric rookie campaign or Kadarius Toney emerges as the clear alpha receiving option?

The process of elimination leads me to the Barkley scenario because I don't foresee Jones making a major leap in Year 4 and Toney has not proved reliable enough to warrant high expectations. At least Barkley has produced like a dominant player, albeit in a rookie season that is becoming increasingly distant in the rearview. The case for a Barkley resurgence is that he's now two years removed from ACL surgery — his decreased production is directly tied to injuries — and his receiving skills should be better used in Daboll's creative offense. — Dan Duggan

New York Jets

Michael Carter had a pretty solid rookie season: 1,000-plus total yards, involved in the passing game, dangerous when healthy. And then the Jets bring in Breece Hall. How will this backfield shake out?

The Jets like Carter a lot. They believe he's a quality back. They've always viewed him as an ideal complement, though, in Mike LaFleur's "running back by committee." Hall, whom the Jets consider a home run threat, is now the Batman to Carter's Robin. The Jets will use both, but Hall is the lead back. — Connor Hughes

Philadelphia Eagles

Despite an uneven 2021, Jalen Hurts finished as a top-10 fantasy quarterback in his first full season as a starter in 2021. With A.J. Brown joining second-year player Devonta Smith in the receiving corps, how realistic is a top-five fantasy QB campaign for Hurts?

If Hurts was a top-10 quarterback last season as an inconsistent passer in an offense with underwhelming weapons, it's reasonable to expect Hurts to make a major jump — and perhaps emerge as a top-five fantasy quarterback — this season. The passing options should be considerably better with Brown, Smith entering Year 2 and Dallas Goedert entrenched as the top tight end. Hurts believes he'll benefit from having the same scheme and play caller for the first time since high school. The Eagles should pass the ball more this season, and they should also run more plays than they did in 2021. Hurts will remain productive running the ball, so the improved passing and offensive efficiency will help his overall statistics. He also missed two games last season and was hindered by an ankle injury in December. If he can stay healthy in 2022, his numbers should also improve. The top-five plateau is difficult to reach, but Hurts' running ability helps his candidacy. — Zach Berman

Pittsburgh Steelers

Will there be enough passes to go around to make George Pickens a decent fantasy play? Or are there just too many mouths to feed before he becomes an option?

If you can afford to do so and especially if you are in a dynasty league, Pickens is a good pick to stash on your roster. He's not going to be Randy Moss or Anquan Boldin as a rookie, especially with Diontae Johnson, Chase Claypool, Pat Freiermuth and Najee Harris clamoring for passes on a team that wants to establish the run first. However, he showed tremendous ball skills and speed during the spring that should get you excited about his future with the Steelers, especially with the uncertain future of Johnson past 2022. Pickens will produce some splash plays as a rookie but not enough to be somebody you blindly start every week. — Mark Kaboly

San Francisco 49ers

Deebo Samuel was the No. 2 fantasy wide receiver in 2021, padding his numbers with 365 rushing yards and eight rushing touchdowns. With work-in-progress Trey Lance taking over for Jimmy Garoppolo at quarterback and San Francisco adding to its depth at running back in the draft, how much of a headwind is Samuel facing in trying to repeat last season's level of production?

Remember that a large chunk of Samuel's production at running back in 2021 came out of necessity, as the 49ers had suffered a plethora of injuries in the backfield. The team has tried to insulate itself against a recurrence by drafting bruising back Ty Davis-Price. Time will tell if that works and if Samuel sees less time in the backfield as a result, but it is likely that more of his action comes at receiver in 2022. Samuel's production should be tied to the chemistry he develops with Lance. — David Lombardi

Seattle Seahawks

DK Metcalf has averaged 72 catches, 1,057 yards and just shy of 10 touchdowns in his first three seasons. How much of a downgrade in those numbers, if any, should fantasy managers expect from Metcalf in 2022 with Russell Wilson now in Denver?

If Geno Smith wins the starting quarterback job, then it wouldn't surprise me to see Metcalf's 2022 numbers look similar to the stats he posted with Smith under center for three weeks in 2021. During that stretch, Metcalf caught 14 of 18 targets for 197 yards and three touchdowns. If you extrapolate those numbers over a 17-game season — which isn't a perfect way to go

2022 FANTASY FOOTBALL GUIDE

about this, but you get the point — then his 2022 stats would look comparable to his career averages despite a dropoff in quarterback talent. — Michael-Shawn Dugar

Tampa Bay Buccaneers

With Antonio Brown out of the picture, Chris Godwin returning from an ACL injury and Rob Gronkowski considering retirement, how much of an impact do you expect free-agent signing Russell Gage to have in his first season in Tampa?

Tom Brady has a lot of mouths to feed in the Bucs' passing game, but especially early in the year while Godwin is still recovering (if not still out), Gage could step in as a solid No. 2 receiver behind Mike Evans. Because Evans draws priority attention from defenses, that's a great spot to be in. So while Gage has never had more than four touchdowns in a season, it would be easy for him to surpass that as part of an offense that has reset the team records for passing touchdowns in the past two seasons with Brady. Late in the year, when Godwin is back to full strength (and it's playoff time in fantasy), he might not have as significant a role. — Greg Auman

Tennessee Titans

If Robert Woods is ready in Week 1, will he be the top receiver, or is that Treylon Burks' role as they look to replace A.J. Brown?

It should be Woods. He and Ryan Tannehill have already been building chemistry, and it would take a setback for Woods to be anything but full go by Week 1. In fact, at this point, Burks realistically projects as WR3 to start, because Nick Westbrook-Ikhine continues to make strides as a playmaker. Burks has had to bail out of some work this spring and has been held out of some things, and wide receivers coach Rob Moore recently confirmed he has asthma. Mike Vrabel said that shouldn't be an issue, but Burks clearly isn't in top shape, and it may take him some time to become a major producer. That said, his Arkansas game film suggests he will eventually get there. — Joe Rexrode

Washington Commanders

Antonio Gibson was the Commanders' top fantasy entity in 2021, but after the team drafted Alabama's Brian Robinson in the third round, there are rumblings that the team is set on trimming Gibson's workload. How much will Gibson's 18.75 touches per game from last season be curtailed in 2022?

"Well, I think for the most part, it's going to be by committee. ... I mean in this league today, you know, you just can't have one primary back," coach Ron Rivera said recently. That's a foreboding comment for those eyeing Antonio Gibson's touches with hammer back Brian Robinson around — and yet less might be more. Gibson, consistently banged up during his first two seasons, was miscast as a workhorse back. Expect less work — that may include around the goal line — and a lower ADP but greater efficiency on 15 or so touches if Gibson remains healthy and Washington feeds him in space. — Ben Standig ▬▬▬

Which late-round QBs could help you win your league? Our experts give their picks

By The Athletic Fantasy Football Staff

Q: Who is your favorite late-round QB for 2022?

Trevor Lawrence, QB, Jacksonville: Trevor Lawrence was the No. 1 pick in 2021, and a bunch of talent evaluators I respect called him a "generational talent." He not only played through the Urban Meyer dysfunction but actually asserted his leadership and publicly revealed he told coaches that James Robinson shouldn't have been benched for long stretches of two games. Now, 2022 brings with it a fresh start — a head coach who isn't grossly overmatched, new pass catchers in Christian Kirk, Zay Jones and Evan Engram, the return of Travis Etienne and hopes that this offense will allow him to run (he had nearly 1,000 rushing yards in college). — Nando Di Fino

Kirk Cousins, QB, Minnesota: Every year Kirk Cousins flies below the radar and each year he seems to improve, last year sneaking into the top 10 within the position. With former Rams offensive coordinator Kevin O'Connell now at the helm of the Vikings, word is that the team is going to run a fast-paced spread offense to get the ball into the playmakers' hands — a group that includes Justin Jefferson, Adam Thielen and returning tight end Irv Smith Jr. Expect more receptions by the running backs, as well. This is only going to pay greater dividends for the upside of the always healthy Cousins. While other fantasy players are rolling the dice on riskier names, I'll lay in the weeds and draft Cousins multiple rounds later. — **Jeff Haverlack**

Another vote for Cousins!

I always look for values at QB because in a game predicated on opportunities, it's the one position that assures a magnitude of them. Cousins is being drafted as QB16 even though in 2021 he was tied for fourth in QBR (103.1) and QB accuracy (77.6 percent), and ninth in QB DVOA (15 percent) while posting a top-12 (QB1) finish in pretty much everything that matters: passing yards (4,221), touchdowns (33), interceptions (7), yards per attempt (7.5), average depth of target (8.5) and PFF's Big Time Throws and Turnover Worthy Plays.

Cousins had six games with more than 315 passing yards and provides more potential than the market is crediting him for. He has a 90th percentile throw velocity (59 mph) and the Minnesota offense operates fast. Maximizing opportunities is paramount in fantasy football and Minnesota was near the top of the league in pace of play, running a snap in under 27 seconds, on average. Don't forget that Cousins also gets Thielen back (63 receptions, 686 receiving yards, 10 TDs in weeks 1-12) and I see an overlooked player who will allow us to wait on our shot-caller in redraft leagues while we stack flex options. — **John Laghezza**

Zach Wilson, QB, New York Jets: Lawrence, Cousins, Jameis Winston, Tua Tagovailoa, I can get on board with all of them. This is why you should be playing SuperFlex. For the sake of putting a new name out there ... how about Zach Wilson? The Jets have built what should be one of the league's best offensive lines to protect last year's No. 2 pick. They added Garrett Wilson and Breece Hall to an intriguing playmaking group that already included Elijah Moore, Corey Davis and Michael Carter. C.J. Uzomah and Tyler Conklin may be marginal fantasy players, but they're both more dynamic than anything Wilson had at tight end last year. He also showed us an ability and willingness to run, racking up 185 yards and four touchdowns on 29 carries last year. Wilson is a true late-round quarterback who gives you the freedom to spend your first 12 to 14 picks elsewhere, while still landing a passer with obvious upside. — **Michael Beller**

Jameis Winston, QB, New Orleans: In 2019, Winston threw 30 interceptions. The narrative that was pushed was one of failure, but fantasy GMs know that he also put up some massive good numbers that season,

including five games with over 25 fantasy points. He even had back-to-back 37- and 33-point outings. Last season, in a little over six games — before he missed the remainder of the year with an injury — Winston threw 14 touchdowns and only three interceptions. He also ran for a score. This season, Winston has another year in an offensive system, another year with corrective eye surgery and a reloaded stable of pass catchers. He should be primed to finish in the top tier of fantasy quarterbacks like he did in 2019. — **Gene Clemons**

Tua Tagovailoa, QB, Miami: Tagovailoa finished the 2021 season as QB18 and is being drafted at about the same level for 2022, with an ADP in the 10th round. Going into his third year with the Dolphins, who have done everything possible to ensure his success, I believe this is the time for Tua to make good on his early first-round promise. Despite playing in a tough division, Tyreek Hill, Jaylen Waddle, Cedrick Wilson and Mike Gesicki supply Tagovailoa with one of, if not the, best receiving corps in the league. The improved defense of the Dolphins is another factor in his favor (early rankings have them around sixth), since getting the opponent off the field provides more offensive opportunities. Tua made relatively small strides from his rookie season to last year, but he is primed to be one of the best 2022 fantasy values. — **Renee Miller**

Justin Fields, QB, Chicago: Nando took my top breakout quarterback for 2022 (justifiably so), which means I'll pivot to my third, Justin Fields. I hear you yelling, "But Jake, they did nothing to help Fields!" Fair point, as Darnell Mooney is a great receiver but better as a team's No. 2, and adding Byron Pringle (free agency) and a 25-year-old rookie slot receiver in Velus Jones doesn't do much to inspire an improved passing attack. However, as with Jalen Hurts last year, I'm not too concerned with that area in fantasy – and don't dismiss the Cole Kmet breakout coming.

Hurts threw for a mere 3,144 yards and 16 touchdowns but finished as QB9 thanks to his rushing (782 yards, 10 TDs). Fields didn't run as much to start the year, but once he settled in, Fields had 52 rushes for 361 yards in his final seven games. That's 6.9 YPC with 7.4 rushing attempts per game. If he maintains that pace over a full season, Fields will easily clear 100 attempts and near or eclipse 800 yards on the ground. If you add in a modest 5-6 rushing touchdowns, those 110-plus rushing points means Fields needs just 3,200 yards and 15 passing touchdowns to reach 300 fantasy points and a top-10 finish. See how easy it is for Fields to be one of the best late-round quarterbacks even with a terrible receiving corps? — Jake Ciely

Daniel Jones, QB, New York Giants: I'm going to go for one of the only dual-threat late QB options, Daniel Jones.

And I'm going to guess that his ADP will stay low all offseason considering the offensive line is consistently ranked as one of the worst in the league (although all offseason they worked to improve it), his surrounding cast of skill players is either inexperienced or beyond what most would consider their "prime" and the team already expressed no confidence by not picking up his fifth-year option. So why am I even mentioning him? Ha! Before his concussion in Week 5, Jones was the QB8 on the young 2021 season. Since 2019, he's averaged 26.3 rushing yards per game (which puts him top 10 at the position). His schedule looks pretty cushy ... I don't like preseason strength of schedule talk, but as of now, seven of his games are against bottom-10 defenses and

most analysts would declare the Giants as the team with the absolute easiest schedule at the QB position.

Brain Daboll as a head coach feels promising, as his former Bills certainly gave Josh Allen a fun-for-fantasy playbook. Jones is not Allen, and will never be. But you do like the coaching history for our fantasy purposes. And I actually like that they didn't pick up his fifth-year option. Motivation. If you're in a SuperFlex and some of the other late-round dual-threat darlings are gone (like Lawrence, Wilson or Tagovailoa), Jones is going to give you some big games when the matchup is right. I would rather have that rushing floor this late in the draft than the non-fantasy friendly choices like Jared Goff, Mac Jones, Carson Wentz, etc. — Brandon Marianne Lee

Matt Ryan, QB, Indianapolis: This one is easy for me. It might bite me in the butt, nevertheless I am still going to go with my gut and take Matt Ryan.

Ryan is the 20th QB off the board with a draft slot of the final pick of Round 12. After loading up with talent early, I will gladly wait until the double-digit rounds to get the veteran leader the Indianapolis Colts have been looking for.

He also has the NFL's top running back and arguably the best offensive line in front of him. He is intelligent, talented and he finally has receivers again – something missing sorely on the Atlanta Falcons of 2021. — Dominick Petrillo ▬▬▬▬

XII. Everything Dynasty

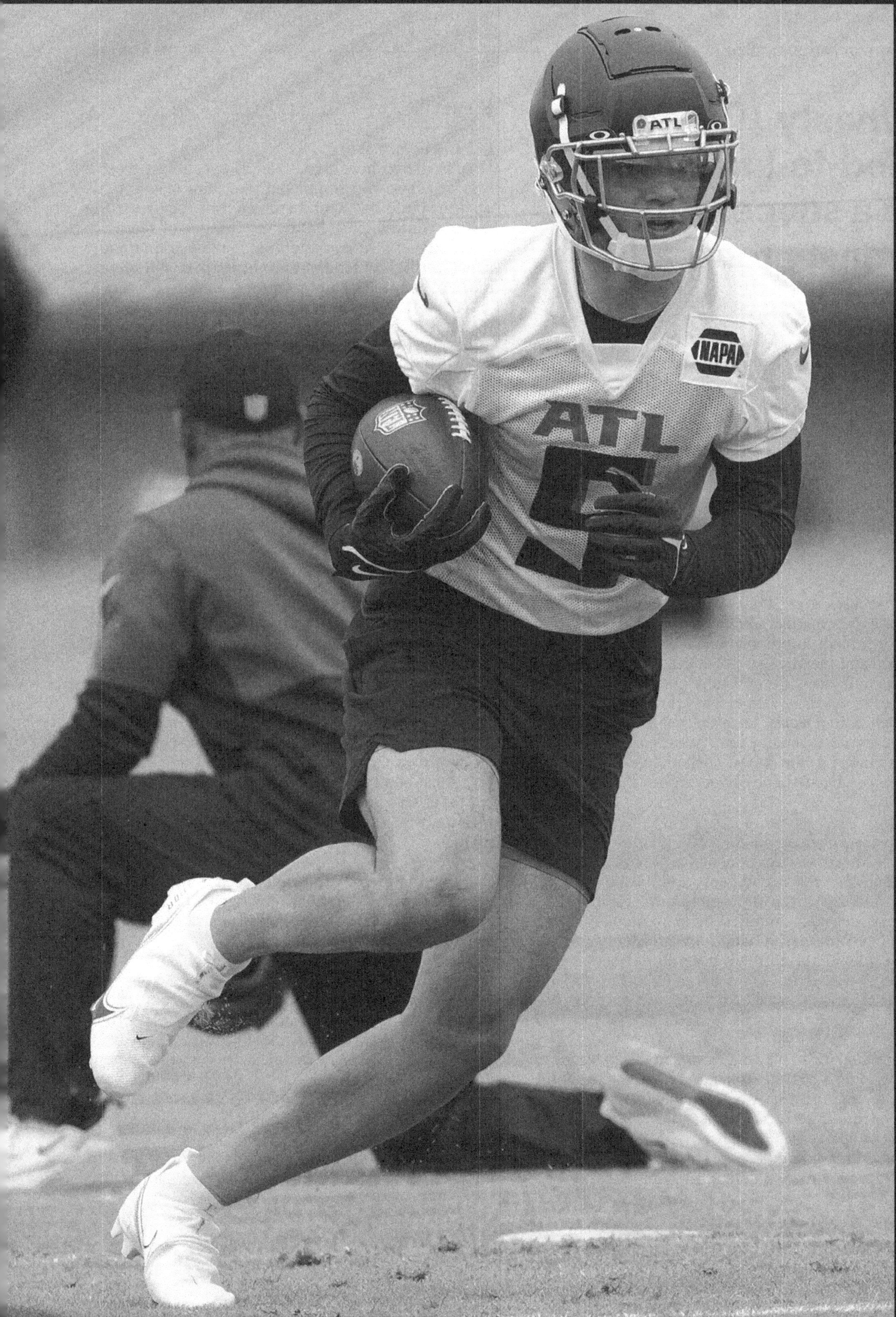

Dynasty 101: Your need-to-know guide for a successful dynasty football league

By Jeff Haverlack

The dynasty format is exploding.

Redraft provides the challenge of drafting for the season ahead with limited fear or frustration of injuries during training camp or at offseason events. Draft the best team possible and, win or lose at the end of the season, wipe the slate clean and do it all again next year.

Those seeking a greater challenge and the desire to simulate the experience of being a general manager of their own team ultimately find their way to dynasty. Drafting and managing a much deeper roster, annual rookie draft and the constant quest to be first to uncover next year's superstar are just part of the experience. In dynasty, once a player is on your roster, there they shall remain until you decide otherwise. That's the key to the dynasty experience — once your roster is established, the players are yours season after season.

The dynasty format provides the greatest challenge possible due to the engagement needed by each coach. Your long-term results will most certainly be impacted by continual research and strategic execution. Follow the news, contracts, injuries, incoming rookies, camp reports and preseason action toward identifying the players who are tomorrow's news stories before your competition does. Luck remains an important variable each season, but it takes a back seat to your due diligence and work ethic as a coach.

Whether seeking to play in your first dynasty league or looking to be a commissioner of a new league, let me offer a few of my primary tenets to being a competitive coach or running a successful league.

Before getting started realize what follows is a very small subset of many different considerations.

Player

Know your format

I can't tell you how many "Help!" questions I receive from coaches who completed their new league start-up draft but didn't spend enough time looking at the roster requirements. From the number of teams in your league, size of rosters and, most importantly, your scoring, understanding the format will dictate much of your initial build strategy.

If your league requires starting two running backs, you must have two quality names to trot out each week. As a general rule in situations like this, I try to prioritize drafting two top-14 backs and neither should have questionable roles. Positional scarcity is a real issue if you misjudge starting requirements or don't secure enough depth in any one position.

The primary action is to understand how all players performed in the scoring format based on last year's production. That, when combined with your starting requirements, will produce your start-up draft cheat sheet.

Know your strategy

I've long said that your strategy for building a dynasty team should only be as strong as your ability to depart from it when needed. You must have an idea about what you are trying to build and how you plan to go about it. When performing your start-up draft, which position will you prioritize before seeking value in other positions? Will you forgo being competitive in the first year or two and build through youth or prioritize veteran production to win now? A balance of both? Perhaps you will seek your favorite players with winning a secondary goal. It's your team, do as you wish.

There is no right or wrong answer in how you wish to construct your roster other than having no strategy at all. Know your format, develop your strategy and stay true to yourself as a coach.

Do the work

There is no substitute for hard work. To be a competitive dynasty coach, you must commit to putting in the time throughout the entire year, not only during the season. In fact, the NFL season is a time for rest and enjoyment of the games. It's the time when you get to take your foot off the pedal a bit and see the work you've put in to that point play out on the gridiron.

Each month of the year presents opportunities to improve your roster now, or in the future. The beauty of the dynasty format is that it's football 7 x 24 x 365. There is no offseason. Rejoice!

Finding and using your resources is extremely important. Whether The Athletic, Dynasty League Football or any of the other mainstream fantasy sites, these resources pay for themselves many times over by performing much of the legwork, allowing you to analyze and process data more quickly, and get a jump on your competition. Support your fantasy sites!

Commissioner

So, you want to want to run a dynasty league? Before you do, make sure you are ready for the commitment and that you've done your homework. Running a dynasty league does possess similarities to that of a redraft league but is much less forgiving.

Getting key decisions correct out of the gate before inviting your first GM will save you from headaches later. To be sure, headaches await in many forms regardless, but if you do your research and prepare properly, you can spend your time on small adjustments rather than trying to patch a sinking boat.

Following are a few key decisions which will serve as the foundation for your league. Think them through carefully and don't be afraid to seek input from others before setting them in stone.

League format

League format is arguably the most important aspect to get right on Day 1 and it's exceedingly difficult to change later. The format will dictate draft strategy for your coaches and a shift in this area in later years could require a redraft, creating some very unhappy coaches.

SuperFlex (SF) formats have dramatically increased in popularity but can create a have or have-not division in your league. This is not meant to scare you away from the format but all coaches need to understand the high priority placed upon quarterbacks in the SF format.

Nuances are present in the other formats including Point Per Reception (PPR) and tight end premium leagues as well. PPR leagues are more well-balanced across all positions while non-PPR overweighs touchdown production, typically reducing the value of wide receivers.

I prefer full 1.0 PPR formats due to the balancing of positions which allows for multiple strategies for coaches to build their rosters but any format is valid as long as every coach understands it ahead of the draft.

League cost

Be very careful as no one likes to throw away money. Prior to the draft, all coaches are filled with excitement and anticipation. But it only takes a year or two until it becomes evident which teams are competitive and which are not. Uncompetitive coaches may become frustrated, disinterested and eventually abandon the league.

Consider keeping the league cost low or use multiple side pots to keep coaches interested and enthusiasm high to reduce abandonment.

Roster size

There are as many thoughts on roster size as there are players in the NFL. My personal desire is to ensure no less than 300 players are rostered. That means at least 25 players per team in a 12-team league assuming no IDP (individual defensive players). My personal preference is for north of 30 players. As an added variable, consider doing away with IR (injured reserve) spots and simply increase roster size.

The reason for large rosters is obvious. You don't want excessive talent on the waiver wire. Talent should be rostered to encourage trading and reward research. For IDP formats, consider bolstering the roster number by 1.5 — 2 times the number of required starters. For example, if you will require four IDP starters, increase the roster size by a total of six to eight.

Starting requirements

Related to "league format" above, the starting requirement for each week is an important determinant for how coaches choose to build their teams. Requiring two running backs means 24 backs will be forced onto the field each week, thus increasing the priority of the position during the draft and beyond. Factoring positional scarcity into your scoring format is a variable in all leagues, but the greater the number of required starters from a position means greater scarcity.

In most leagues, I favor starting one running back and two wide receivers while allowing for 2-3 Flex players. The reason for this is to allow for maximum flexibility in roster construction. Dynasty GMs must decide whether to overweight running backs, invest more heavily in wide receiver or be positionally agnostic.

Trade deadline

This is a hotly debated topic and discussing it openly is akin to a dinner party for the Hatfields and McCoys of the 1800s.

The primary battle lines are drawn around which week the trade deadline should be placed. Many favor an "as late as possible" (Week 12-plus) deadline while others favor earlier (Week 8). A later deadline allows coaches to shape their teams late into the season in preparation for, or even during, the playoffs, while an earlier deadline requires more forethought and preparation by coaches, potentially allowing for second-half injuries to play a larger role.

I strongly favor a Week 8 deadline. The reason is because I'm a passionate believer of coaches needing to perform the work necessary to prepare their teams and allowing injuries to be part of the game which will challenge depth. Furthermore, I'm firmly against later season trades by coaches with no chance of making the playoffs for draft picks and younger players in return for productive veterans. This can upset the balance of the league late in the season. In my view, trades need to occur earlier in the season when the playoffs are still on the line.

I've seen too many situations where an average team "sells out" late in the season via a roster dump which unbalances the league playoffs in a way which would not have played out otherwise.

Commissioner psychology

Commissioner behavior brings down more leagues than any of the other items on the list in my estimation.

A heavy-handed commissioner may be seen as meddling and overreaching his/her authority. A completely hands-off commissioner who doesn't set expectations for sportsmanship, team management and league operation may be overrun by more assertive coaches. It takes a very even-handed commissioner to strike the right balance between fun in the league and proper/expected coach behavior.

Encourage your coaches to propose and respond timely to trades, engage in "healthy" trash-talking, actively participate in making their teams better and engage in league operations by voting in polls, adhering to roster rules and voicing disagreement privately as opposed to in an open forum. Good sportsmanship must be encouraged for the fun of all.

Again, it's a fine line between being a dictator and a milk toast. Set the expectation early with your coaches, get their buy-in and then stay active to keep it. And addressing conflict immediately must be practiced!

In conclusion, I hope you found this "brief" foray into the dynasty league informative and helpful. It's a challenge to properly cover such a deep topic in a single article.

If you haven't taken the dive into dynasty yet, you won't regret it. Once you do, you'll never go back. ▬▬▬

Dynasty league futures: How far ahead should fantasy managers be planning?

By KC Joyner

When fantasy managers in dynasty leagues head into drafts, their primary goal is to upgrade their team in the short term. After all, what fun is fantasy football if you aren't building a roster that can contend for championships?

The nature of the dynasty format means these managers also have an important secondary goal of building for the long haul. No fantasy manager is thinking in terms of a 10-year plan like NFL general managers do, but how long should they be thinking about? What's a reasonable goal for the number of starter-caliber years a dynasty fantasy manager should expect to get when selecting a highly rated rookie?

To answer this question, we will use the career points ranking system I created for the best-ever fantasy players for every NFL team series that can be found in The Athletic's fantasy football section.

The career points ranking system compiled era-adjusted fantasy rankings that rewarded players for various season-long achievements. The base accomplishment was scoring enough points to rate as a fantasy starter, but bonus points were also given for racking up a quality season, which was defined as scoring 50 percent more points than the lowest-rated starter at your position. Additional bonus points were also granted for impact and elite seasons, but these were rare achievements, so this study will focus on starter- and quality-caliber campaign volume.

The best-ever series covered the entirety of NFL history, but this analysis will look at performance for each fantasy position since the AFL-NFL merger in 1970.

Quarterbacks

It is incredibly difficult to find a long-term starting quarterback in fantasy; in the 52 seasons since the merger, only 52 quarterbacks have posted five-plus starter-caliber campaigns. The number doesn't spike much if the span is lowered to four years, as only 66 quarterbacks have tallied four-plus starter seasons.

Dynasty managers wanting quality-caliber campaigns will find this search even more difficult. Here are the only quarterbacks to post five-plus quality-caliber seasons since 1970:

Player	Quality
Peyton Manning	14
Dan Marino	10
John Elway	10
Tom Brady	9
Aaron Rodgers	9
Roger Staubach	8
Fran Tarkenton	8
Drew Brees	8
Brett Favre	8
Steve Young	7
Joe Montana	7
Ken Anderson	6
Warren Moon	6
Randall Cunningham	6
Terry Bradshaw	5
Boomer Esiason	5
Dan Fouts	5
Jim Kelly	5

That's 18 quarterbacks who reached this level in just over half a century's worth of seasons. These trends suggest dynasty managers should hold on to solid quarterbacks as long as possible, as good long-term candidates are hard to find.

Running backs

There have been 90 running backs with five-plus points-per-reception (PPR) starter seasons since 1970 and 85 who have tallied five-plus starter campaigns in non-PPR. That is a higher volume than quarterbacks, but since there are twice as many starting running backs on fantasy teams as there are quarterbacks, it is

clear that long-term value is even harder to find at this position.

Since the NFL is a much more pass-happy league than it was in the 1970s-90s, one question that comes to mind is whether long-term value is getting harder to find at this position.

The numbers don't support that notion, as the distribution of these long-term starters has remained consistent. For example, there have been 37 running backs with five-plus non-PPR starter seasons since 2000. Both of those account for just over 40 percent of their respective totals in this entire analysis, thus indicating the volume of long-term RB starters isn't declining. It might actually be increasing, as there have been 11 running backs with five-plus starter seasons in non-PPR since 2011.

Long-term production at the quality-caliber campaign level is difficult to find, as evidenced by the list of only 17 running backs with five-plus quality seasons in the PPR format since 1970:

Player	PPR Quality
Walter Payton	9
Barry Sanders	9
Ricky Watters	8
LaDainian Tomlinson	8
Emmitt Smith	8
Marshall Faulk	7
Curtis Martin	7
Roger Craig	6
Tiki Barber	5
Thurman Thomas	5
Shaun Alexander	5
Ottis Anderson	5
LeSean McCoy	5
Edgerrin James	5
Herschel Walker	5
Eric Dickerson	5
Adrian Peterson	5

Wide receivers

In fantasy football, the wide receiver position is the easiest to find long-term value in. There have been 129 wide receivers with five-plus PPR starter-caliber seasons and 128 to reach this level in non-PPR formats.

Everything Dynasty

Part of this is due to the wide receiver position having more starting slots than the other positions (this analysis rates any wide receiver in the top 30 at this position as a starter), but the reality is the long-term value holds up even if one raises the bar to seven-plus seasons. There have been 73 wide receivers who have reached that bar in PPR formats, and 72 did so in non-PPR environments.

That shows the relative depth at this position, but the competition that depth provides has a downside in that only 17 wide receivers posted at least five quality-caliber PPR seasons. That number moves a bit higher in non-PPR, as 20 wideouts have hit that mark.

Player	Non-PPR Quality
Jerry Rice	11
Steve Largent	9
Terrell Owens	8
Marvin Harrison	8
Randy Moss	7
Cris Carter	7
Gene Washington	6
Antonio Brown	6
Torry Holt	5
Steve Smith Sr.	5
Tim Brown	5
Michael Irvin	5
Larry Fitzgerald	5
James Lofton	5
John Stallworth	5
Harold Carmichael	5
Fred Biletnikoff	5
Brandon Marshall	5
Calvin Johnson	5
Charley Taylor	5

Tight end

The fantasy football world has been lamenting the lack of tight end depth for years, but that dearth of good players has an upside in that it makes it easier for a tight end to tally multiple years as a starter. This is why there have been 45 tight ends with five-plus PPR starter seasons since 1970 and 44 tight ends with five-plus starter campaigns in the non-PPR format.

The shortage of elite talent shows up in the volume of quality-caliber seasons, as there have been only 10 tight ends with five-plus quality seasons in non-PPR. Here are the 11 who racked up five-plus in PPR:

Player	PPR Quality
Tony Gonzalez	11
Shannon Sharpe	9
Keith Jackson	7
Travis Kelce	6
Todd Christensen	6
Kellen Winslow	6
Ben Coates	6
Ozzie Newsome	5
Jason Witten	5
Antonio Gates	5
Brent Jones	5

Summary

So, how many starting-caliber years can a fantasy manager expect from a good rookie? The typical answer is less than five years, as that bar has been surprisingly difficult to reach at every fantasy position. This means dynasty managers should play for the short term except in rare instances when it is clear a prospect is likely to be one of those rare players capable of posting five or more starting-caliber campaigns. ▬▬

2022 SuperFlex dynasty league fantasy football trade values chart

By Alex Korff

I am back this preseason to bring some fresh, hot dynasty trade values. For your perusal, I have rookies, rookie pick slots, positional tiers and some new, funky colors. Trade values charts are a great tool for evaluating players and looking for potential trades. As always, these are more of a guideline and should not be used as a bible. I will go over what is special about these charts, how to use them and how I make them.

But first, let's dive right into the chart!

What is special about this chart?

I was able to partner with the experts here at The Athletic to make a special chart by generating exclusive values. Then, I compared them to the calculated values of the aggregated expert consensus ranks (ECR). The ECR (+/-) column can be used to find which players the experts here want you to buy or sell and to help identify some key market deficiencies. That way, you can really get an edge on your league-mates.

For example, Jalen Hurts' trade value is calculated to be 66, a full 19 points higher than consensus. That is a lot of potential value you might be able to gain if you can trade for him at a value of 47-55. Use this chart to look for those buys or sells, and then make some offers.

Another special feature of this chart is that the rookies are broken out into their own column next to a corresponding pick. Make sure to check them out because they are a little different than ECR.

How to use a trade values chart

These are tools to make your life easier! The left-most column is the assigned trade value for a row. All players and picks in a row have the same value and, in theory, could be traded for one another. Players are separated into columns by position. The ECR column is calculated based on my "Reddit Adjusted" column that I publish on Patreon, Twitter and Reddit. A plus value means the trade value is above ECR; minus is the inverse.

If you are looking at larger trades (2-for-2 or 3-for-3), you just sum the sides of each trade to get an idea of fairness. Make sure to account for consolidating depth and trying to acquire stud players by overpaying. These are really a guideline to look for reasonable trades.

How I make these charts

The backbone of my model is seeded by the expert consensus ranks I aggregate from as many published sources as I can find. The goal is to try to average as much of the market

The Athletic — The Athletic Dynasty Trade Values
Superflex (2 QB) Dynasty Trade Values — June 2022 — /u/PeakedInHighSkool · @PeakedInHS_FF

Trade Value	2022 Picks	2023 Picks	2024 Picks	Running Back	ECR (+/-)	Wide Receiver	ECR (+/-)	Tight End	ECR (+/-)	Quarterback	ECR (+/-)
83										Josh Allen	0
81										Patrick Mahomes	0
80										Justin Herbert	2
78						Justin Jefferson	2				
77						Ja'Marr Chase	0			Lamar Jackson	3
73				Jonathan Taylor	-7					Kyler Murray	6
72				Najee Harris	-2						
69				Christian McCaffrey	3					Joe Burrow	0
68						Cooper Kupp	3				
67						CeeDee Lamb	1				
66										Dak Prescott	7
66										Jalen Hurts	19
64				Javonte Williams	-3						
61				D'Andre Swift	-10			Kyle Pitts		Deshaun Watson	-1
59						A.J. Brown	-3				
58	2022 1.01					Davante Adams	1				
57	Breece Hall (RB)									Trey Lance	9
56						Deebo Samuel	0			Trevor Lawrence	0
54				Joe Mixon	-5					Justin Fields	12
52				Austin Ekeler	-8	Stefon Diggs	-1				
51										Russell Wilson	1
50						Jaylen Waddle	0	Mark Andrews	-3	Matthew Stafford	9
47	2022 1.02			Dalvin Cook	-7						
46	Drake London (WR)			Antonio Gibson	7	Tyreek Hill	-5			Aaron Rodgers	9
45						Tee Higgins	-11				
44				Saquon Barkley	-1	DK Metcalf	-8				
42	Jameson Williams (WR) / 2022 1.03			Cam Akers	-2	Diontae Johnson	1				
41				Alvin Kamara	-8					Derek Carr	6
40				Nick Chubb	-8					Mac Jones	8
39						DJ Moore	-5				
38						Chris Godwin	-1				
37				Derrick Henry	-5			Travis Kelce	-2	Tua Tagovailoa	2
36						Terry McLaurin	-2				
35						Michael Pittman Jr.	-1			Zach Wilson	3
33	Ken Walker III (RB) / 2022 1.04 · 1.05	2023 1st				Elijah Moore	-1	George Kittle	-4	Kirk Cousins	7
32	Treylon Burks (RB)			J.K. Dobbins	-8	DeVonta Smith	0				
32				Travis Etienne Jr.	-7	Mike Evans	-2				
31				Aaron Jones	-1	Jerry Jeudy	-1				
30	Garrett Wilson (WR) / 2022 1.06 · 1.08			David Montgomery	-3	Amari Cooper	0			Tom Brady	6
29	Chris Olave (WR)					Courtland Sutton	3				
29	Malik Willis (QB)					Rashod Bateman	-5				
28				Elijah Mitchell	1						
28				Leonard Fournette	-2						
28				Josh Jacobs	-2						
28				AJ Dillon							
27				Ezekiel Elliott	-1					Ryan Tannehill	3
26			2024 1st	James Conner	1	Keenan Allen	-3				
26						Amon-Ra St. Brown	1				
25						DeAndre Hopkins	0				
25						Michael Thomas	2				
25						Darnell Mooney	0				
25						Mike Williams	0				
24						Brandon Aiyuk	1	Darren Waller	-4		
23				Clyde Edwards-Helaire	0	Allen Robinson II	1				
23	2022 1.09			Miles Sanders	0	Gabriel Davis	4				
23	Skyy Moore (WR) / 2022 1.10			Michael Carter	3			T.J. Hockenson	-4		
22								Pat Freiermuth	-1		
22						JuJu Smith-Schuster	1	Dallas Goedert	-2		
22						Kadarius Toney	3				
22						Marquise Brown	-3			Davis Mills	0
20		2023 2nd		Kareem Hunt	-2	Brandin Cooks	0				
20				Damien Harris	-1	Chase Claypool	0				
20				Tony Pollard	-2						
20				Chase Edmonds	1						
19				Devin Singletary	1	Tyler Lockett	-1	Dalton Schultz	-3	Matt Ryan	0
19						Christian Kirk	3				
18	2022 1.11 · 1.12			Rhamondre Stevenson	-1	Hunter Renfrow	-1				
18						Michael Gallup	1				
18	Christian Watson (WR)					Calvin Ridley	1				
18	Dameon Pierce (RB)					Rondale Moore	2				
17	Jahan Dotson (WR)					Tyler Boyd	2			Carson Wentz	-2
17	George Pickens (WR) / 2022 2.01 · 2.06		2024 2nd	Rashaad Penny	-1	Alexander Mattison	0			Daniel Jones	1
16	Desmond Ridder (QB)							Dawson Knox	-4		
16	Isaiah Spiller (RB)							Noah Fant	-2		
16	Matt Corral (QB)					Tim Patrick	3	Mike Gesicki	2		
15	Tyler Allgeier (RB) / 2022 2.07			James Robinson	0	Terrace Marshall Jr.	5	Irv Smith Jr.	-1		
15	Rachaad White (RB)			Melvin Gordon III	1	Kenny Golladay	1				
14						Odell Beckham Jr.	1				
14	2022 2.08			Ronald Jones II	-1	Adam Thielen	-1	Cole Kmet	-1		
14				Khalil Herbert	-1	Robert Woods	0	David Njoku	1		
13	James Cook (RB)					DJ Chark Jr.	1				
13	Brian Robinson Jr. (RB) / 2022 2.09					Jakobi Meyers	0	Albert Okwuegbunam	-3	Drew Lock	9
13	David Bell (WR) / 2022 2.10									Jimmy Garoppolo	5
13						Corey Davis	1			Marcus Mariota	7
12						Laviska Shenault Jr.	-1			Sam Darnold	8
12	2022 2.11 · 2.12			Kenneth Gainwell	-2	Russell Gage	-1				
12				Sony Michel	1	William Fuller V	1				
12	Alec Pierce (WR)			Gus Edwards	1	Curtis Samuel	2	Hunter Henry	-3		
11	Sam Howell (QB)			Chuba Hubbard	1	Jarvis Landry	0	Zach Ertz	-3		
11	John Metchie III (WR) / 2022 3.01 · 3.04			Cordarrelle Patterson	-3	Van Jefferson	1	Evan Engram	-2		
11	Wan'Dale Robinson (WR)			Chris Evans	4	Allen Lazard	2				
10	Zamir White (RB)					Joshua Palmer	1				
10	Trey McBride (TE)					Marquez Valdes-Scantling	0	Brevin Jordan	-1		
10	2022 3.05	2023 3rd				DeVante Parker	-1			Jordan Love	10
10				J.D. McKissic	-2	Robbie Anderson	2				
10						Nico Collins	0				
9						Donovan Peoples-Jones	0				
9						Mecole Hardman	0	Logan Thomas	-3	Teddy Bridgewater	9
9				Trey Sermon	-1			Rob Gronkowski	-1	Taysom Hill	9
9				Chris Carson	-1			Tyler Higbee	-5		
8				D'Ernest Johnson	-1					Gardner Minshew II	8
8				D'Onta Foreman	-1	Parris Campbell	2	Gerald Everett	-1	Tyler Huntley	5
8				Nyheim Hines	-4						
8			2024 3rd	Jamaal Williams	-4	K.J. Osborn	0				
7						Julio Jones	0				
7				Ke'Shawn Vaughn	-1	Sterling Shepard	0	Adam Trautman	-2		
7				Raheem Mostert	-2	Marquez Callaway	0	Jonnu Smith	-2		
7				Kenyan Drake	-1						
7				Myles Gaskin	-1						
7	Pierre Strong Jr. (RB) / 2022 3.06 · 3.12			Darrel Williams	-1						
7	Tyrion Davis-Price (RB)					Kendrick Bourne	-2	Austin Hooper	-1		
6	Keaontay Ingram (RB)					Zack Moss	0	Robert Tonyan	-4		
6	Khalil Shakir (RB)					Jeff Wilson Jr.	1	Hayden Hurst	0		
6	Jerome Ford (RB)					Mike Davis	2	Marvin Jones Jr.	-1		
6	Danny Gray (WR)							Harrison Bryant	-1		
6	Hassan Haskins (RB)										
5						K.J. Osborn	-2				
5				James White		Jamison Crowder	-2				
5				Marlon Mack	-3	Dyami Brown	-1	C.J. Uzomah	-1		

as I can into one analysis. I feed the ranks into my database (clean up the names) and average positional ranks before running them through my model. Next, I assign rank-based trade values built on historic values as a function of positional scarcity. In all my models, running backs are the backbone. Wide receiver, tight end and quarterback values are determined based on a function of nearby RB values.

The dynasty rookie picks are a lot more complex. So, I manually go through crowd-sourced data (Twitter polls, KTC, etc.) and create a high- and low-value range for groups of picks (early, mid, late). Post-NFL Draft, the current-year rookie picks get a little easier to add to the chart. I will compare picks to other players at all positions to try to dial in the placement.

The 2023 picks are higher than normal n+1 rookie picks would be because of all the hype. The 2024 picks are about where I would expect n+2 picks to be located. They lose value due to not being relevant for another two years. I like scoring points and winning this year!

Let us know which trades you are working on this offseason. Trading makes fantasy fun! ▬▬

Dynasty league fantasy football: Top 24 rookies from the 2022 NFL draft class

By Jeff Haverlack

Nothing excites dynasty league players like a rookie draft!

The 2022 rookie class long carried the stigma of being a down year for talent and depth but, as the dust settled following the NFL draft, an intriguing group of receivers found their way into upside situations, and combined with just enough talent at running back, it has elevated the class enough to keep things interesting.

For those teams needing quarterback help, 2022 was one of the weakest classes in recent memory, and tight ends left much to be desired as well. While many

remain focused on the promise of 2023, we shouldn't overlook the potential of the 2022 class.

Let's take a look at the Top 24 rookies for 2022 as found at DynastyLeagueFootball.com (DLF), the Internet's largest and oldest dynasty-centric fantasy football site.

1. Breece Hall, RB, NYJ

5'11/217 lbs. — Age: 21

Hall is a potential carry-the-load back who is as adept as a receiver as he is productive as a runner. With over 3,000 rushing yards and 41 touchdowns in his final two years at Iowa State, he easily separated himself from all other rookie runners in 2022 and he's the overwhelming favorite as 2022's 1.01 pick in dynasty rookie drafts.

2. Drake London, WR, ATL

6'4/219 lbs. — Age: 20

London amassed 1,084 yards and seven touchdowns before a broken ankle ended his junior season at USC. Selected No. 8 overall, he inherits a true WR1 role and should be a volume option for the rebuilding Falcons. Atlanta's quarterback play remains a concern but London's targets are all but guaranteed.

3. Treylon Burks, WR, TEN

6'2/225 lbs. — Age: 22

Burks disappointed at the combine with a 4.55 40-yard dash, but tape shows plenty of speed combined with physicality, strong hands and an NFL build. He'll step right into the shoes of traded receiver A.J. Brown (PHI).

4. Garrett Wilson, WR, NYJ

6'/183 lbs. — Age: 21

Selected No. 10 overall, Wilson is a silky-smooth route runner with legitimate 4.38 wheels who should step into the starting lineup immediately for the Jets. Target share will remain a concern until sophomore quarterback Zach Wilson proves he can distribute the ball effectively, but Garrett Wilson has the ability to a top receiver for the next decade once chemistry is present.

5. Ken Walker, RB, SEA

5'9/211 lbs. — Age: 21

Walker was a surprise selection by the run-first Seahawks and, without superstar Russell Wilson at the helm, it's a rebuilding year for the team. It's a full room in Seattle with Rashaad Penny and Chris Carson (if he's cleared medically) all in the mix for carries, so dynasty managers may need to be patient.

6. Jameson Williams, WR DET

6'1/179 lbs. — Age: 21

Selected No. 12 overall, if not for an ACL injury suffered in the national championship game, Williams may have been the first receiver off the board in the NFL draft. Williams could start the season on the PUP list but all reports are that his rehab is going well. Detroit has quietly assembled an impressive collection of young playmakers on offense, and Williams is arguably the most dynamic receiver in the 2022 draft class.

7. Chris Olave, WR, NO

6'/187 lbs. — Age: 21

Olave blazed a surprising 4.39 40-yard dash at the NFL combine and is widely believed to be the most polished and NFL-ready rookie receiver. Like other receivers in this year's class, quarterback play is a concern.

8. George Pickens, WR, PIT

6'3/195 lbs. — Age: 21

Pickens tore his ACL in spring practices during 2021 but returned late in the season to help Georgia win the national championship. Big, fast and with strong hands, Pickens will have every opportunity to make an early-career impact in Pittsburgh.

9. Jahan Dotson, WR, WAS

5'11/178 lbs. — Age: 22

A capable receiver at all levels, Dotson has the dynamic ability to be an immediate impact player for the Commanders and should see volume targets immediately. Look for Dotson to be used all over the field.

10. Skyy Moore, WR, KC

5'10/195 lbs. — Age: 21

Moore's 4.41 40-yard dash a the combine impressed and his landing spot in Kansas City following the Tyreek Hill trades makes for an extremely intriguing late-first round rookie selection in dynasty. It's a full room in KC but Moore should have every opportunity to shine early.

11. Christian Watson, WR, GB

6'4/208 lbs. — Age: 23

Watson has the speed and profile to be a top NFL receiver in time when considering he'll be receiving passes from MVP Aaron Rodgers. He's raw, but patience could be well rewarded.

12. James Cook, RB, BUF

5'11/199 lbs. — Age: 22

It's all in the family as Cook's brother, Dalvin, plays in Minnesota. While not possessing the early-down size of his brother, James Cook will see immediate time as a receiver and has the ability to work into an early-down role over time.

13. Rachaad White, RB, TB

6'/214 lbs. — Age: 23

He's older for a rookie but White's receiving ability suggests he could see field-time early in his career while Leonard Fournette plays out his contract.

14. John Metchie, WR, HOU

5'11/187 lbs. — Age: 21

Another standout receiver for Alabama who tore his ACL during the team's playoff run. Fast and fluid, Metchie needs to work on refining his routes but has the tools to be an impact player at the next level with the rebuilding Houston Texans.

15. David Bell, WR, CLE

6'1/212 lbs. — Age: 21

What Bell lacks in long speed and suddenness he makes up for with crafty route running and frame positioning to complete receptions. He's a candidate to start in the slot for Cleveland.

16. Wan'Dale Robinson, WR, NYG

5'8/178 lbs. — Age: 21

Robinson is a candidate to start immediately in the slot for the Giants, bringing a combination of agility and elusiveness to a team badly needing both at receiver.

17. Jalen Tolbert, WR, DAL

6'1/194 lbs. — Age: 23

If he can see field time early in his career to generate chemistry with quarterback Dak Prescott, Tolbert could be a sneaky second-round dynasty rookie selection.

18. Dameon Pierce, RB, HOU

5'10/218 lbs. — Age: 22

Underutilized in his time at Florida, Pierce is a dynasty second-round rookie steal who figures to have a more productive NFL career than collegiate. A great consolation prize for those needing running back help.

19. Alec Pierce, WR, IND

6'3/211 lbs. — Age: 22

Pierce is built for the NFL and flew under the radar though he possesses size, speed and a drafted situation to be an early-career producer. Veteran quarterback Matt Ryan should aid Pierce's development.

20. Isaiah Spiller, RB, LAC

6'/217 lbs. — Age: 20

Spiller turned in a disappointing pro day but his collegiate tape shows power, durability and production. He's a fine selection in the late second round of dynasty rookie drafts.

21. Trey McBride, TE, ARI

6'4/246 lbs. — Age: 22

McBride headlines a weak 2022 rookie tight end class and lands in a perfect situation in the desert, learning behind Zach Ertz. Patience should be rewarded in time.

22. Brian Robinson, RB, WAS

6'2/225 lbs. — Age: 23

A five-year player at Alabama and somewhat of a one-year wonder, Robinson is built for the NFL but landed in a disappointing situation for early-career impact.

23. Zamir White, RB, LV

6'/214 lbs. — Age: 22

White projects as an early-down producer in time but dynasty managers will need to remain patient while waiting for current starter Josh Jacobs to move on in free agency in 2023.

24. Kenny Pickett, QB, PIT

6'3/220 lbs. Age: 23

Headlining a weak quarterback class, Pickett falls to an ideal situation and is an odds-on favorite to be starting in the later weeks of the 2022 NFL season. ▃▃

Want to draft Drake London? Do it — data shows that rookies win fantasy football leagues

By Michael Salfino

Since 2018, 29 rookie RBs and WRs have cracked the 170-point mark in PPR, according to Pro Football Reference. That's a little more than seven per year and equates to about a top-70 non-QB (in other words, a top-six-round value).

A top-48 (first four rounds) pick scores at least 200 PPR points, and 16 rookies have done that since 2018, an average of four per year. Six have been "boom" players, meaning 250 points or more (about a top-20 pick), and one, Saquon Barkley, was a league winner at nearly 400 points (385).

THE ATHLETIC ———————————————————————————— 2022 FANTASY FOOTBALL GUIDE

Of the 29 total fantasy-relevant rookies with 170-point PPR performances, 10 have been real-life first-round picks. Ten have been second-rounders. And seven were taken in the third round or later in the actual draft. Two — 2020's James Robinson and 2018's Phillip Lindsay — thrived as undrafted free agents. Last year, a fourth-round real-life pick, Amon-Ra St. Brown, was the eighth-highest-scoring rookie in the four-year period.

Top rookies in PPR since 2018

Rank	PLAYER	YEAR	POS	DRAFT	PPR
1	Saquon Barkley	2018	RB	1-2	385.8
2	Ja'Marr Chase	2021	WR	1-5	304.6
3	Najee Harris	2021	RB	1-22	300.7
4	Justin Jefferson	2020	WR	1-22	274.2
5	Jonathan Taylor	2020	RB	2-41	252.8
6	James Robinson	2020	RB	UDFA	250.4
7	Jaylen Waddle	2021	WR	1-6	245.8
8	Amon-Ra St. Brown	2021	WR	4-112	227.3
9	Phillip Lindsay	2018	RB	UDFA	222.8
10	Miles Sanders	2019	RB	2-53	218.7

This is what the numbers tell us: Two to three first-rounders on average pop, as do about three second-rounders (remember, more RBs are taken in the second round) and about two "others," including free agents.

But what are the denominators? There were 22 first-round (real NFL Draft) RBs and WRs in the period, so 45.4 percent of them hit. Let's call it half. There are 36 second-rounders, for a hit rate of 28 percent. There are 158 in the third round or later, for a hit rate of about 3 percent (excluding the undrafted players).

Here is the pool of candidates and their teams this year:

First-round rookies

Drake London (WR, Falcons), Garrett Wilson (WR, Jets), Chris Olave (WR, Saints), Jameson Williams (WR, Lions), Jahan Dotson (WR, Commanders), Treylon Burks (WR, Titans).

So about half of these guys are going to be fantasy relevant. The early ADP market is not betting on these WRs very heavily; London is about WR40, Wilson WR45, Olave WR47, Williams WR56, Dotson WR65, but then Burks is way out of order, all the way up to WR38. Since round correlates to success, it's logical that draft order should, too. Why expect so much out of the lowest-drafted first-round WR?

The value here is obviously Dotson. Always gamble when you are paid to gamble. Do not pay to gamble, as you'd be doing with Burks. I'd stay away from Williams because of his ACL injury and the likelihood he's not even active to start the season. I see no problem with where the other rookies are drafted, but no bargains, either.

Second-round rookies

In the second round this year we have 10 players, including three running backs: Christian Watson (WR, Packers), Breece Hall (RB, Jets), Kenneth Walker (RB, Seahawks), Wan'Dale Robinson (WR, Giants), John Metchie (WR, Texans), Tyquan Thornton (WR, Patriots), George Pickens (WR, Steelers), Alec Pierce (WR, Colts), Skyy Moore (WR, Chiefs), James Cook (RB, Bills).

Two or three of these guys will pop. Breece Hall is the obvious choice, as he's slated for a heavy workload. View his floor as 2021 Javonte Williams (though he's more comparable to Jonathan Taylor as a runner). So there are maybe one or two more guys (at most) who will be real assets. Draft order here is not much of a help. Of course, Walker is a candidate to be the starting RB for Seattle with draft capital in the top third of the first round. However, the Seahawks staff does not have a reputation for giving highly drafted running backs commensurate touches. Walker is RB26 vs. RB17 for Hall. I think that's right. But Walker is at least cheap. Cook is RB37, and I think that's also right for a guy who is probably limited to being a receiving back on a team that does not throw much to RBs, historically.

As for the second-round receivers, the market is betting the most on Moore, and it makes sense given the Chiefs need to replace Tyreek Hill. But you have to expect Moore to be the third WR and fourth receiving option behind JuJu Smith-Schuster, Marquez Valdes-Scantling and Travis Kelce. Historically, we need a guy who steps into a starting (top two) WR role. At the respective prices, I like Alec Pierce as a player who can do that in Indy, alongside Michael Pittman. And he's been going off the board at WR72, which is a free roll. (In a dynasty format, of course Moore is the play; there's just so much long-term upside with Mahomes as his QB.)

Later picks/free agents

I don't want to ever say never, but the odds of a pick from the third round or later popping are so low that you should not burn draft capital on them. If they emerge in-season, that's why we have the waiver wire. Of course, if a later pick falls into a starting gig on the eve of your draft, by all means take him. Then draft capital hardly matters. You just don't want to bet on any of these later-round guys or free agents emerging from obscurity. ▬▬

2023 fantasy football rookies: CJ Stroud and 7 more names to get to know now

By Dane Brugler

Two players at each offensive skill position who figure to factor into your 2023 fantasy football draft analysis — especially for dynasty leagues:

Quarterback

CJ Stroud, Ohio State

Replacing Justin Fields was no easy task, but Stroud grew up quickly last season and showed impressive progress with his steady heartbeat and outstanding passing anticipation. Stroud has a chance to cement himself as QB1 and the favorite to be the No. 1 pick if he continues to improve in key areas in 2022.

Bryce Young, Alabama

Young, the reigning Heisman Trophy winner with 4,872 passing yards and 50 touchdowns, is undersized and doesn't fit the prototypical physical traits that every NFL team covets. However, he remains poised versus pressure, processes quickly and creates plays, which will translate to any level of football.

Running back

Bijan Robinson, Texas

Running back was shut out of the first round in the 2022 NFL Draft, but there is a good chance Robinson will make sure that doesn't happen next April. The former five-star recruit is 220-plus pounds yet moves like a sub-200-pounder with his elusive feet and vision to match.

Devon Achane, Texas A&M

Isaiah Spiller is now in the NFL, but the Texas A&M backfield will be in good shape this season. A two-sport star for the Aggies, Achane led the FBS in yards per carry (7.0) last season as a backup and ran a blistering 10.12-second 100-meter sprint this spring for the track team.

Wide receiver

Jaxon Smith-Njigba, Ohio State

Ohio State produced a pair of top-15 wide receivers in this year's draft (Garrett Wilson, Chris Olave), and it might add another one next April. Coming off a record-setting 347-yard receiving performance in the Rose Bowl, Smith-Njigba isn't a burner with his average speed, but he plays with outstanding coordination and ball skills.

Kayshon Boutte, LSU

Though not on the same level as Ja'Marr Chase as a pro prospect, Boutte shows flashes of the former top-five draft pick, including similar power and acceleration after the catch. He missed most of last season after his second right ankle surgery, so staying healthy in 2022 will be paramount to his draft projection.

Tight end

Michael Mayer, Notre Dame

No, Mayer isn't on the Kyle Pitts level as an NFL prospect, but he is a clear upgrade over any tight end in the 2022 draft class. He already looks like an NFL starter with his size, strength and physicality to line up anywhere across the formation and create separation as a pass catcher.

Sam LaPorta, Iowa

Iowa asks its tight ends to do everything, so it doesn't take long to understand LaPorta's value to the Hawkeyes offense. He needs to be more consistent as a point-of-attack blocker, but he makes himself available as a receiver with his soft hands and toughness over the middle and down the seam. ▬▬

Fantasy football mailbag: Where to take Cooper Kupp, TE draft strategy and more

By Brandon Marianne Lee and Gene Clemons

Welcome to the fantasy football mailbag, supersized 2022 edition. Our in-house experts Brandon Marianne Lee and Gene Clemons picked the nine most interesting questions from our readers and put their own spin on the answers. Enjoy!

Jalen Hurts clearly has a very good opportunity to be a top QB this year, but how do you sort out the ambiguity around the Eagles' pass catchers — specifically, A.J. Brown, DeVonta Smith and Dallas Goedert? — Eoin R.

Gene: Last season, the Eagles had seven receivers with 30 or more targets. Five of the seven had 50 or more, and two of the five had over 75 targets. Goedert had 76 targets, and Smith had 104 targets. Expect Brown to suck up a lot of the targets that went to Quez Watkins and Jalen Reagor last year. I don't foresee Smith and Goedart's targets diminishing, but Brown's physicality makes it easy to foresee him working well underneath and on the intermediate routes. He should end up with the most targets of the three top Eagles pass catchers.

Brandon: I think you already have the players in the correct order: A.J. Brown, DeVonta Smith, Dallas Goedert. All three will be strong picks, with Goedert a standout at the super murky tight end position. Jalen Hurts as a top QB is a strong 2022 narrative, especially since he improved as a real football player at the end of the 2021 season. He was always killing it in fantasy, but in real football, some of those games were rough. But now, I'm totally digging him even more based on his hard work and improvement. I'm bullish on the whole crew.

For redraft: Which current RB2 has a strong chance to emerge as their team's RB1 this season? — Michael B.

Brandon: I'm really liking the landing spot for Tyler Allgeier. The Atlanta Falcons took him in the fifth round, which typically isn't a great sign, but as of now it's just Cordarrelle Patterson officially ahead of him on the depth chart. Damien Williams and Quadree Ellison are also there, but I really like Allgeier's versatility and size, which were on full display at BYU. He worked his way up from a walk-on there, and I could see him doing it again.

Gene: Last season in Denver, Melvin Gordon was actually RB1. He started 16 games for the Broncos and had an impressive 918 yards on 203 carries. But the writing seems to be on the wall that Javonte Williams will be the RB1 this season. He received the same number of carries as Gordon and almost matched his yardage (903). He was also more productive as a pass receiver. The difference was in the touchdowns; Gordon reached the end zone 10 times compared with Williams' seven. With Packers offensive coordinator Nathaniel Hackett taking over as head coach, expect him to showcase his newest weapons more to complement new quarterback Russell Wilson. The difference may not show up in the rushing statistics but may actually bear more fruit through the passing game, where you could see Williams used more like Packers RB1 Aaron Jones.

Is Travis Kelce still a late-first-round pick in a 12-team PPR draft with Tyreek Hill gone, allowing defenses to focus on Kelce more? — Brian H.

Gene: With the depth of top-scoring running backs and receivers, it is difficult to go with any tight end in the first round. It has much less to do with Tyreek Hill, because Kelce has performed well without Hill in the past. In 2020, Kelce was the equivalent of WR4 — behind only Davante Adams, Tyreek Hill and Stefon Diggs — and a top 10 non-QB overall, but things have definitely changed. On any given week, could he be a top-12 performer? Absolutely. But on a week-to-week basis, he is probably not going to net you more points than the top-10 running backs or wide receivers. That still puts him firmly as a second-round pick, and therefore extremely valuable, but probably not a top-12 pick overall.

Brandon: I'm totally with Gene on this one. If he's not scoring more fantasy points than the other options in the first round, then he doesn't belong there. Position scarcity be damned, you have to score points. That first-round pick needs to hit big, and if Kelce is just "toward the top of his position" and not "toward the top of the league," then that isn't going to cut it.

This year feels like a tough year to go two RBs at the turn. Do you think it's still a lucrative strategy? Or would you rather grab a WR, or maybe even two, with those top two picks? — Samuel H.

Gene: Until they start allowing running backs to score points only off rushing attempts, there is still a reason for them to be taken in multiples in the early rounds of the draft. With all of the advancements in the game and even as the paradigm shifts away from run-intensive teams to pass-happy squads, teams have also added more backs with elite skills as runners and receivers. Backs like Austin Ekler, Cordarrelle Patterson, Aaron Jones and Alvin Kamara affect the games in many ways, and that is reflected in the numbers. They may not rush for over 100 yards but the combination of rushing yards, receptions, receiving yards and touchdowns gives them consistent production for fantasy managers. Load them up and ride them.

Brandon: Let the draft come to you. I have some leagues where running backs are so heavy at the top of the draft that sometimes I can get two super-elite wide receivers, then I plan to reach for the sleeper running backs a little earlier than ADP to make sure that I get them as the draft goes on. At that point, everyone else is stocked at running back, so they end up fighting over the meh wide receivers left while I ignore that position and get depth everywhere else. Know your league and know your settings. But if you do go WR/WR or WR/TE, you need to do extra homework when it comes to later-round running backs. And honestly, it's hard to argue with WR/RB or RB/WR, because balance is a nice place to start.

In your experience, what's the best way to handle or limit corrupt trades? Is the voting system the best bad answer, or is there something that's worked well for you? These leagues are mostly for fun, and this has always been a difficult part of the game. — Eric F.

Brandon: An unpopular opinion, perhaps, but I don't veto anything. I take radical responsibility. If I play in a league with cheaters, year after year, then that's on me. And if these leagues are for fun, then you are saying that you find cheating fun. Or you would stop playing with them. Because, I'll be honest with you, I've never seen a trade that was truly corrupt. And the lopsided trades that did happen, ironically, would blow up in the "winner's" face often enough that it's easy for me to let it go. In terms of rules, almost all of my leagues have a rule that if over half of the people vote to veto, then the trade can't proceed. I would enact that and

then re-evaluate the leagues you're in. Harsh? Maybe. But now's the time to be discerning, not when it's Week 8 and you're in a big playoff push and you look like a toddler throwing a tantrum (even if you're right). I have a toddler, and the struggle is real. Ha!

Gene: There is no one perfect way to eliminate corrupt trades, and it does not matter if your league is for fun or serious money. I believe the best system needs to be two parts. The first is the commissioner's veto. This first step will normally put a halt to corrupt trades, as many times most guys are just trying to test what they can get away with. Once it is established that trades that make no sense for one side are rejected, the requests dwindle. On occasion, when the two parties really feel that a trade should be made, that's when a league vote is called upon to decide whether it will be accepted. Now everyone has a say, is aware of the outcome and can adjust accordingly.

Do you think you should be able to stash a player listed as "out" on IR even though they're not on the injured list? I kind of don't get why you can. — Sheldon G.

Gene: Yes, I definitely do. Sometimes you are hindered from making a weekly roster acquisition because of something like this. That almost forces you to drop a player you don't want to drop. By stashing him on IR, you get to fill a need that particular week but it doesn't allow you to have an ongoing interchangeable advantage because you must release one of them once the player is active.

Brandon: I don't love this situation, but it sort of cuts both ways. If a player surprisingly does play (especially in a Thursday game) and you don't remember to move him, then you are screwed the rest of the week because you can't move him. The IR position almost always ticks everyone off for different reasons. Most important, establish clear rules now.

How many RBs would you take before you'd take the first WR (Cooper Kupp)? — David A.

Brandon: Right now I would take Jonathan Taylor, Derrick Henry, Austin Ekeler and Najee Harris before Kupp. Some would switch in or out Christian McCaffrey and Dalvin Cook (yes, I know I'm low on McCaffrey, and I reserve the right to change my mind during the preseason — ha!). Overall, I'd say those are the top six running backs coming off the board potentially before Kupp. But then it's Kupp. I wouldn't even mind if you went Kupp before some of these backs in full-PPR formats. Barring injury (which could happen to any player), Kupp is as safe a pick as any of those backs. It's just about your team construction and the scarcity of the bell-cow back with the argument that these are the only backs with the bell-cow potential (although I would also label Alvin Kamara, Joe Mixon and D'Andre Swift as potential big-time players at the position, and you can get them after Kupp).

Gene: Probably four or five! Last season was skewed because of injuries to a lot of the top backs. It was probably an anomaly for Cooper Kupp to be the second-highest-scoring non-quarterback in fantasy. Regardless of last season, the shift has definitely begun. The very elite receivers are now just as important as top running backs, except in most cases you need more of them. The question has to be asked: Would you rather have the fifth-best running back in a draft or the best receiver? If you are thinking logically, you will probably say the receiver. Especially today, with the number of targets the elite receivers command, they are invaluable to your team regardless of the format.

Which team's coaching change will most positively impact fantasy scoring? Which change will most hurt fantasy scoring? — Doug C.

Gene: Just the consistency in New York should improve the offense of the Giants this season. The combination of Brian Daboll trying to re-create what he accomplished in Buffalo and Mike Kafka trying to sprinkle in some of that Kansas City magic will definitely benefit Saquon Barkley, Daniel Jones and all of the receivers.

Brandon: Love the New York Giants call. I don't love the coach shuffling that happened in New Orleans. I'm in the minority on this, but the team is going from an offensive-minded head coach who called the plays to a defensive-minded coach who went 8-28 during his only stint as a head coach (to be fair, the Raiders set him up to fail, but that's for another article). Sure, the offensive coordinator, Pat Carmichael Jr., has been with the team since the 2009 Super Bowl season. Still, I don't know if I like all the comfort of people being with the organization for a long time but now missing their captain. A good change for fantasy would be the Denver Broncos. Head coach Nathaniel Hackett had a ton of success in Green Bay with Aaron Rodgers. Now he gets a talented Russell Wilson with a strong supporting cast and an organization that just broke records with a sale in a town that's sizzling hot when it comes to sports teams. I am a Denver homer, I'll admit that. But come on … sometimes facts are facts.

Can we talk about TE drafting strategy this year? To what extreme do we prioritize the top guys, or do we forget about the position until the end, or is there a gem who you're pounding the table for at a reasonable ADP? — Eric F.

Brandon: If you want the big three (Travis Kelce, Mark Andrews, Kyle Pitts), then you'll have to use the second pick of your draft (or first if you are really committed to them). George Kittle and Darren Waller typically go in the third round. Everyone else is in the fifth round or later, so that's probably where I'll draft my guy(s). I'm more inclined to wait for a Dalton Schultz or Dawson Knox and then pair them with a sleeper at the end of the draft, like Cole Kmet or Irv Smith Jr., and then play the matchups. Mark Andrews seems to be the least scary of the top picks, then Kyle Pitts (although that QB situation in Atlanta is brutal). But honestly, I really like the teams where I wait. I feel like I get enough value from the picks at the other positions early on.

Gene: I think you never forget about tight ends. The fact that there are not as many productive ones and that, in many circumstances, their success can be week to week, you need to make sure you prioritize grabbing a good one or else you are shopping for penny stocks hoping to get lucky. The fact that the top two tight ends in 2021, Mark Andrews and Travis Kelce, were equivalents to top-10 WRs means that if you are able to grab them at the right time for the right price, they can be difference-makers for your team every week. ■

XIV. All the Strategy You'll Ever Need

Fantasy football auction draft strategy: Stars and scrubs the only way to fly

By Michael Salfino

There's but one fantasy football auction strategy: stars and scrubs.

Do not fear rostering a bunch of $1 players in 12-team, one-QB formats.

Paying for stars and taking on a bunch of $1 scrubs is the only way to auction. If you want to "spread the risk," just draft.

So committing to stars by paying whatever it takes for top-tier players is the first strategic decision to make. The only way around this is to add a lot of starters, Flexes and SuperFlexes. Also, you can get rid of kickers, which is just another $1 streaming spot. Perhaps make your league 14 teams instead of 12. Then, you have shaken things up to the point that "spread the risk" is a viable winning strategy. This is why 12-team (or, God forbid, 10-team) auctions in standard one-QB formats are super boring — the analytics have spoken, and there is exactly one way to play.

The second related question is how to budget the onesies — quarterback and tight end.

If you auction, you should use a SuperFlex. You want people to have to make more decisions on $1 players and not make the strategy for success so obvious. But few leagues have a SuperFlex (the number is growing, though!). So we will proceed with the assumption you are a standard, one-QB league. In this case, your quarterback has to join your defense and kicker as $1 starting positions. Now you have $197 left for (let's call it) 13 players. But only seven are starters: two running backs, three wide receivers, a tight end and the traditional RB/WR/TE Flex.

Am I nuts for even listing TE as a possible Flex? The traditional stars and scrubbers might say: "All onesies are $1." But I see an alternate path. In 2018, my advice was a premium tight end. It proved successful, generally. I don't want to fight 2018's war and just by default say you should go premium tight end again, but I repeat: TE1 equals WR10, and TE5 equals WR25, on average. The cost of these tight ends is generally far less than it is for those commensurate receivers. So I like a strategy where you pay for, say, George Kittle but also for a mid-range option and have two equivalent top-25 receivers at TE and Flex. The cost for them will be well below the expected value, generally. And the reason is that half your auction probably is handcuffing themselves to a $1 TE strategy before they even enter the room.

Prioritize the RBs. I like getting a couple of RB5 types who I think can finish at RB1.

I want to go a little cheaper at WR because I already am super strong at TE and have my Flex filled (with that second TE). Plus, I want two or three backup RBs who are not $1 players. The backups should not be more than $5, and $3 is perfect. Two backup $1 WRs is fine. So now instead of $66 for three WRs, I have $60 — but probably more because the room likely is not going to make me pay market prices for tight ends.

I want a top-15-projected guy with upside. Say he costs $29, leaving me $31 for two WRs. Your mileage might vary, but this is the idea: decent floor, high ceiling. The other key point is you're not targeting specific players, just similar players in the same tier.

Remember: This isn't about the individual picks. It's about constructing a budget — minimum bids at QB, K and D/ST. Premium for RBs (costly in auctions) and TEs (undervalued in auctions). A little spare change for better backup RB options. If you want to go 1EliteRB (instead of possibly two) and put the remainder into a true No. 1 receiver, fine. You can easily win this way, too.

Finally, in terms of auction gamesmanship, a few big points:

- Do not make a plausible bid to drive up the cost of a player (price enforcing). This makes you a chump since you are assuming all the risk for a benefit you can only share with the entire room.

- Tether bid. What this means is let's say you want Kittle but don't know what he's going to cost and would like clarity. Toss Kelce, and then Kittle's price is tethered to Kelce's. It will be "Kelce's price minus X." It will not be more. If there's a WR15-ish you like, nominate a consensus one you do not want for a minimum bid and see what he goes for; then you know your guy is definitely not going to go for more and could go for less.

- Jump bid after tethering. For example, you toss Kelce and he goes for $42. Someone else immediately nominates Kittle for $15. Jump right up to the average discount, which is (for this example) Kelce minus $12, and say $30 immediately. Now someone who likes Kittle can't just walk him up slowly and talk himself into simply just a little more than the room seems to think he's worth. They have to make a purchase decision based on only one bid: yours. And if your leaguemate does say $31, just say $33 after "going once" to close the deal. Nothing is more meaningless in an auction than the $2 you saved not bidding on a player you want. This is the "jump and plus-two strategy" I just named. ▬▬

Snake draft strategy: Zig when others zag, follow the data and wait on QB

By Michael Salfino

In snake drafts, draft order is destiny.

This does not mean you are destined to win or lose based on where you pick. It means the shape of your roster will be determined by this. If you catch a top-six pick, you can plan to implement a 1EliteRB strategy — basically a variation of zeroRB, where you take a plausible top-scoring running back with your first pick, then target wide receivers and tight ends with your other premium picks. (Note: We are assuming a format with three wide receivers and a Flex – 10 starters.)

The math behind getting a late pick

However, if you are handed a late pick, you're probably going to have to audible. My data suggests if you make the RB8 or RB10 your first-round pick, you should expect to be 50 points behind everyone unless that running back just crushes it (which is unlikely). So this is a Top 1-5 WR/Top TE slot (factoring in the immediate second-rounder). You're going to have to scramble for running backs, hope to catch lightning (or at least

something serviceable) on the waiver wire early, then stream backs who happen to be starting that given week. But at least you'll have as many or more expected points after two rounds as all your league-mates.

From 2019 to 2021, the 10th-best running back in points per reception (PPR) finishes the year with 231 points on average versus an expected 285 for the fifth-best wide receiver (and you will be able to draft two, probably, at the turn — or opt for the likely TE1s in Travis Kelce/ Mark Andrews). Yes, I know drafting the WR4 and WR5 doesn't guarantee top-five wide receiver scoring (that guy might be WR25 for all we know). But we're just drafting expected points, not players. You might have to lie down after reading that, but this is the core principle of fantasy analytics.

Plus, the variance is much greater at running back than at wide receiver. The data shows running backs are less likely than wide receivers to meet their average draft position (ADP) and more likely to be a complete bust when you compare end-of-season rankings to ADP.

Maybe Nick Chubb falls to you in the second round and you think he can be the RB1. If that's the case, draft him. But if you're taking the RB11 hoping he'll be RB11, you're losing a lot of ground. The default pick in the second round is a wide receiver or a top tight end, just like the default pick in the first round is a running back.

Considering a tight end early

"Premium tight end" is a winning strategy. We can pretty much guarantee it's going to be Kelce or Andrews. Maybe George Kittle if he stays healthy (unlikely). Maybe Kyle Pitts if the quarterback play is serviceable (unlikely). Those last two guys are fine, but they're not going to be 300-point scorers like Kelce and Andrews are likely to be. If you draft one of them, you have your league in a stranglehold at the position; you'll likely destroy them at tight end week in and out. Historically (2019-21), TE1 equals WR5. TE5, though, equates to just WR30. So if you don't get Andrews or Kelce, I'd sit the position out and try to take two guys at TE10-15 who might rise, something you can do deep into the draft (the tight end finishing the year third in points scored is generally the 10th to 15th tight end drafted). Tight end is basically "go big or go home." I get that Pitts is an ethereal talent, but he doesn't have the QB or the offense, so the receivers where he's being picked are probably going to beat him.

Of course, in a one-quarterback league, you don't want to take a quarterback early, meaning not in the first five rounds. Looking at the data, on average,

QB5 is a 300-point player and QB10 finishes with 270 points. You'd rather have the former than the latter, of course. But at what price of draft capital? QB10 can be had about 75 picks/five rounds later. And QB10 (think Jalen Hurts, for example) can easily end up as QB1. You know who's not likely to be QB1? The top drafted quarterback. That hasn't happened once during the past decade.

The middle and late rounds

Once you have a running back, three or four wide receivers and a tight end locked up, it's time to swing for the fences. You can't do this on every pick. Maybe with your second running back you want someone with a clear role but little path to bell-cow status, like Chase Edmonds. Taking WR50 because you think that's his floor is a losing approach. Don't focus on floors when the rounds approach the double digits. Think instead about players who can shatter projections, traditionally younger players with established roles who play with top quarterbacks (like Allen Lazard).

Even at quarterback, why take Derek Carr for his floor when you can swing for the fences with Hurts? If you're wrong, so what? You can pick someone safe (Kirk Cousins, who can lead the NFL in passing yards) with your other quarterback pick.

Why am I telling you to take two quarterbacks in a one-quarterback league? Well, Yahoo research I pulled when I wrote there said that across its platform, teams draft 1.9 quarterbacks per team — and they roster slightly more on average each week of the season. If this isn't your league, draft one quarterback. If it is, you have to protect yourself with a second pick because your streaming options are going to be severely limited. This data even persuaded one of the industry's leading advocates of streaming quarterbacks that you have to adapt to your league's reality:

"That 1.92 number is ... something else," said C.D. Carter, co-host of the "Living the Stream" podcast that is built around punting quarterbacks. "Hard to believe that many people find it necessary to have a damn backup QB. That would change my approach a bit. I would be compelled to take someone in the 10th- to 12th-round range unless there were screaming WR or RB values there because so many people used so much draft capital on QB."

Of course, you could just convince your league to go with a SuperFlex option and then have a quarterback position that somewhat reflects its importance on the real gridiron.

But we play the fake game, an upside-down one in which running backs are lusted for, quarterbacks are meaningless and you can never have enough receivers who command the football. ▄▄▄

From 'No Bad Offenses' to zeroRB: The 2022 fantasy football draft strategy field guide

By Michael Salfino

In the game of picking players, no person is king. Sure, you may have a great year with your projections and crush your league. But the data says this skill is not repeatable. To consistently make the playoffs in your leagues, you need structural strategic advantages that can be more reliably leveraged.

Then, of course, you have to pick the right players on top of this, as no strategy can overcome bad forecasting and bad luck on the player side (just as no strategy is bad if you happen to pick the right players).

However, a good strategy can significantly increase the odds of good picks, because you are continuously selecting from a plus-expected-value pool (and avoiding the minus-EV ones).

But what strategies are optimal, either by themselves or in combination? There are so many to choose from: zeroRB, 1EliteRB, zeroWR, Premium TE, late-round QB, second-year breakout, no bad offenses. ... Let's review them all!

Note: I am assuming a "Flex-10 league," meaning three WRs and a Flex (equaling 10 starters).

ZeroRB is dead, they say. The popularizer of zeroRB, Shawn Siegele (The Athletic's Chris Vaccaro is credited with creating the strategy), said on a podcast before the 2020 season that his research proved that 14.7 percent of GMs who did not draft a running back in the first five rounds won their leagues (the expected rate of winning a 12-team league is 8.3 percent). No other strategy, he said, came close to this win rate. However, in recent years, that win rate has cratered, and it's likely because the strategy went mainstream. Even teams that draft RBs early are avoiding them in the third, fourth and fifth rounds. So the idea you can go zeroRB and land four top-25 receivers (in ADP) and a top-five TE with your first five picks is no longer realistic.

I don't want to overreact to recent trends. Overall, since its inception, zeroRB has been a tailwind to building a playoff team. It's a strategy for leveraging in-season transactions and the free RB loot that will inevitably be on the waiver wire. Running backs who get jobs through the attrition of injury or the failure of starters have very projectable touches in an upcoming game and thus can reliably be started. Conversely, waiver wire receivers may score as much in total, but their variance in touches is so extreme you cannot start them with confidence.

Verdict: This is a strategy for a late draft slot in which you can double tap two top-five WRs and maybe get two more top-25 WRs at the 3/4 turn. It is a way to make lemonade out of the lemons of a suboptimal draft slot in which the most likely top-five RBs are long gone.

No Dead-Zone RBs: One thing zeroRB does is avoid the worst picks in every draft: the second-tier running backs. From 2019 to 2021, RB15 scores 51 percent of the fantasy points of RB1, a massive decline. But RB35 scores 67 percent of RB15's point total. Even RB50 scores 51 percent of RB15's points. So RB50 is to RB15 what RB15 is to RB1 — this is to say how suboptimal it is, generally, to draft the 15th RB in your league. And these points do not even account for streaming. The fantasy GM who drafted RB15 and is getting ADP value is going to play him every week, while the RB35 GM is going to rotate that back out for a starter he finds on the waiver wire (which is increasingly easy as the season proceeds, and especially in the fantasy playoffs). You don't lose that much sitting out RB15 to 25 and loading up on RB35 to 50 instead.

Even teams that draft a running back or two in the first two rounds today generally just pound the WR queue versus taking these dead-zone RBs (the ones going 15 to 25 or so in the draft). And why not? WR10 is there when RB15 goes, on average, and beats RB15 since 2019 in PPR, 253-207. (These are end-of-season ranks, not where a player is drafted; but the whole idea of structural drafting is that you just need to get expected value.) Even later, when things invert and RB20 is there when 20 or even 25 WRs are off the board, a WR finishing the year 25th in his position easily beats the 20th RB, 209 to 193.

Verdict: 100 percent avoid RBs here.

1EliteRB is simply taking a back you think can be the best back — or at least a likely top-five scoring back — and then reverting to the zeroRB rules after the first round. It's a hybrid strategy and is the strategy of choice for most sharp drafters today. You get an anchor who, if he stays healthy, will likely propel your team to the playoffs while also staying out of the dead zone of running back in rounds 3 to 5. These teams will only take an RB in Round 2 if they think he has a chance to be a top-five RB. But since at least 10 to 12 RBs will be gone at most points in Round 2, the play is to take a top-five RB there (or the TE you think can lead his position in scoring, as TE1 equals WR5 on average the past three years).

Verdict: Not too hot and not too cold, and thus just right for the Goldilocks drafters.

Five WRs by Round 10: This provides maximum flexibility. You have the option of drafting RBs early, even three in the first five rounds if you want. But then WR becomes the overwhelming priority. By the end of Round 10, on average, about 50 WRs are off the board. By the end of Round 8, on average, about 40. To get five WRs in the top 35 of ADP, you need to draft them by round 6 or 7.

Let's look at the difference in scoring, and again, if you are a genius drafter who can get WR35 end-of-year value by taking the 50th WR in the draft, like picking an apple off the tree — you don't need structure. But we mere mortals want to lean into structural advantages that increase the odds of maximizing points. So, WR35 is 177 points and WR50 on average, finishes the year with 143. Satisfying this requirement by taking three WRs in the eighth, ninth and 10th rounds just does not move the needle enough.

Verdict: It's just checking a box. Five WRs by Round 8 has my attention, though. But then that's basically 1EliteRB.

ZeroWR is a strategy designed to foil the zeroRB leagues that exist only in our imagination. If everyone is doing zeroRB, then go zeroWRs and draft all the RBs! Brilliant, right?

Nah. This is like if everyone in the world decided to go to your favorite diner for blueberry pancakes Sunday morning. Sure, then the smart play would be to avoid the life-threatening chaos and simply go to another diner. But the odds of everyone in your league drafting zeroRB and everyone in the world going to your diner and ordering the same breakfast are roughly the same.

All the Strategy You'll Ever Need

It's undeniable that the RBs 15 to 25 are minus-EV picks. Why would you want to lean into making bad picks?

I get the rationale here — RBs get hurt and I'll be fine! No, you won't be fine. There's nothing more useless in fantasy football than RB15 or RB20.

Verdict: This is the bizarro zeroRB … meaning the opposite, in that it's absolutely a terrible idea. Not enough people avoid RBs early to make this strategy remotely tenable.

Elite TE is a personal favorite structure. This is just simple math. TE1 at the end of the year equals the scoring output of WR5. The cost of the two or three tight ends who have a chance to be the TE1 is generally far less than it is for those commensurate receivers. And remember, your third-best TE may actually be the fifth taken in your draft.

Verdict: Value-based picking, and it is easily implemented during the draft when your league gets WR happy at the expense of bettable TEs. Half the GMs in every league reflexively view TE as a position you essentially ignore.

Late-Round QB is such an obvious strategy in one QB league. But the streaming ability that often accompanies it is very league specific. If your league is average in rostering 1.9 QBs per team at the draft, according to Yahoo research (and that actually goes UP in-season in one-QB leagues relative to draft day), you can't wait THAT LONG. I advocate not taking a QB in a single-digit round, but then double-tapping the position with ideally a high floor (more of a pocket passer) player on a winning team (top-five QBs almost uniformly come from winning teams, though that may be a chicken-or-the-egg issue) and then an upside/running QB (even a super athletic one with a very low floor like a Zach Wilson). This lowers the draft capital you spend at the position but doesn't leave you exposed to a waiver wire generally bereft of signal callers.

Verdict: The top QB drafted is almost never the top-drafted QB. That player often comes out of the QB10-15 (in ADP) bucket. So lean into this reality.

Second-year Breakout is a cheat code for finding players who are more likely to significantly beat projections. Let me emphasize, this does not mean "likely" period, it just means you're increasing the odds of finding dramatic surplus value if you pick from the pool of second-year players. And you do this regardless of their rookie performance — you just factor in draft capital and expected roles.

In 2022, this group includes the QBs who were rookies in 2021. I like Wilson's environment and skills the best, but of course Trevor Lawrence, Justin Fields or Trey Lance can be QB7 or so with a little imagination — we can pretty much guarantee that one of them will be.

In early 2022 drafts, people are leaning into this too hard, with Javonte Williams coming off the board in the first round despite the continued presence of Melvin Gordon. Additionally:

- Travis Etienne didn't even have a rookie year but is still pick 50 to 55 in early drafts.

- Jaylen Waddle is going to cost you a third- or fourth-round pick; so you're paying for the breakout there, too, basically.

- Amon-Ra St. Brown can be had about pick 60 or so. I'm not excited about that, even though St. Brown already broke out as a rookie; there were just too many receivers added by the Lions.

- DeVonta Smith at WR35? That's fine. Not a bargain given the presence of A.J. Brown and expected subpar passing volume in Philly.

- Give me all the Rashod Bateman at pick 90 or so.

- Elijah Moore was WR2 in PPR his last five games — this is not a misprint. But he's going early in drafts about WR25, and I'd rather wait forever and take a flier on Corey Davis, who has a chance to lead the club in targets.

- Kyle Pitts is being drafted like he can be the TE1.

Verdict: Not very actionable in 2022 outside of Bateman.

No Bad Offenses (also called QB-centric drafting) but the latter term is confusing because it suggests we're drafting QBs where, really, we're drawing skill positions from the offenses who have the quarterbacks in which we believe.

There's such a changing of the guard at the position that it's hard to implement. The five rookie QBs last year could be good or bad — or just boring/in a vanilla offense like Mac Jones. Which teams definitely have QBs that we want to avoid? Giants, Commanders, Falcons, Lions, Seahawks (as we go to print), Texans (though Davis Mills was a five-star recruit), Browns (I'm assuming Deshaun Watson has a long-term suspension), Steelers, maybe the Dolphins, maybe the Colts. That's it. And really only the Giants, Commanders, Falcons, Lions and Steelers seem definite.

Verdict: Generally viable but difficult to implement this year. ▬▬

'I was JUST about to take him!' A neuroscientist explains how to stay cool when your draft goes awry

By Renee Miller

What's worse than finally getting in your fantasy draft, having thoroughly prepped by reading all the great stuff, tweaking rankings to develop your own foolproof plan for the season ... only to get your guy stolen at every perfectly lined-up pick?

Well, a lot of things are worse, if we're being honest, and furthermore, if you still think there's such a thing as a foolproof plan, I'll have what you're having! But nevertheless, it does suck.

Have you ever heard that the planning of an event usually brings more joy and happiness than the event itself? Your perfect wedding, your luxurious vacation, moving into your new house — just as with planning your best-ever fantasy football draft, sometimes the expectation and your imagination exceed the actual lived experience. Hopefully, the discrepancy is so small as to be overlooked and forgotten. The months or even years spent in anticipation of something great do provide a lion's share of good feelings, and some experts go so far as to say that the planning is more important than the doing, in terms of well-being.

Getting a guy stolen from your virtual grasp during a live draft, in person or online — especially if a timer is involved and especially if it happens to be by the person drafting immediately ahead of you — is simply no fun. Many a prayer has been sent to the fantasy gods to "please don't let him or her pick Hunter Renfrow

here." Having your best-laid plans go for naught in an instant is disappointing and frustrating.

Here's how the experience of getting a player stolen goes for me. Initial shock upon seeing MY PLAYER'S NAME called by the drafter in front of me. Heart plummets, maybe a bit cold and shaky, head totally blank. This is followed by panic, then heat returns, especially to the face, heart races, brain tries to analyze 50 possible alternative moves at once, until ultimately a decision is made. I'm a bit bewildered and exhausted after that 60 or 90 seconds.

All of these physical and physiological events are triggered by changes in the neurochemicals in our brains and bodies (peripheral nervous system). Very generally, all the neurotransmitters that make us feel good — dopamine, serotonin, norepinephrine — drop when we sense disappointment. This not only hurts (pain is sensed emotionally and physically) but also doesn't exactly make our brains work any better, smarter or faster. In fact, it does just the opposite. Not a good spot to be in with that clock ticking.

The good news — and of course there is good news! — is that the brain's response to disappointment can be modulated, and modulating that response is something you can practice and prepare to do.

The strength of the neurochemical response depends in part on the magnitude of the surprise. Therefore, the simplest thing you can do during a draft is EXPECT to get your player stolen at every pick. Expecting to have to rely on a backup plan does two things. It forces you to have a backup plan, and it reduces the shock of being put in a position to use it.

There are a few possible knee-jerk reactions to this happening without a backup plan. One response, depending on how long that blank brain lasts, is to just draft the next player in the site's ADP. Another is to take the next available player at the position you were targeting. The other — the one I'm most susceptible to — is to reach for the next round's planned pick now, ensuring that I don't get my player stolen again. Let's be super clear: None of these moves will cripple your fantasy team and none will prevent you from getting clear on your next move(s) during the wait until your next pick. The issue is that making a decision in the heat (or cold) of a moment — a disappointing moment, at that — will never deliver the most logical decision you could make. I know that fantasy football is an emotional game (and it wouldn't be so popular if it weren't) but the best players try to base their moves on clear, rational, justifiable logic. Especially if you know you're the kind of person whom logic deserts in a pinch, having a backup plan (or two or three) will keep your head in the draft.

So mindset adjustment No. 1 is to prepare to be pickpocketed and plan accordingly. The other aspect of having things not go according to our wishes or plans is that we can lose confidence in our ability to make good plans or expect good things to happen. On the scale of real life, this is a devastating state to be in, and repeated disappointments can lead to depression. In fantasy football, however, when you get a player stolen it's almost like getting a compliment. At least one other person thought your idea was brilliant! Framing the sniping in this way can keep you from getting too down and disappointed and let you trust that your next idea will be just as good. This is mindset adjustment No. 2. If you keep losing out on players, you must have had a good plan. The corollary here is that if it never happens, you are either very lucky or you're on an island with your player rankings.

If you draft enough, you get used to getting players stolen, you get used to making backup plans, and it isn't until all three of your Round 5 queued picks get swiped from your hands that you start to panic with frustration. If you're in this category of player, you'll want to take a couple of additional steps.

First and foremost, know every scoring rule your league has. You have to understand what is most valuable in your league. Next, when it's not your pick, study the other teams' drafts so far. Who needs a QB or a TE, and who has zero running backs? This will give you an idea of where the people in front of you might look to draft, and therefore your likelihood of draft disappointment. Alternatively, in a one-QB league, if you and the guy drafting ahead of you in Round 10 are the last two teams to take a QB, and he takes the one you were eyeing this round, there is absolutely no need to take the next best available QB with this pick. The next tier of QBs should be available for a while since everyone has one but you. Knowing other peoples' teams can also help you bolster your future trade market.

The bottom line is that if you and your league mates are well-prepared, you'll probably get your target taken riiiight before you pick once or twice. You'll probably be the takee on occasion, too. Being prepared for this eventuality can force you to have backup plans, limit the destructive disappointment mentality and view it as a compliment and opportunity to make an even savvier move. Worst case: If you do fall into panic mode and draft the next guy on the site's list

with two seconds remaining, it's not the end of your season. Take a deep breath, remember that you read this article and get on with the logical, rational draft you know you can have. ▬▬

Drafting for the floor: Using Warren Buffett's investment strategy to win at fantasy football

By KC Joyner

Fantasy managers are always looking for the most profitable draft-day strategies. Since profit is on their minds, it might be a good idea to take some advice from a duo who knows a thing or two about getting a strong return on investment.

Warren Buffett and Charlie Munger are two of the greatest investors in the history of the world, as their decades of directing Berkshire Hathaway has resulted in a company with close to $700 billion in market capitalization.

One of the ways they achieved this remarkable success is by pursuing what Munger calls the lollapalooza effect, which is when two or three or more forces are operating in the same direction and cause a cascade of effects.

It's not easy to find lollapalooza effects, but a key factor in doing so is avoiding negative elements. Munger and Buffett know that any notable downside factor in a company, be it in management, product quality or a change in customer wants, will almost immediately preclude that company from being able to benefit from a positive lollapalooza effect. If there are enough downside factors in a business, it can actually cause a negative lollapalooza effect that can be disastrous to its employees and stockholders.

So, how does all of this apply to fantasy football? It's pretty simple, as fantasy managers should apply Buffett and Munger's lollapalooza philosophy on draft day by taking a draft-to-the-floor approach.

Drafting to the floor means that a fantasy manager should always find a reasonable floor value for a player and almost never draft that player any higher than that. For example, if a fantasy manager determines that a running back has an RB2 floor and RB1 ceiling, that player should only be drafted as an RB2 and not as an RB1.

To illustrate why drafting that player as an RB1 is a bad idea, look at this chart that shows the 2021 PPR point difference between players in the middle of each scoring tier for running backs and wide receivers.

Position tiers	Tier pt. spread
RB1 to RB2	48.8
RB2 to RB3	35.3
RB3 to RB4	35.4
RB4 to RB5	21
WR1 to WR2	62.2
WR2 to WR3	28.9
WR3 to WR4	43.2
WR4 to WR5	22.5

To clarify, this chart shows that the difference between a mid-tier RB1 and a mid-tier RB2 last season was 48.8 points. That is a nearly three-point-per-week difference over the course of a fantasy season, which is a huge downside element. The downside point totals for the other tiers at RB and WR aren't as impactful outside of the 62.2-point decline from a mid-tier WR1 to a mid-tier WR2, but even the lower point levels here indicate that it doesn't take many draft mistakes of this nature to crush that roster's chances of competing for a title.

The preferred option would be to find an RB2 candidate with RB1 upside and draft him at the RB2 level. The initial benefit of this might seem obvious but consider what happened to fantasy managers who did this when drafting Najee Harris last season.

Harris had an average PPR ADP of 18 for much of the 2021 fantasy draft season. That means he could have been selected in the third round in an eight-team league, near the end of the second round in a 10-team league, and midway through the second round of a 12-team league. In other words, nearly every fantasy manager had this option available to them at one time or another.

It was clear that Harris was likely to have RB2 floor value as the lead back in the Steelers offense, but there were also numerous signs that he had RB1 upside. Harris set Alabama career records in rushing yards and rushing touchdowns and set the all-time single-season record for receiving touchdowns by a Crimson Tide running back. He was also going to a Pittsburgh team whose head coach had a track record of leaning on a bell-cow approach to carries whenever possible.

That confluence of events resulted in Harris ranking third in RB PPR points, so he did provide the RB1 return, but the real value in selecting him at the RB2 level is how that single successful pick impacts the rest of the fantasy roster by doing the following:

- It gave the team RB1 depth if the drafted RB1 got hurt.

- The team could produce RB1-caliber points during the drafted RB1's bye week.

- Any running back slotted as an RB3 or lower could now be fully dedicated toward filling a flex roster spot rather than having to occasionally fill in as a matchup RB2.

- If the RB3-or-lower running backs end up being capable flex candidates, the entire WR corps could be focused on generating value at that position rather than dividing starts between the WR and flex positions.

- The handcuff player to a bell-cow back costs very little in terms of draft or free-agent capital.

That is the definition of a lollapalooza effect for a draft pick, as it increased the potential value of players across the roster. This level of cascading impacts doesn't just work with RB1 candidates, as a cross-roster production spike can occur when selecting players for any roster slot.

In addition to the upside benefits of the draft-to-the-floor strategy, there is built-in downside insurance if the player doesn't hit his ceiling. Using the Harris scenario as an example, had he ended up producing RB2-caliber points as an RB2 draft pick, it would mean that his draft pick returned expected value. That wouldn't produce a lollapalooza effect, but it also means that it wouldn't prevent one, which can be just as important.

In the end, fantasy managers should take heed of the advice Munger gave when he said if you eliminate every negative element, all you will have left are the positive ones. That's what the draft-to-the-floor concept helps fantasy managers do. ▰▰▰

The 'true' value of running back touches: Adjusting ranks based on receptions and runs

By Michael Salfino

Touches are your enemy in projecting the running back position. The reason? Rush attempts (we'll call them "runs" for the rest of this column) have an expected value far less than receptions, even in leagues that employ standard/non-PPR (points per reception) scoring.

All rushing touches are the same in expected value regardless of scoring format: .431 points, assuming one point every 10 yards (excluding rushing TDs). But the top 70 PPR-scoring running backs in touches averaged 7.6 yards per reception last season.

Let's illustrate with D'Andre Swift, who was 24th in raw touches among running backs last year. He had 213 touches, but 62 of those were receptions. Since a reception is worth 7.60 yards on average for a running back, it's worth 1.76 runs, even in standard scoring. So Swift's 213 touches had the same expected value as 260 runs only, even in leagues with zero PPR scoring. That means Swift was the 16th best volume back in non-PPR leagues (again, ignoring touchdowns, which are hard to project anyway).

In half-point PPR, a reception is worth about three times a run. So Swift's 213 touches, so heavily weighted in catches, translate in half-point PPR to the expected value of 332 runs, which would rank 12th.

And in full-point PPR, a reception is worth 4.08 times a run, making Swift's touches worth 404 runs, 10th most, ahead of David Montgomery and just behind Ezekiel Elliott. (To be clear, we're taking all the expected value of a back's touches and translating it into the currency of runs only, in all of the major scoring formats.)

So a reception is worth nearly two times a run in standard, three times as much in half-point and four times as much in full. Here are the top 20 when we adjust for equivalents and true touch value.

This is why Christian McCaffrey has often been the No. 1 pick in leagues that reward receptions. With McCaffrey out most of the past two years, the closest thing we had to him in 2021 — a player whose value soared because of the weight of his receptions among his total touches — was Leonard Fournette. In standard, he was 10th. But in PPR, he was the RB5 (he was also RB5 in half-point PPR). Which other RBs are likely to be undervalued based on 2021 touches adjusted for the value of receptions?

First, let's take a little air out of the Swift balloon. His season was unbalanced. In his last six games, both before and after missing four games with an injury, he had 61 yards on 20 catches (26 targets). Is he likely to get the receiving volume he averaged in 2021 in light of this declining efficiency, in addition to the upgrades the Lions made in the offseason to their receiving corps? That falls outside of this model, though I'd wager he will not. Plus, his receiving efficiency in 2022 might be below average, as it was — decidedly — in that last-six-games sample.

Najee Harris has a case to be the No. 1 running back in 2022. All he needs is average efficiency, given 307 runs and 74 catches. The Steelers offense might be different with Ben Roethlisberger retired, but given the value of Harris' touches, he seems like the classic guy you draft happily at RB5 thinking he can be RB1.

Very cheaply, Darrel Williams (adjusted as the 19th running back in PPR due to the value of his receptions) could be a playable option for teams looking for double-digit expected points out of a late-round running back. Yes, he's on a new team (the Cardinals), but he should have the same role as the primary receiving back in Arizona. This is more valuable in standard and massively valuable in full PPR.

Aaron Jones could be the rare back who's actually worth a third-round pick, where he was often available at the start of the draft season. He was 20th in touches and has AJ Dillon to contend with. But a lot of targets have become available with the departing Davante Adams and Marquez Valdes-Scantling. Last year, Jones' expected touch value in full PPR ranked 13th — and he missed two games — so it's reasonable to boost him to 10th or so in PPR-equivalent runs. Jones has also displayed solid efficiency in his career, so that could get him easily to No. 8 or so. This seems like solid value at RB12 or later.

Conversely, Derrick Henry looks like a terrible pick among the top five running backs. Last season, the mixture of his touches — actually the paucity of receptions — made the PPR value of his touches lag

Touch Rank	Player	Rush Att	Rec	Actual Touches	Standard Equivalent Runs	Standard Rank	1/2 PPR ER	1/2 Rank	PPR ER	PPR Rank
1	Najee Harris	307	74	381	437.24	1	523.08	1	608.92	1
2	Jonathan Taylor	332	40	372	402.4	2	448.8	2	495.2	2
3	Joe Mixon	292	42	334	365.92	3	414.64	3	463.36	4
4	Antonio Gibson	258	42	300	331.92	4	380.64	6	429.36	8
5	Alvin Kamara	240	47	287	322.72	6	377.24	7	431.76	7
6	Ezekiel Elliott	237	47	284	319.72	7	374.24	9	428.76	9
7	Dalvin Cook	249	34	283	308.84	9	348.28	10	387.72	12
8	Austin Ekeler	206	70	276	329.2	5	410.4	4	491.6	3
9	Josh Jacobs	217	54	271	312.04	8	374.68	8	437.32	6
10	David Montgomery	225	42	267	298.92	11	347.64	11	396.36	11
11	Leonard Fournette	180	69	249	301.44	10	381.48	5	461.52	5
12	Nick Chubb	228	20	248	263.2	14	286.4	20	309.6	24
13	Javonte Williams	203	43	246	278.68	12	328.56	13	378.44	14
14	James Conner	202	37	239	267.12	13	310.04	16	352.96	17
15	Derrick Henry	219	18	237	250.68	20	271.56	24	292.44	28
16	Melvin Gordon	203	28	231	252.28	19	284.76	21	317.24	23
17	Sony Michel	208	21	229	244.96	22	269.32	25	293.68	27
18	Devin Singletary	188	40	228	258.4	18	304.8	18	351.2	18
19	Elijah Mitchell	207	19	226	240.44	24	262.48	28	284.52	32
20	Aaron Jones	171	52	223	262.52	15	322.84	14	383.16	13

All the Strategy You'll Ever Need

greatly behind the raw number. He needs unreal yards per rush and TD efficiency to make up for that. But you want efficiency to be the bonus. You don't want to pay for it. It's really hard to be that good/lucky with touchdowns. Drafting Henry ahead of Harris, which is generally the case in full PPR, seems very unwise.

The same issues are in play for Nick Chubb. His touch mix and lack of receptions are just not conducive to top scoring. If you think he's going to average 5-plus yards per carry (and fine, he has generally done this) and score about a TD per game, then go for it. You should bet against this level of production 100 times out of 100, however — always expect highly efficient players to regress.

It's never the player, it's just the price. And the price for these low-reception guys is just too high. In the case of Elijah Mitchell — yes, we love 49ers runs, which are likely to have higher-than-expected run-only value, but you can bank on a lack of catches for 49ers running backs, too — his raw touches were 19th last season, but his PPR run-only-equivalent touches were just 32nd. So even if you think he'll finish 10th in touches this season, that's really the equivalent of finishing about 17th.

Though PPR was created to devalue running backs relative to wide receivers, what it's really done is just revalue RBs among one another. Receptions are even more important than touchdowns because they are more stable and easier to project. ▬▬▬

Renee Miller's Brain Games: A primer on cognitive science for fantasy football

By Renee Miller

Everyone has access to the same player stats, narratives and other data with which to make their fantasy lineup decisions, whether we're talking about drafting, weekly sit/start or DFS. The information is there, but people will vary widely in how they interpret it and use it, which of course is why we play the (fantasy) game. There are three elements of cognitive science that I incorporate in my weekly advice columns in the regular season: cognitive bias, valuation and game theory. Today we'll talk about my favorite, cognitive bias.

A cognitive bias occurs when we make a decision based on subconscious factors rather than in a completely logical way. One common misconception is that cognitive bias is always bad. It's not. In fact, sometimes bias drives you to the exact same place as logic.

Sometimes, however, it misleads you and you're left wondering how you didn't see this outcome coming.

Let me explain more about what bias is. It's a shortcut, basically. A way for your brain to assess a situation and make a decision quickly. It doesn't consider "all the facts" but rather uses superficial, often emotionally driven information to drive an action. As an aside, most decisions, maybe all decisions, come down to two choices: approach or avoid. Bias arises in the oldest parts of the brain, bypassing the neocortex (of which the prefrontal cortex is most important for our purposes) altogether. Some people refer to this evolutionarily old circuit as "lizard brain." Evolution is important here; not only were ancient people lacking the modern neural capacity the prefrontal cortex provides, they didn't have the luxury of taking their time. Approach that new potential food source? Avoid that strange slithering animal coming at you? Approach that new girl at the watering hole? Avoid the guy that brought her? Bad or even slow decisions could result in missed opportunities to eat, or procreate, or death.

The mere fact that we can readily identify cognitive biases in modern humans attests to their virtue and utility. If bias didn't work, we wouldn't be here (or it would have been lost to natural selection over the years). Take first impressions, for example. We're wildly accurate in our assessment of people based on still photos, a few seconds of video, in-person meetings. One famous study showed that college students will decide whether they think a teacher is good based on a photo or short video, and those ratings correlate strongly with year-end ratings by those same teachers' students.

Primacy bias

Since first impressions are related to primacy, we'll start here. Primacy bias is the practice of giving more weight to the first item in a sequence than subsequent items when performing a task related to the sequence of items. In a laboratory, this might mean that if subjects are given a list of words and told to remember them for a recall test later, they will overwhelmingly remember the first word on the list better than any of the others. In terms of fantasy football, it means that your Week 1 impressions will drive decision-making on a player for the entire season. Primacy bias is why it's nearly impossible to change your first impression. The brain thinks it has seen enough after one outing, it has formed its decision— approach or avoid — based on that outing, and the shortcut is in place. It takes a lot to alter that, and the first step is knowing that it's happening.

But if we're so good at making snap judgments, what's wrong with a little primacy bias? When it comes to a full season of football, we're relying too heavily on the first week to make ongoing player evaluations. Logic might say to simply average a player's performance over the first seven weeks to get an idea of what he might do in Week 8, but primacy sneaks in a weighted coefficient on the Week 1 numbers. So if two running backs each have five TDs by the end of Week 7, we're more likely to more confidently start or roster a guy who scored three TDs in Week 1, rather than the guy who scored one TD each in Weeks 2-6. We believe the first guy is a three-touchdown player.

Just watch the waivers after Week 1. Solid players who fail to perform are dropped, random boom performances are overbid on and held onto for far too long in most cases. One week of the NFL season doesn't determine who a player is. Week 6 is, by all logic, just as important as Week 1 (of course, nuances of matchups, teammates, etc., may lead us to slightly different conclusions) so be wary of setting your opinions in stone after the first outing. I've come to believe, too, that our heightened emotional state during Week 1, after waiting so freaking long for it, contributes to the primacy effect. The brain, and particularly those "lizard" circuits, is on high alert thanks to floods of norepinephrine and dopamine being released to the anticipation and reward of the beginning of the regular season.

Recency bias

If there's one bias I think people are recognizing more and more, and hopefully I've had something to do with that, it's recency. Very closely related to primacy, recency refers to the process of weighting the most recent event in a series more highly than any other event in the series. Evolutionarily, this makes sense. If you take the same path today that you took yesterday which led to a patch of raspberries, there's a great chance you end up at the berry patch again today. In sports, recency bias has value, too. What a player has been doing is one of the best indicators of what he will do. But there are caveats.

Asking "why?" is a good way to be on the right side of recency bias. Why was he so good last week? Why didn't he score at all last night? Why were his targets down this week? Seeking the answers to these questions instead of blindly trusting that the first-round running back you drafted will never score because he hasn't scored in the first two games or that the wide receiver you grabbed off waivers after he scored twice with 150 receiving yards will supply you with 30 fantasy points every week is a much smarter approach.

You'll see the backlash of recency bias in sports, too. Regression? Being due? These are the antitheses of recency and are rooted in our impressions of who a player is. They can be dangerous, too, because players and circumstances and opportunity and even talent DO change. One of the goals of my regular in-season article will be to sort these things out and help you believe in or eschew (approach or avoid), or at least properly weight, recent performances for the coming game.

Novelty bias

There are so many biases out there, but novelty can affect our fantasy judgments in a lot of different ways, so we'll conclude with this simple idea. Newer is better. What we have no experience with is more attractive than what we have been exposed to in the past. This holds true of every single organism that it can be tested in, from the simplest soil-dwelling nematode and annoying fruit fly right up to us and the chimpanzees. Something new, with no context, itself evokes a surge of dopamine release in our brains, signaling reward

and reinforcement. In other words, the dopamine makes us feel good, increasing the likelihood of repeating whatever we did to get it. The novelty effect is so strong that it is frequently used as a memory test in people and animals with dementia — if the subject fails to choose the novel thing in a two-choice test, it is assumed it is because they can't remember having ever experienced the familiar thing.

By now you should be thinking about rookies, right? They are our novelty in fantasy football. They've never burned us (unless we played college fantasy football, which is a relatively small number), they have tons of hype, especially coming off the preseason, and we selectively remember all the rookie success stories of seasons past while conveniently forgetting all the rookie failure stories of seasons past.

I always come back to the idea that fantasy football is fun, and drafting rookies is fun — remember the novelty-induced dopamine surge — so if you're taking a risk, and you know it and you want to do it anyway, I'm not stopping you. But, if you are reaching for a rookie based on novelty and high hopes when you could be drafting or starting an established veteran, you might not be making the best decision.

One thing I see year in and year out is people drafting for what they think "should" happen, or will happen at some point during the season. Drafting for my vision of Week 9 isn't the way I do it. You have to expect the league, and your fantasy roster, to change a lot during the season, so draft for the most likely Week 1-4 scenarios.

In the regular season, novelty bias can pop up in weekly start/sit decisions, DFS lineups, and it doesn't need to merely involve rookies. We have old players on new teams, old players getting a chance to start due to midseason injuries and more. I'll aim to analyze the facts behind any newness as the weeks wear on and try to limit deciding to use a player based on novelty alone. ▬▬

Scan here for up-to-date content on TheAthletic.com

The 5 injuries that can derail a fantasy season — and what they mean for your team

by Virginia Zakas, Inside Injuries

Fantasy football can be fickle. One day you're riding high with a team destined for a playoff run, the next you're getting served Facebook ads for local podiatrists because of all the Googling you did on a Jones fracture.

To know injuries — what they mean, how long a recovery is, and how someone bounces back from it — is an underrated edge for the typical fantasy player. We asked Virginia Zakas of Inside Injuries to explain the five most unfortunate injuries, and what to expect as a player heals.

1. High ankle sprain

What It Is: A high ankle sprain, or syndesmotic sprain, indicates damage to the ligaments that hold the two lower leg bones together. This is called the distal tibiofibular joint, and it's a completely different joint than the ankle. It sits just above it where the tibia and fibula meet and is held together by three ligaments. When this type of sprain occurs, one or more of these ligaments are damaged. This leads to widening between the bones at the ankle mortise and a lack of stability. High ankle sprains often occur when a player gets rolled up on or hit from the side as their leg is firmly planted. Many low ankle sprains happen without contact, but a syndesmotic sprain often involves some sort of a collision and a twisting motion to the lower leg.

Why It's Tough to Recover From? These ligaments tend to be slower to heal than the ligaments in the low ankle because of blood flow. It's also tough to keep those lower leg bones from separating any time weight is put on the leg, so a significant amount of rest is needed. Surgery isn't usually needed unless it's a severe ligament tear.

How Much Time Will They Miss? A majority of athletes who suffer a high ankle sprain will miss at least four weeks. Even a "mild" high ankle sprain isn't really a mild injury. Athletes often feel like it isn't that bad early on, but then it just doesn't seem to progress. We've seen players return in as few as two weeks from this injury, but it's one that significantly hurts performance if they return before it is 100 percent. That's especially true for positions such as wide receiver and running back that do a lot of cutting. The expectation for most high ankle sprains should be a minimum of three to four weeks out, but realistically it will take even longer to fully recover. A moderate to severe sprain can lead to a six-to-eight-week absence.

Players Who Recently Suffered This Injury: Michael Thomas, Jerry Jeudy, Adam Thielen.

2. Hamstring strain

What It Is: The hamstring is a group of muscles in the back of the thigh. A grade 1 (mild) strain indicates small tears to the muscle fibers, but a grade 2 to 3 strain means there is more extensive damage to the muscle.

Why It's Tough to Recover From? The hamstring is often damaged during quick, powerful movements. These happen on every play, especially for positions such as wide receiver and running back. That makes it a very common non-contact injury. It often starts as just some tightness that the athlete feels like they can handle without rest. Then they try to play through it and it turns into a more serious strain and a lengthier absence. The muscle is left weaker even once it feels like it is healed, so aggravations are common.

How Much Time Will They Miss? A mild strain can heal in two to three weeks, although we often see players return within a week. A grade 2 (moderate) strain takes around a month, and a more significant strain can take six to 12 weeks.

Players Who Recently Suffered This Injury: Christian McCaffrey, Mike Evans, Julio Jones, DeVante Parker.

3. MCL sprain

What It Is: The MCL, medial collateral ligament, is one of four knee ligaments that provide stability to the joint. It runs along the inside of the knee and is typically injured when the leg is planted and hit from the outside, forcing it inward. MCL injuries don't usually require surgery and tend to heal well on their own, although it can still lead to a lengthy absence. This ligament is important for preventing the knee from moving too far inward and provides stability during twisting and lateral movements. It is the most common injury to the knee.

Why It's Tough to Recover From? Though the MCL heals well on its own, it can take a lot of time. Complications aren't too common once that ligament is healthy again, but a lengthy period of rest is needed to get to that point. We often see athletes try to return too soon, and one hard cut leads to a significant setback. The MCL is heavily involved in lateral movements and sharp cuts. Any sort of twisting motion or quick change of direction adds stress, so it's tough to play through.

Players Who Recently Suffered This Injury: Aaron Jones, Clyde Edwards-Helaire, Jarvis Landry.

4. Turf toe

What It Is: Turf toe indicates damage to the large joint at the base of the big toe, called the metatarsophalangeal (MTP) joint. It might not sound like a big deal, but every lower-body movement starts with this joint. Turf toe occurs when the big toe is forced into hyperextension, damaging the ligament. It can be an acute injury or one that slowly appears and gets worse over time. It is more common on artificial turf (hence the name) because the surface can be a lot harder, putting more stress on the joints.

Why It's Tough to Recover From? Every time you push off and hyperextend the toe, which happens when doing something as simple as taking a step or more strenuous like cutting and jumping, the MTP joint is involved. Turf toe often becomes a chronic injury that needs continuous management to reduce inflammation. When playing football, it's impossible to avoid the constant pounding to this area when scrambling, running routes or trying to power through a tackle.

How Much Time Will They Miss? We often see athletes try to play through turf toe, but even a mild case needs at least three weeks to fully heal. Many football players won't recover until they have the offseason to truly rest. Playing through turf toe will significantly hamper performance. More serious cases of turf toe can also lead to surgery or cause a more serious injury, like a fracture to the first metatarsal.

Players Who Recently Suffered This Injury: Josh Allen, Josh Jacobs, Patrick Mahomes, Antonio Gibson.

5. Jones fracture

What It Is: A Jones fracture is the name for a fracture at the base of the fifth metatarsal, located on the outside (pinky side) of the foot. The metatarsals are the long bones that run from the toes to the arch. This location is vulnerable to injury when the ankle is forced inward. It can be an acute or an overuse injury.

Why It's Tough to Recover From? Blood supply to this location in the foot is very poor, so the bone doesn't heal well on its own. That's why surgery is typically needed to have a screw inserted for stability. Even then it often isn't a straightforward recovery. The hardware inserted during surgery can lead to aggravation and needs to be removed months later. There is also often a reason the fracture occurred in the first place — this can be due to the way that athlete moves or the shape of their foot. Something about their running mechanics puts stress on that location, meaning they are vulnerable to injuring it again if they aren't able to change how they run.

How Much Time Will They Miss? Most athletes come out of surgery with an expected recovery time of six to eight weeks, but in reality, they won't be ready to play that quickly. Eight to 10 weeks is much more realistic to return to the field, although even then the bone isn't always strong enough yet. There's a high risk of re-fracture in those first few months back, so multiple lengthy absences are common.

Players Who Recently Suffered This Injury: Derrick Henry, Deebo Samuel. ▄▄▄

Hacking the draft room: How to take advantage of the ESPN, Yahoo and CBS rankings biases

By David Gonos

In the 21st century, we love life hacks, cheat codes and shortcuts. We want positive results with minimal effort, and we want it now!

Did our great-grandfathers need cheat codes to storm Normandy? (Well, I guess they did use spies.)

Did our grandfathers need shortcuts during the tumultuous '60s and '70s? (Then again, I suppose Watergate was America's greatest cheat code.)

OK, let's start over. As a human race, we've always loved cheat codes and shortcuts! Viva la hack!

Hacking a fantasy football draft room using Average Draft Position (ADP) can be greatly beneficial for your team. Granted, using ADP in general is already a hack, as we rely on the wisdom of the crowds that have already done tens of thousands of fantasy drafts before we step up to the mic for pick No. 1.

What we're talking about, however, is hacking "Average ADP" to help us make better picks on the specific fantasy draft site we're using.

Understanding how your draft room's rankings work

I wrote at CBS Sports for most of the 2000s, and our preseason rankings for every sport, which were based on our projections, helped populate the order of the rankings in the draft rooms. Our opinions on which players would have better or worse seasons than other players affected the draft room's recommendations for the next available picks.

That means our rankings directly affected CBS Sports' ADP

Think about your past drafts. When an uninjured player remains at the top of the "Available Players" list for 10 picks or so, doesn't it subconsciously eat at you, causing you to wonder whether your own ranking of that player was too low? Eventually, someone succumbs to the draft pressure (or just decides his value is where it should be) and picks him.

Back to the writers' rankings that affected the draft room rankings. Imagine that same scene going on at ESPN, Yahoo, NFL.com and all the other content sites that offer drafting services. Even the sites that don't have writer rankings, like My Fantasy League and Sleeper, still must create an initial set of draft room rankings; otherwise, the first couple hundred drafts on those sites would be chaos.

Now imagine drafting on ESPN while using a set of rankings from CBS. The best available players are going to be different, especially after the first couple of rounds. As you get into the middle rounds, the separation of the CBS list compared to the ESPN draft room "best available" rankings is going to get greater. The site experts influence the rankings and ADP, and you need to treat it all as noise.

Now imagine — there's a lot of imagining in this article — you use an aggregate list of fantasy rankings among all the other major sites that you are not drafting on, to find great values and avoid great mistakes on the site you are drafting on!

Hack!

By using FantasyPros' ADP rankings, which brings in ADP from most of the major drafting sites, you can look at each position singularly to see which players are ranked much higher on one site compared to the other sites. These are outliers that can help you determine the players you can wait on (players whose ADP is much lower on the site you're drafting on compared to the other ADPs).

Hack!

It can also help decipher which players you might have to draft earlier if you want them (players whose ADP is much higher on the site you're drafting on compared to other ADPs).

One could also consider these "sleeper" and "bust" lists — the sleepers being the players your draft site has ranked higher than other sites, and the busts being the players they have ranked much lower than everyone else.

Hack! (Sorry, that one was just a hairball.)

Does this draft hack work?

I know what you are saying. You're saying: "Daniel, how big of a difference can this possibly make? I mean, if one wide receiver is ranked 32nd on my draft site and the other sites rank him as the 37th-best WR, so what?"

First, my name is David, not Daniel.

Second, that's exactly right: So what?! You're really looking for the wide receiver they rank 32nd and other sites rank 44th. That's generally a difference of three rounds in a 12-team league! While others draft that guy too high, you can get the wideout the other sites rank 28th and your draft site ranks 40th. You zig while others zag! (Unless you're in Australia, where you will zag while others zig. It's like how their water flows backward down the drain.)

Looking over the past few years, we've uncovered some serious bargains for those who used overall ADP versus their draft site's ADP:

You avoided drafting Tom Brady several rounds too early on ESPN in 2018, the year he finished as QB12, after a QB2 2017 season.

You got to draft Derrick Henry and Joe Mixon two rounds earlier than others would have on Yahoo in 2018, the year of their breakout seasons.

You would have learned in 2019 that Yahoo's draft rooms had Russell Wilson ranked nearly four rounds higher than all the other draft sites, in a year when Wilson finished as the fourth-best QB.

Other big players you were tipped off on early that the site you were drafting on had either much higher or much lower than other sites in the past four seasons, included:

- 2018 Nick Chubb before his big rookie year.

- 2018 Brandin Cooks before his top-12 WR season.

- 2020 Justin Jefferson before his big rookie year.

Those are just some of the big swings your draft can take when you compare your site's draft rankings (usually fed by that site's ADP) to all other draft sites' ADP.

Something you must be careful about, though, is being mindful of the scoring systems for the ADPs you are using. Your draft site might be a points per reception (PPR) league, but if you're looking at average ADP on a non-PPR site, that will throw a huge wrench in your draft plans.

Also, don't wait too long for sleepers you want because not all the teams you are going up against are driving their drafts based on that site's best-available-players list. Some will have their own rankings, and some might be using ADP from another site altogether! Use this exercise as a guide to learn which players might go higher or lower based on the site you are drafting on. And to see if certain positions are going to be promoted in the draft room more than others, like quarterbacks and tight ends.

In the end, information is king — and having an idea of what others might do can help you decide what you should do. It's like playing rock-paper-scissors against someone you know is already allergic to paper and scissors! (Analogy? Nailed it!) ▬▬

Why a SuperFlex league? It's time to give quarterbacks the respect they deserve

By Michael Beller

Take yourself back to October 2019. You remember October 2019. The Nationals were busy completing their run to the franchise's first World Series title. The Chiefs were holding their breath over Patrick Mahomes' dislocated kneecap. And many of us were sitting down to draft our fantasy basketball teams.

If you can, try to remember what those ADP charts looked like. Giannis Antetokounmpo, the reigning MVP, was the second player off the board in a typical draft, just behind do-it-all center Anthony Davis. Steph Curry, who was getting ready to score about 3,000 points with Kevin Durant and Klay Thompson injured, was third, and James Harden, the league's 2018 MVP, was fourth.

Now take yourself forward a few months to March 2020, and fantasy baseball draft prep before the entire country went off the rails. Mike Trout (2019 AL MVP, on track to retire as the best player of all-time), Christian Yelich (2018 NL MVP), Ronald Acuña (2018 NL Rookie of the Year), Cody Bellinger (2019 NL MVP) and Mookie Betts (2018 AL MVP), were top 5 hitters by ADP. The two top pitchers by ADP were Gerrit Cole, who went 20-5 with a 2.50 ERA and 326 strikeouts in 2019, and Jacob deGrom, who had won the last two NL Cy Young Awards. By and large, the best players in both baseball and basketball are the top picks in the fantasy versions of those sports. As they should be.

Bring yourself back to the present day, and the heart of fantasy football draft prep season. Consider the top of the fantasy football ADP charts. Whither Josh Allen? Whither Lamar Jackson? Or Mahomes? Surely the league's most exciting QBs should be among the first players drafted if fantasy value reflects real-life value. Whither Justin Herbert and Joe Burrow and Kyler Murray? They're all nowhere to be found.

All the Strategy You'll Ever Need

The very best in any other fantasy sport still appear near the top of the draft board, but elite quarterbacks appear only after the top running backs and wide receivers have been taken. The rest, meanwhile, are consigned to the middle and late rounds, complementary pieces to fantasy teams and afterthoughts on draft day. This, clearly, is a problem. The good news is there is an obvious and, more importantly, fun solution.

Play SuperFlex.

It's time for SuperFlex fantasy football to be the standard. In case you're unfamiliar, SuperFlex is actually the name of a position, but its prominence in leagues that use it has made it the name of an entire format. The SuperFlex position is like the Flex spot you know and love, but with one caveat. Quarterbacks are also eligible to fill the position, in addition to running backs, receivers and tight ends. SuperFlex leagues are effectively two-quarterback leagues, though they give GMs the flexibility to play a non-QB in the spot in case of injury or bye-week woes, or by strategic choice.

There is, quite literally, no downside to converting your league into a SuperFlex one.

First and foremost, SuperFlex leagues elevate quarterbacks, especially the great ones, to their rightful place in the fantasy pecking order. Allen is a first-round pick. So is Jackson. Several quarterbacks come off the board in the first round.

Why is this an objective good? That question brings us to point No. 2. Quarterbacks should matter. Even the shallowest fantasy leagues start at least 20 running backs and receivers, and most are in the 24 to 36 range for those positions. Why should we be starting one-half or one-third or one-fourth as many quarterbacks? The answer? We shouldn't.

And now we arrive at the third, and most significant, point. SuperFlex allows for a range of draft-day strategies that you aren't going to see in a traditional one-quarterback league. Waiting on a quarterback is standard practice in typical leagues, and for good reason. First, consider the numbers. A 12-team league has 12 starting quarterbacks every week, despite the fact that there are 32 starting quarterbacks in the NFL. In other words, there's always a starting option available, and replacement level only requires that option to be as good as QB12, which is hardly a stretch to find from week to week. That same 12-team league asks its members to start at least 24 running backs and 36 receivers, plus a Flex spot that is going to be populated mostly by backs and receivers. Replacement-level value at those positions is much harder to find, which makes them far more important on draft day.

Season-long quarterback scoring is relatively challenging to predict in the summer, but weekly quarterback performance is relatively simple to predict during the season. There's a reason why so many quarterbacks have ADPs of 90 or later. There's a reason why streaming the quarterback position from week to week is viable. So little distinguishes the non-elite quarterbacks during draft season, that being the first one to jump into that pool is a waste of draft-day capital when you can still grab startable backs, receivers and tight ends who could be real difference-makers. Predictable quarterback scoring based on matchup, expected game flow and point-spread and over/under factors makes it easy to find a quarterback de la semaine during the season.

SuperFlex turns the late-round quarterback strategy on its head. Now Allen is the above-replacement-level asset in fantasy that he is in real life. Same goes for Jackson, Mahomes and Herbert. The older guard may all be beyond their peaks, but they go from being back-end starters in traditional leagues to comfortable QB1s in SuperFlex leagues. Matt Ryan, Jameis Winston and Mac Jones go from the post-draft waiver wire to solid QB2s who open the year as easy starters.

Would you rather have one of the elite quarterbacks or receivers? There's no question in a standard league, but it isn't so easy to answer in a SuperFlex league. Instead of everyone being on the late-round quarterback path, some people will attack the position early, others will try to approach it evenly, and still others will gamble that they can find two starting options after the first 10 or 14 quarterbacks are off the board. Those diverse strategies take your draft from autopilot to active, cookie-cutter to engaging.

I know, trying something new can be uncomfortable. I admit, I didn't dive in headfirst to my first SuperFlex experience. But "that's the way we've always done it" is the worst reason to do anything. This is the year to try something new. This is the year to make quarterbacks matter. This is the year for SuperFlex to become the standard. ▬▬

A road map for the perilous wait-on-QB SuperFlex league draft strategy

By Michael Beller

Warning: This content is suitable only for people who want to get unhealthily risky in SuperFlex leagues.

Nailing the quarterback position is crucial in SuperFlex leagues. And drafters can take multiple paths to achieve this goal. There's my preferred method of targeting two mid-tier quarterbacks, which combines a foundation of backs and receivers with plenty of stability and upside at quarterback. You can also build around the position, targeting two elite quarterbacks with your first two picks. You can modify and combine those two, taking a Josh Allen or Lamar Jackson early, then pairing him with a mid-tier quarterback anywhere in the Tom Brady to Trevor Lawrence range.

One potential plan of attack is conspicuously absent in the above paragraph. Waiting on a quarterback in traditional one-quarterback leagues isn't exactly a strategy any longer. Rather, the efficacy of waiting on the position increasing your chances of winning a championship is an axiom of fantasy football. It's fair to wonder, then, whether a tweaked version of the same strategy would work in the SuperFlex format.

My instinct is to tell you to stop wondering, and put it out of your mind forever. It's not that the strategy can't work. It's that the margin of error is so minuscule that it almost doesn't exist. You're asking yourself to thread a needle with an eye the size of a grain of sand. Remember, part of the reason the late-round quarterback strategy works in one-QB leagues is that there are always reinforcements at the position on the waiver wire. Derek Carr isn't working out? Guess what, Matt Ryan or Jameis Winston or Tua Tagovailoa, or even all three, are sitting there for you on the wire. That isn't the case in SuperFlex leagues. Not only will all 32 starters get drafted, but so, too, will high-profile backups. Forget about being readily available. Replacements may not be available, period. Why put yourself through that when you can get two mid-tier quarterbacks, or two elite quarterbacks, or some

combination of the two groups? The short answer? You shouldn't.

However, I am a fantasy football realist, and I know some of you out there will be tempted enough by the late-round quarterback apple — "Just think of all the backs and receivers I can get," you're telling yourself — to take a bite. Some of you, too, will accidentally fall into it, rolling the dice one too many times before staring down a reality of Kirk Cousins as your QB1. And so, as any responsible counselor would do, I will help guide those of you who want to get crazy on draft day through this scheme. This flawed, wild, but just-so-wild-it-might-work scheme.

Don't get too cute

This is Step 1, and if you miss it, you're toast. Inherent in this harebrained strategy is the idea that you are passing on, at the very least, the top 15 or so quarterbacks.

At this point, you should see the potential for a massive problem formulating. If your QB1 comes from that second tier of quarterbacks, who would your QB2 be? Well, it would be someone in that group, or someone from the next tier, which comprises the final starting quarterbacks on the board.

You want your QB1 to come from either the first tier, or the top half of the second tier, but that's not what we mean by "don't get too cute." Again, you've already decided that you're comfortable playing it fast and loose at the quarterback position if you're employing this strategy. When we say "don't get too cute," we're referring to your QB2. Remember, your QB2 is an every-week starter in SuperFlex formats. If you pursue this path, you won't have a Patrick Mahomes to balance out uneven play from a Davis Mills or a Mitch Trubisky. Your QB2 absolutely has to come from the second tier.

Get four QBs

If you're going this route, you also have to allow for the possibility that your QB2 won't be any good. You have to face the reality that your QB1 may not be as reliable as you dreamed he'd be on draft day. In short, you're going to need options at the position and, again, there will be major competition on the waiver wire for anyone who becomes a starting quarterback during the season. You need to plan for all of this coming to fruition.

Think of this as the standard zero-RB strategy, adapted to quarterbacks and SuperFlex leagues. Zero-RB leans on a few pillars, but the operative one for our purposes is that an injured or underperforming back is generally replaced by one player. Dalvin Cook gets injured, Alexander Mattison takes over. Simple, right? That one-for-one trade is even cleaner at quarterback because teams can literally only play one quarterback.

The late-round QB drafter in SuperFlex leagues needs immediate post-draft options, and a zero-RB mentality helps bring that goal into focus. You already know that coming out of any SuperFlex draft or auction with at least three quarterbacks is a must for anyone, even someone who takes top-tier QBs. You, however, need a fourth at all costs. That fourth quarterback may never start a game for you, but the insurance policy is an absolute must if your QB1 and QB2 are outside the top 15 at the position.

Get an elite tight end

There's an element of zagging while the rest of your league zigs in this strategy. If you're going against the grain, you have to be strong in as many places as possible where your league-mates are weak. I don't mean to belabor the point, but you are almost certainly going to have the worst starting quarterbacks in your league if you head down this path. You have to make up that ground wherever possible, and nowhere is it more possible than at tight end.

Let's not beat around the bush here. When we say "get an elite tight end," we mean "get Travis Kelce, George Kittle, Mark Andrews, or Kyle Pitts." One could argue that grabbing someone from this top tier at ADP will give back in value at running back or receiver whatever you've picked up at tight end. That ignores the fact running back and especially receiver are far deeper than the tight end position. Those pools become even deeper for you, the late-round QB SuperFlex drafter, when you factor in all the quarterbacks coming off the board that you're ignoring.

Getting a top-tier TE will give you a sizable advantage over even the next-tier TE drafters. You'll have a monster advantage over everyone else. Given the deficit you're facing at quarterback, you're going to need it.

You know what? I've almost convinced myself that this is the way to g ...

Nahhhhh.

But, if this is your desired path, let the above be your road map. ▰▰▰

35 pretty sweet ways to run your fantasy football draft lottery

By David Gonos

Draft lotteries are some of my favorite moments of the fantasy football season. It's like opening a pack of football cards. Before it's open, there's so much promise!

"I could get five rookie cards in this one pack – it's possible!"

But then after the lottery, after you found out you got the 11th pick, you have that same remorse as when you are done opening a pack with 10 Jets players who have already been cut.

I would also like to take this time to pitch this alternative league rule:

Do a lottery for every single round of your draft

We used to do this for my league in the '90s and it was pretty fantastic. We only stopped because the league moved to an online service, and we realized no one else was doing it this way.

But, if you do a draft lottery for every round, starting from the last round and going forward, it does a few things that add to the greatness of the draft lottery:

1. It adds a lot more suspense and buildup to the actual first-round lottery.

2. It helps everyone win one or two rounds, which makes them feel a little better when they get hit with that 11th pick in Round 1. "Hey, at least I'm picking first in Round 9!"

3. It begets a TON more trades. Suddenly, you see that if you trade this pick and this pick, you can move up six spots in this round to grab the guy you believe will be there.

True, it doesn't make the draft lottery fair down the line, but when was the last time something was fair?

THE ATHLETIC ———————————————————————————————— 2022 FANTASY FOOTBALL GUIDE

I mean, even the midway games at the state fair aren't fair – and "fair" is right in their name!

Eight boring ways to do your draft lottery

So how can we make the draft lottery even more fun? There are a few dozen ways – but first, let's review some relatively boring, if not effective, ways to determine your league's draft order. Boring isn't always horrible. Some people love saltine crackers!

1. Use the league's online service
Are you a commissioner who just doesn't have time to do a cool draft lottery? Or do you just barely care? Then just let the league randomize the draft order. Make sure you only do it once because if it sends out an email and the other GMs get it, then you randomize it again and they get a second email – some will think it's a little fishy, including me.

2. Have two GMs email you separately
Ask one GM to mix up the numbers 1 through 12 (for a 12-team draft) and send them to you in any order he wants. Then ask another GM to mix up all the team names and send them to you in any order he wants. Then make a master email, combine both of their emails and match the first number with the first name — that's where that team is picking. Do the same with all the others, and that's your draft order! Then send out that email that includes both of their emails, so others can audit how you did it, and voila! This method works especially well when you all don't live close enough to each other to get together for the draft lottery.

3. Pull paper out of a hat
If all the managers are together at one time, write down numbers from 1 through 12 and place them in a hat, cup or a margarita pitcher (an empty one!), whatever. Then have each GM pull their number out. It doesn't matter who goes first or last, the odds are the same they'll get the top pick.

If everyone's not together, then you can put everyone's team names in the hat and draw the team names out. But make sure you mention that you are starting with the 12th pick first! Don't announce that after you pull a name out or else you run the risk of receiving a beatdown.

4. Draft your draft picks
I've always liked giving the GMs who win the lottery the option of saying where they'd like to pick. While the first few teams might want the first five picks, you'll eventually reach a spot where an GM is happier drafting his first pick late, so that he can draft his second pick earlier. He might value two of the top 15 players more than having one top-five player.

5. Draw cards
Separate one suit from a deck of cards, ace through queen, and shuffle them and have the GMs pick one card each. That card is their pick! (A queen is the 12th pick and the jack is the 11th.)

6. Use an online dice roller
For one league I've been in dating back to the mid-2000s, we use the dice roller at RPGLibrary.org, which has some specific settings you need to use.

Roll 1 d 100 +0, and Sum them all (normal roll).

then roll and subtract 0 d 6 +0, and Sum them all (normal roll).

Roll 0 Fudge (or FATE) dice.

Roll this set of dice 1 time.

Send the signed results of this roll to yourself: [your email address]

and the GM: [Your commissioner's email]

with this subject: [2022 Fantasy League Name].

I don't know what any of it means, other than it sends my commish and myself the number I rolled.

Nerd alert!

7. Roll a many-sided die ... or 5 regular-sided dice
Either bust out that Dungeons and Dragons game you've been dying someone to ask you about or just grab your Yahtzee box. Each GM gets one roll of all five dice — highest total wins the top pick! (But they have to yell, "Yahtzee!" That's the rules.)

8. NBA Draft Lottery style
Sometimes, the best thing to do is just to follow what the NBA does. It's classic. Ask everyone for team logos, print them out on a sheet of paper, tape them to thicker card stock or a foam core board. Then put them in big envelopes and mix them up. Have each manager come up and mix them up, too! Shuffle, shuffle!

Then ask your server, or an innocent bystander, or a wife, or a hitchhiker you picked up for this very task, to open each envelope, one at a time, to reveal the picks — going backward, from 12 to 1.

All the Strategy You'll Ever Need

27 much more exciting ways to determine your draft order

Inject a little energy into your draft lotteries with these ideas!

9. Run a Tecmo-like 100-yard dash simulation

I love this because rather than just watching team names revealed, you get to watch an actual simulated race between cartoon football players on the website 100YardRush.com. Imagine cheering on your team representative as he's racing 100 yards down the field against the other participants. (I feel like this is how people from that movie "WALL-E" watched the Olympics.)

First, choose how many teams are in the league, and then on the next page, name all the managers (I like to name the teams, so the team name is shown with each pick at the end, instead of the manager). You can even change the colors of each little running back to show off your team's favorite color if you like.

You'll then see the team names listed by their running back on the left side, so you can hit the shuffle button as many times as you like to mix up where the runners start from (I like three!). Then you can assign "Higher Luck Values" to teams that should be weighted with better chances to win (like if they were the worst team last year, etc.).

Choose "Yards travelled per rush," "Seconds per rush" and "Speed" — or just leave it all on the default setting like I do. Then it gives you one final page to review your settings — and then you hit "Start Rush"! There's a short countdown and then they're off! (Should work well for Zoom participants, too!)

10. Take an online sample Wonderlic test

Get everyone to take the same test college players take before the NFL Draft, and give the top picks to the highest scores! Each manager gets 12 minutes to take this free sample Wonderlic test, and someone should be there to help administer it and make sure they don't cheat or use their phone.

11. Start a draft lottery rewards program

If you're going to do a draft lottery, with the ability to add more balls in the hopper for certain teams, then consider starting a lottery rewards program that allows team GMs ways of earning more balls in the hopper for their team. For instance, a team can get extra balls in the hopper for any of the following:

- Paying their league fee before the draft.

- Writing a good article/doing a good video for the league last year.
- Having the best player knocked out due to injury the year before (voted on by the managers at the end of the previous season). For instance, Christian McCaffrey's manager would get an extra ball in this year's draft lottery.
- Being the highest scoring non-playoff team from the previous season.
- Owning the last pick of the first round in last year's draft.
- Drafting the Fantasy MVP from the previous season (voted on by GMs).
- Drafting the Rookie of Year from the previous season (voted on by GMs).
- Drafting the Sleeper of the Year from the previous season (voted on by GMs).
- Picking up the Waiver-Wire Pickup from the previous season (voted on by GMs).
- Earning the Best Regular Season Record from the previous season.
- Bringing food and drink to this year's draft party
- Making a significant contribution to the league in some fashion (voted on by the commissioner).
- Being the commissioner.
- Breaking any league records the previous year (highest weekly score, highest total points, most wins, etc.).
- Suggesting a new rule that gets passed by the league.

12. Weighted draft lottery in order of last year's finish

I like weighted lotteries for dynasty or large keeper leagues, giving the worst teams one year the best chance at good picks the next year. I usually like to give four balls to the worst team from last year, three balls to the second-worst team and two balls to the third-worst team.

FantasyDraftLottery.com allows you to do a weighted draft lottery for free, and it's a pretty sweet setup. They allow you to enter your team names and how many balls go into the hopper for each team. Then you hit the button and it brings you to a page with all the picks listed (and you can turn on the NFL music to play in the background — which is amazing!). Then you go down and click on "Pick 12:" to see who got it, and then Pick 11, and then Pick 10, etc., all the way down to the final reveal. (You can also just hit the "Show All" button to see everyone's picks immediately.)

One thing I thought might be cool is to reveal the middle picks first, like Pick 8, then Pick 7, then Pick 6, so there's an even higher depth of drama, leaving Pick 1 and Pick 12 for the final two reveals. That means whoever is left either has the very first pick in the first round — or the very last. Then you reveal the first pick and leave the 12th pick for last, which I believe ignites the drama at the most precise moment. (Should work well for Zoom participants, too!)

13. Fantasy Nerds' LIVE random draft order tool
This is a pretty great draft order generator. Fill out your league's team names (create a free account first or you'll have to do this all over again), schedule when you want the draft lottery to be held, choose how long you should wait between when the picks are revealed (they default to four seconds, but I found that was too fast, I would say choose 15-20 seconds for some drama!). Then you have it email you the results, and click the Schedule the Live Draft Order button. You can then email the link it provides to all of the managers who might not be present. A countdown clock appears, building the suspense! Then the picks are randomized and revealed. I enjoyed this — not as much as the 100yardrush game, but still, this was fun. (Should work well for Zoom participants, too!)

14. Paper airplane distance competition
Give everyone 15 minutes to make the absolute best paper airplane they can make, then write their team name on the wings. Mark a line on the ground, then see who can throw their airplane the farthest. Draft order is determined by the length at which each plane is thrown!

15. Free-throw contest at a local basketball court
I'm not suggesting a game of 21, as we all want everyone still alive at the end of the draft. But bring everyone to the court for a free-throw competition. Have each person shoot, and if they make it on their first try, they keep shooting until they miss. Whoever makes the most in a row gets first pick, whoever makes the second most in a row gets second pick, etc. For those that miss, they all move on to Round 2 with the same setup. (When it's all over, play a game of H-O-R-S-E to see who gets to eat and drink for free at the draft that year!)

16. Cornhole tournament
Same concept as above, with each manager getting one throw, and if he makes it, he keeps throwing until he doesn't. You could make this tougher by having everyone throw with their opposite hand, also.

17. Family fun center tournament
If you have a Dave and Buster's or another similar-styled place, you can have all your GMs get together for a handful of competitions. Have each do a Pop-a-Shot basketball game, and rank them by finish. Have them do a Skee-Ball game, then rank their scores again. Choose a racing game, and rank their timed finishes. Just make it a great day of nostalgic awesomeness.

While I like the idea of having each contest as a separate event, you could also just have everyone buy $10 or $20 worth of playing time, then the player with the most tickets at the end wins the top pick – and all the tickets!

18. Left-handed darts tournament
Understand that when I say "left-handed," I really just mean opposite-handed. Each GM gets three throws, totaling all the points for a final score. You should allow everyone to practice, just so it's not a billion throws that just hit the wall and drop. Cats should definitely be put away.

19. Skills competition: Punt, Pass and Kick
Head out to the local park — and bring a football. Rank everyone for each effort, then use the average rankings for the draft order. If there are women or kids in this league, consider creating some "red tees" for them to hit from.

20. Hold a fantasy football combine
If you like the idea of the punt, pass and kick contest, try this one out! Combine several of the above events for a Fantasy Field Day.

Do a 40-yard dash, long jump, shuttle race, punt, pass and kick, and whatever else you want to add to the day's festivities. Make sure you get someone to video the whole thing and take some pictures because you're going to want to revisit these pics/videos at draft parties for years to come!

21. Football trivia exam
I think this is one of my favorites, and I might just have to create one of these exams for the site for everyone to use for drafts — or just for fun. Have whoever scores highest on a football trivia test win the top pick. This trivia exam should be a mix of fun trivia about NFL rules, team origins, fantasy facts and more, preferably designed by a third party. Like me!

22. Your server ranks your league's team names
I saw this one on Reddit, but the Redditor said to have your server rank your real names. That's interesting, but I like the idea of having them rank your team names. This makes your leaguemates try to name their team better than usual. I can see me naming my team something like, "Jessica Rules!" if our server's name is Jessica. I'm smart like that. Just make sure all the team names are written down, and Jessica just puts numbers by each one. Then have her read off the draft order backward, from 12 to 1. Then order some cheese fries.

23. Fantasy NFL preseason weekend

On the weekend before your draft, have everyone pick a QB, RB and WR from all the preseason games that week. Tabulate the scores and the highest scores win the top picks. Teams can have the same players, breaking any tie scores using last year's finish (highest finish wins).

24. Royal rumble in video game wrestling on WWE 2K

Another entrant from Reddit (thanks Meta_Franko!). He suggested plugging in an Xbox at a bar and setting up a wrestling video game to run a Royal Rumble wrestling match, with the computer controlling all players, and each time someone gets tossed out, their draft pick is the last available from the first round. He said have people choose their characters to make it more fun. He said it takes about 30 minutes, but it gets pretty exciting – and the rest of the bar even got into it, too!

25. Modified beer pong

Write the draft pick numbers on the bottom of 12 cups, then mix them up and pour some beer in there. Then each GM takes their turn at throwing one pingpong ball into a cup. Once you make it, drink, then look at what pick you earned!

26. Beer guzzling competition

Staying with the beer theme, set up a phone to do slo-mo video of everyone drinking a full cup of beer as fast as possible. Go to the tape to figure out the exact draft order! Plus, you can use the tape to see if anyone jumped the gun!

27. Play laser tag

Everyone goes to your local laser tag spot and fights for the highest score!

28. Poker hands dealt out

Get two decks of cards together and deal each person five cards — and only five, no draws! Deal them face up, and the person with the best poker hand wins the top pick. Keep doing it until the second-to-last pick and last pick are decided.

29. Race go-karts

Don't race and hurt each other in a 12-car pileup, but instead, do time trials to see who can finish two laps the fastest.

30. Pick entrants in a race

Head to a horse track and have everyone pick a horse in a race (you might have to split the GMs into two races). You can also have everyone pick a driver in an upcoming NASCAR race (note if you do this: Read our NASCAR writers first, they're awesome).

31. Bowling tournament

Make sure you make this event fair, though, by making everyone throw the balls opposite-handed or between the legs for the entire game.

32. Miniature golf tournament

Rather than just a regular round of miniature golf, try this out. My wife and her family do this every year, and it's a hoot. A hoot, I tells ya! Everyone can only use ONE hand on their golf club, and the other hand must have an alcoholic beverage of their choice — for the entire round. One-handed putting is tricky!

33. Video game tournament

Whether it's Mario Kart or just playing an old Nintendo game, like Tetris or Super Mario, have everyone play to try to get the best scores.

34. Bids placed on picks

This was another great one taken from Reddit (thanks champion_underdog!). Have each GM bid or choose secretly what pick they want. Then the commissioner goes through the bids, and if an GM bids on a pick that no one else bids on, then he/she gets that pick. If multiple people bid on that pick, then their names go in a hat, and one person's name is drawn out. After all winning bids are assigned, all the extra names go in a hat to fill out the lottery. Do you put a bid on the first pick, with the knowledge that everyone wants that pick, so you might be drawing against a bunch of people? Or do you try to outsmart everyone and choose the second or third pick, hoping to be singular? Strategy!

Hopefully, some of these methods to determine your league's draft order work for you and your leaguemates. My suggestion is to rotate what competition you use every year so people can't practice! ▰▰

Scan here for up-to-date content on TheAthletic.com

Drafting a quarterback: Why waiting … and waiting … and waiting is the key to fantasy football success

By Michael Salfino

Is the era of waiting forever on a QB over? Is the sharp move now to pivot and take the QB early, given the massive points that can be compiled by the ones who run enough where those stats can actually be projected/expected?

Nah.

It would be so much fun to say that everything has changed and what's old is new and what's viewed as smart is actually dumb. Heck, that's most of my articles. If I have a brand, that's it. But waiting on a QB is still the plus-expected value (+EV) play.

First, let's say why we historically have waited on quarterbacks. It's a "onesie" position (meaning you only start one QB — unless you play SuperFlex, which I recommend). You can just wait until every team but yours has a starter and take QB12 in a 12-team league. That's a long wait, typically. And what have you lost? Do you know the average spot among quarterbacks where the top-scoring QB each year since 2018 has been drafted is 13.3? That's not a QB1 but THE QB1.

Indulge me with further explanation that hopefully will get you to understand positional value more generally (and why wide receivers should be prioritized). Every team has a starting QB and that player has a very high touch floor. So there is a very low variance of opportunities for the quarterback to score, league-wide. Every one of them is going to be projected for 30-to-40 attempts-plus-rushes. (The same is true for starting running backs, given almost every team has one primary RB.) So just about any of them could be at least a top-five and even the top overall scorer in any given week.

Consider all the starting QBs and count how many definitely can't be an average fantasy starter, meaning they finish overall QB6 or QB7? Maybe your list is more expansive. But there are 25 QBs and certainly no fewer than 20 who can do it.

The GM who finds that fantasy-winning QB late will be accused of being lucky; but it's a skill to know where the luck can be leaned into in our game. And that's at QB for sure.

My "Breakfast Table" podcast partner and Yahoo scribe Scott Pianowski always asks the early QB drafters: "What problem are you trying to solve?" Even if you whiff on the quarterback, you can probably find one on waivers. I wrote an article about how public leagues (as opposed to expert ones) draft an average of about two QBs per team. And they hold that many throughout the season, too. But even with 22 off the board, you can find gold on waivers. Odds are that the two you draft will be more than fine.

Bottom line: We don't lose our leagues because our QB wasn't good enough.

What about the "Konami Code" QBs who are basically cheat codes for our game since they are hybrid RB/QBs? Well, Josh Allen was that in 2020 and he was drafted QB11 on average. Plus, it's getting harder to name the QBs who don't run than the ones who do. The point is, you don't have to pay retail to even get a running QB. And we don't need 1,000 rushing yards. A top passer with 400 rushing yards and six rushing TDs can do it.

What if you wait and teams start taking second QBs? It happens. I remember thinking there is no point in taking a QB in my first fantasy draft and the guy who took Dan Marino first overall (for some reason) took Vinny Testaverde with his second-round pick. It was a one-QB league. He got creamed. I waited forever for a QB and took Boomer Esiason, who was fine. (I stacked him with Eddie Brown, Tim McGee and even James Brooks when no one even had a word for that. But I did not even make the playoffs.) If that happens, big deal. Then you get like QB13 and QB15.

So please, unless you're building a specific stack, just chill out at QB. Give yourself the chance to be the team that gets difference-making production at little or no cost. ▰▰

Shadow cornerbacks, and why you shouldn't fear your receiver facing them in fantasy football

By KC Joyner

During their incredibly successful tenure running the Oakland Raiders, Al Davis and John Madden used to have frequent discussions about the value of cornerbacks. They knew that cornerbacks were highly valuable and that games could be won or lost based on how strong a team was at that position.

Fantasy managers are often of a similar mindset, as many of them adhere to the idea of significantly downgrading wide receivers if those pass catchers are due to face a potential shutdown shadow cornerback who will follow the receiver around the field all game.

It's understandable to want to avoid that caliber of matchup, but is it wise for fantasy managers to adopt this approach? Are these matchups tough enough to warrant significant value in making start-sit decisions?

I've been studying cornerback performance for years, having been a pioneer nearly two decades ago in highlighting the value of yards-per-attempt (YPA) totals in grading cornerbacks, and along the way have been able to garner some insights into the matter.

(Please note that in my fantasy football matchup grading system, a red-rated cornerback designates a defender whose metrics indicate that he is a very difficult matchup and thus would potentially land in the shadow cornerback category.)

Most receivers see red-rated coverage on a small percentage of targets

For many years, I tracked the number of times a wide receiver would face different levels of cornerback competition and found that red-rated coverage was nowhere near as prevalent as is generally thought.

In a typical 16-game season (we don't have enough 17-game-season data yet), there will be anywhere from 85 to 90 wide receivers who see 48 or more targets in that campaign, or an average of at least three targets per game.

Among that group, roughly half of them will face a red-rated cornerback in direct coverage on fewer than 10 percent of passes. Around 20 to 25 percent will see a red-rated cornerback in direct coverage from 10 to 15 percent of the time. That leaves about 30 percent of qualifying wide receivers seeing red-rated coverage more than 15 percent of the time and only about a third to half of those will usually see that type of coverage at least 20 percent of the time.

One might think that the latter group would be chock full of top-flight wideouts, as they should be red-rated coverage magnets, yet the reality is even among those players it is often subpar wide receivers who have high-percentage levels in this area.

For example, in the 2018 season, here are the nine wide receivers who saw red-rated cornerbacks in direct coverage between 20 to 35 percent of their targets (no one saw more than 35.6 percent): Robby Anderson, Kelvin Benjamin, Antonio Brown, Corey Davis, Devin Funchess, A.J. Green, DeAndre Hopkins, John Ross and Taywan Taylor. Only Brown and Hopkins rated as WR1 candidates in fantasy football that year, and the highest-rated wideout among the other seven was Davis, who was a high-end WR3.

Red-rated cornerbacks are rare

A primary reason that receivers don't see red-rated coverage very often is that red-rated cornerbacks are rare.

Heading into the 2021 season, there were only 25 cornerbacks who earned a red-rated designation in my matchup grading system. To put this into perspective, consider that there are 32 NFL teams and that each has two starting cornerbacks in a base defense. Add to that a nickel cornerback who most teams would also consider a starter since three-wide-receiver sets are quite common and it makes for 96 starting cornerbacks.

This means that we start the year with around one-quarter of cornerbacks in the red-rated category. That number could move up based on the play of cornerbacks who have other color-grade designations, but it is just as, and maybe more, likely to drop due to injuries over the course of a 17-game season.

Offenses have a lot of tools to avoid red-rated cornerbacks

Another reason this type of coverage doesn't impact wide receivers as often as generally thought is that offenses have a ton of tools to get players open. Pick-route combinations, flooding zones, sight adjustments, bunch and stack-wide-receiver sets, motion — the list of ways that offensive coordinators use to get coverage off eligible pass catchers is nearly endless.

It is also quite difficult for a defense to adopt shadow coverage on a regular basis, as using something other than man-to-man coverage to do this requires many defensive play-calling adjustments.

Even when a team has a red-rated cornerback, there is no guarantee the player will line up against the opponent's top wideout. This is often the case with the Patriots, as Bill Belichick will frequently have New England's best cornerback face the opponent's second-best receiver. He surmises this will lead to a shutdown in that individual battle and thus allow the rest of the defense to double cover the top receiver.

Now that we've covered (pun intended) all these factors, it's time to address the question of how should fantasy managers handle potential shadow coverage situations?

Know the limit of matchup points

It's the type of factor that will typically move a player's weekly ranking by only roughly a tier in the most extreme cases. That means a blue-rated (elite) WR1 will at worst drop to green-rated (strong starter) WR2 status when facing an extremely difficult matchup and thus will still be an automatic start candidate.

A green-rated WR2 could drop to the WR3 level in this case, but that would leave him in the starter's tier in many three-WR leagues as well. The only time a red-rated matchup would be likely to move a wide receiver out of the starter's tier is if the player is normally a WR3. In that case, he would generally be subject to bench consideration depending on several factors anyway, so the matchup won't necessarily be the deciding factor in starting or sitting the player.

Pay more attention to red-rated defenses than red-rated cornerbacks

It's also worth calling attention to the fact that the toughest matchup points totals occur against teams with many red-rated defenders in the secondary.

This is the case with the Baltimore Ravens, as they started the 2021 campaign as the only club with three red-rated cornerbacks in their starting lineup. Any wideout facing a platoon like this has to deal with red-rated coverage more frequently than they might see in any other matchup, thus making this a situation to consider avoiding for lower-tier wide receivers.

It is also a coverage hindrance if a team has two red-rated safeties, as was the case in 2021 with the Los Angeles Chargers, New England Patriots and New Orleans Saints. Fantasy managers in leagues with long-touchdown point bonuses should factor that in when deciding start candidates. ▬▬

Soph situations: How offseason moves impact Jaylen Waddle, Najee Harris and more

By Brandon Howard

If your favorite team acquired a highly touted offensive player in the 2021 NFL Draft, it would behoove it to select players in the 2022 draft to support last year's key acquisitions. Despite whether last year's pick was a quarterback, running back or wide receiver, we must remember that football is the ultimate team sport. Each player relies on others to do their job well for the team to have success.

During the 2022 draft, some teams helped last year's rookie offensive players more than others. Teams also utilized other avenues to help their 2021 picks elevate their play. One area that was explored to improve the play of last year's draft picks was coaching, and another was free agency.

Whether offseason additions to the roster or changes to the coaching staff result in greater success for heralded 2021 prospects remains to be seen. However, it's not too difficult to look at some of the top players from the 2021 draft class and begin grading their team's offseason. Depending on the moves made by their respective teams, we can determine whether their arrow is pointing up or down heading into the 2022 NFL season.

Trevor Lawrence, QB, JAX

After finishing the 2021 season with a 3-14 record, it's hard to imagine things getting any worse for Trevor Lawrence and the Jacksonville Jaguars in 2022. The Jaguars have brought in Doug Pederson to replace embattled head coach Urban Meyer. Pederson has a track record of success and is known for helping quarterbacks reinvent themselves by designing offenses that best suit their skill sets.

In free agency, Lawrence gained pass catchers Christian Kirk, Zay Jones and Evan Engram. Each player has tremendous run-after-catch (RAC) skills. Kirk is shifty, while Jones and Engram can use their speed to turn upfield and maximize yards. These are traits that will enable Lawrence to improve his completion percentage, which sits at just 59.6.

In the 2022 draft, the Jags selected just one skill position player: running back Snoop Conner out of Ole Miss. At 5-foot-10, 220 pounds, Conner has an excellent blend of size and quickness. He's more of a one-cut back who can also catch the football out of the backfield. With Travis Etienne and James Robinson returning from injuries next season, Conner offers Jacksonville a great insurance policy in case something goes awry with either recovery. The Jaguars also drafted offensive lineman Luke Fortner out of Kentucky. The former Wildcats center has played every position along the interior offensive line and will be a welcome addition to the Jaguars roster.

Given Jacksonville's existing pieces, new coaching staff, free-agent acquisitions and draft picks, expect Lawrence to complete over 63 percent of his passes this season while upping his touchdown total to 22-plus.

Justin Fields, QB, CHI

When we speak of Justin Fields, we must discuss how he was acquired. The Chicago Bears moved up nine spots in the 2021 draft to select him, giving up the No. 20 pick in 2021, along with a first-rounder in 2022 and a fourth-round pick in 2023. For this reason, the Bears are somewhat hamstrung when it comes to building around Fields. They simply do not have the resources to put adequate talent around him. The organization hired a defensive-minded head coach in Matt Eberflus when offensive coordinators such as Pep Hamilton and Byron Leftwich were available.

The Bears finished No. 24 in the NFL in total offense last season and haven't added pieces that would help drastically improve their offensive output. Chicago signed receivers Byron Pringle and Equanimeous St. Brown to one-year deals. Pringle played 61 percent of his snaps in the slot last season, but with Darnell Mooney already on the roster, someone will need to spend more time on the outside in 2022. On top of a dearth of talent on the perimeter, the Bears are also lacking game-breaking ability out of the backfield, with the exception of Darrynton Evans.

If you were looking for the 2022 draft to yield more offensive help for Fields, think again. Chicago's highest-rated offensive selection was Velus Jones Jr., who graded out as my No.7 slot receiver. Jones is ultra-explosive but needs to become accustomed to reading leverage on the fly during training camp. He also needs to frame the ball better with his hands and eliminate focus drops.

In short, you can't send a soldier to war with no ammo, and that's exactly what the Bears are poised to do in 2022. For that reason, I do not see Fields becoming a top-15 quarterback in 2022.

Jaylen Waddle, WR, MIA

It's not every day you see a rookie receiver go for 1,015 yards and six touchdowns on 104 receptions. Jaylen Waddle managed to lead the Dolphins in receiving yards in 2021, and despite Miami adding more weapons this offseason, it's possible he'll top those numbers with fewer receptions in 2022. Let's remember: Waddle was coming off a broken ankle coming into his rookie season. Now he's two years removed from injury and will likely be more explosive than he was just a season ago.

The Dolphins fired head coach Brian Flores and brought in San Francisco 49ers offensive coordinator Mike McDaniel to become their head coach. McDaniel is known for his creativity in the run game and his ability to cultivate positive relationships with his players. As far as free agency is concerned, the Dolphins seemingly acquired all the best talent on the market. They solved their problem at left tackle by signing Terron Armstead of the New Orleans Saints. To continue along the theme of more protection for quarterback Tua Tagovailoa, Miami also signed guard Connor Williams. The run game was far from productive last season, so Miami decided to pick up two new backs in Raheem Mostert and Chase Edmonds.

The Dolphins signed Teddy Bridgewater as an insurance policy for Tagovailoa and also acquired

THE ATHLETIC ———————————————————————————————— 2022 FANTASY FOOTBALL GUIDE

Cedrick Wilson Jr., an outstanding slot receiver with tremendous RAC ability. Last but certainly not least, Miami traded a first-, second- and fourth-round pick in the 2022 draft in exchange for Tyreek Hill. Teams will double-team and bracket Hill, which means Waddle will be singled up more often than not. He'll also benefit from Miami's improved run game, which will allow the Dolphins to take more deep shots off play-action.

While it's true that Miami will likely spread the ball around a bit more in 2022, don't be surprised to see Waddle eclipse his yards and touchdown numbers on fewer receptions than a season ago.

Najee Harris, RB, PIT

Najee Harris might've rushed for 1,200 yards and seven touchdowns last season, but it took him 307 carries to do it. The most impressive thing about his game was how reliable he was. Harris racked up 467 yards and three touchdowns on 73 receptions. Though I fully expect his production to continue, I have a hard time believing he'll go over 1,000 yards on the ground next season.

Pittsburgh added center Mason Cole and guard James Daniels to its offensive line. Outside of that, the Steelers have done little to fortify an offensive line that struggled at the point of attack just a season ago. In the 2022 draft, the Steelers neglected to address the offensive line there as well. They got cute on offense and selected a quarterback and two wide receivers they didn't necessarily need.

One thing to keep in mind is that the team's No. 1 quarterback is Mitchell Trubisky. In the past, Trubisky has struggled to get through progressions in a timely fashion. If pressure is in his face, he's inclined to panic, as opposed to using his athleticism to get out of harm's way. If Trubisky is pressured and unable to get the ball to his weapons on the perimeter, opposing defenses will simply drop another run defender into the box and stop the run on their way to the quarterback.

Due to a lack of protection up front and suboptimal quarterback play, Harris' production might take a dip in 2022. ▄▄▄

Vampires, throwbacks and more: 10 alternative fantasy football leagues for your consideration

By David Gonos

These days, everyone loves specialization. We have stores that specialize in many different things, from running shoes to yoga clothes to video games to things that cost $1 or less. Someday, there will be a specialty store that sells specialty stores!

Yet, even with all this specialization, it doesn't negate the fact we still need grocery stores and department stores.

Fantasy football is similar — there are many different types of leagues people can join, but it doesn't make them leave their tried-and-true standard leagues they play in with their pals. We just want more, and we want them to be different.

10 alternative fantasy football leagues

We're going to assume you already play in different versions of standard leagues, from PPR to IDP, from drafts to auctions, and we believe you likely already know the options there. These are ALT leagues that are for veteran fantasy players. You must be THIS tall to go on this ride.

1. 2-QB leagues

In the early 2000s, this type of league started to gain traction, specifically on MyFantasyLeague.com. Basically, each team must start two quarterbacks in its lineup. Obviously, just like how adding a third wide receiver to your lineup makes the WR position more important, 2-QB leagues make that quarterback position very important on draft day.

It's not uncommon to see 15-20 quarterbacks drafted in the first five rounds. Nobody wants to be stuck with a desperation, bottom-of-the-barrel starter, even if

All the Strategy You'll Ever Need

you have Patrick Mahomes at No. 1. Unlike the other valuable positions (running backs, wide receivers and tight ends), NFL starting quarterbacks are relatively finite. By that, I mean it's pretty uncommon for more than 32 quarterbacks to offer fantasy value in a given week, unlike the other positions, where a third-down back or a slot receiver can still pick up points as a non-starter.

This league harkens back to the late '80s when quarterbacks were more valuable because of TD-only scoring formats.

2. SuperFlex leagues

On the heels of a 2-QB league is the SuperFlex fantasy setup, which allows teams the option of starting two quarterbacks in their lineup — or they can start a running back, wide receiver or tight end in that lineup slot. This makes for some huge changes in strategy — both in draft prep and certainly as the draft is going on. But listen to our Michael Salfino, who believes you should always treat SuperFlex leagues as if they were just straight 2-QB leagues.

"In a SuperFlex league, quarterbacks are like running backs minus the expected injury attrition — so there is no fragility to lean into; no steady supply of weekly starters continuously coming online via waivers." — Salfino

3. Retro TD-only leagues

I mentioned this earlier in the article, but in the old days, when we only got to watch a couple of games a week on TV, fantasy football was all about TD-only scoring. What that meant was the only way for players in your lineup to score (excluding kickers) was to score a touchdown (4 points for passing TDs, 6 points for rushing/receiving TDs). This included defense/special teams, so the only way they could get you points was to return a kick or a turnover for a touchdown, or a safety. Try out a six- or eight-team league with this setting and see how much more interesting life gets when NFL teams get into the red zone.

The whole concept of yardage scoring might have only come around because Barry Sanders was regularly destroying teams between the 20s for billions of yards, but he wasn't racking up many touchdowns in Detroit's run-n-shoot (from 1992-95, he averaged just seven TDs per season). People were angry! Fantasy villagers took their torches into town and called for fantasy heads to roll!

4. Survivor leagues

First, let me explain there are different types of survivor leagues, but I'll mention the most common one to start — guillotine leagues.

This fantasy survivor format eliminates one team each week — the lowest-scoring team — and continues to the end of the season when it comes down to just two teams. If you do the math, you can figure out that you can do an 18-team league if you wanted to, with the ability to eliminate one team each week until it comes down to a Week 17 championship game.

Another type of fantasy survivor league I've played in is where you fill out a different lineup every week (there was a tournament called Fantasy Football Tournament of Champions that used this setup). You get to start a player just once all season, so you had to be selective on when you would use superstars or save them for later. The trick about saving them for later was that half the field is eliminated after each week. So saving Saquon Barkley for later might not work out if you are no longer in the game!

(Note: We'll discuss the third type of survivor league when we get to the DFS section.)

5. Bizarro leagues

These are fun mostly because you can finally enjoy some bad fantasy players, as opposed to cursing their existence. Each GM drafts a lineup that consists of 1 QB, 2 RBs, 2 WRs, 1 TE and 1 DEF. The idea is that the worse these players do, the more points they score for your team. If they do well, your team loses points. The trick is — scoring is set up to reward players who play poorly … a lot. In other words, you can't just draft backup players who never play.

Fantasy points are awarded for fumbles, incomplete passes, interceptions thrown, low yards per carry and missed field goals.

6. All vs. one and one vs. all

A commissioner can set up the scheduling so that each team plays against all the other teams each week, and its record carries on throughout the year. So if you are the top-scoring team in a 12-team league, you go 11-0 that week. If you are the lowest-scoring team, you go 0-11. Imagine this played out throughout the fantasy regular season, then the top six teams win playoff spots. Once the fantasy playoffs start in Week 15, the top two teams get byes, and the top two scoring teams in Week 15 move on. The top two scoring teams in Week

16 move on to face each other in a one-game playoff for the league title!

7. Rotisserie leagues

Fantasy baseball players are familiar with rotisserie scoring, which awards points in categories, rather than head-to-head play. It's nerd sports. I know. There were moments when rotisserie scoring in fantasy football picked up steam, including in the late '90s when fantasy sports was moving to online management. But it faded away as the head-to-head format started snowballing. This is still a viable alternate fantasy league format, but the scoring has to be weighted, in my opinion, with double scoring for some categories. Here are my 10 categories for Roto football:

5 Double-scoring categories

- Passing touchdowns
- Passing yards
- Rushing and receiving touchdowns
- Rushing yards
- Receiving yards

5 Secondary categories

- Receptions
- Turnovers (Fewest wins the category)
- Field goals
- Defensive yards allowed
- Defensive points allowed

8. DFS leagues

Daily fantasy sports took over the fantasy world for a minute about eight years ago, and now it seems to have leveled off. I love the concept of marrying both seasonal leagues with DFS leagues, and that's what we're talking about here.

Take your regular fantasy league's GMs, enter them into a weekly DFS contest and keep track of the standings from week to week. It's basically a complementary league to your regular league, and it helps keep those teams that suffered major injuries from losing interest.

9. Survivor DFS league

This is that third fantasy survivor league I was talking about, and it's more like the CBS TV show "Survivor" than any other setup.

Get 18 teams together for this league. Each week, every team fills out a DFS lineup, and the worst scoring team gets "kicked off the island." The highest-scoring team gets an Immunity Idol.

The next week, the surviving 17 teams fill out lineups (as well as the eliminated team). Once again, the highest-scoring team wins the Immunity Idol (even if it already owns one, it can win another), and the lowest-scoring team gets eliminated — unless it has an Immunity Idol! In that case, the second-lowest scoring team gets the boot after that Immunity Idol is used. If the previously eliminated team scores the highest points overall, it is added back into the field, and TWO non-immunity teams are eliminated.

Immunity Idols are awarded every week through Week 10, then it's down to just the lowest-scoring team going home no matter. Any leftover idols are useless.

I started a league like this in 2009 when I worked with OPENsports.com and it was a huge success — the game, not the site. You started scoreboard watching the top and the bottom of the leaderboard to see who would get the Immunity Idol and who would get kicked out. And when you saw a formerly eliminated team near the top of the leaderboard, you understood — two people might get eliminated from the bottom this week! And if one of them had an Immunity Idol, then the third-worst scoring team would get booted!

10. Vampire fantasy leagues

This is an interesting concept I saw on Twitter several years ago. Take a 12-team league and mark one of those GMs as the "vampire." The fantasy draft happens with the 11 non-vampire teams. They will draft like regular, but during the season, they're not allowed to make any waiver wire moves or trades. They are stuck with the team they drafted for the entire season.

The vampire team gets to pick up his team from the leftovers, of course. Each week, the vampire team faces an opponent, and if he beats them, he gets to trade one of his starters for one of their starters, essentially siphoning off the best players off each team he beats.

I've never played in this league, but when we tried to get one going last season, we realized — it's only really fun for the vampire. Everyone wants to be the vampire. ▬▬▬

All the Strategy You'll Ever Need

The 139 best team names for fantasy football

By David Gonos

Writing a column about naming your fantasy football team is like bringing beer to a friend's tailgate party. You really think they don't already have beer? Of course, they have beer. Yet, they're happy you brought beer — and they intend to drink it all!

No one really needs help coming up with a fantasy football team name. Yet, it's impossible to not read an article about fantasy football team names. See? You're reading it now.

Outside of just jumping headfirst into awesome 2022 fantasy team names, we thought we'd share some different ideas surrounding this exercise.

I used to call these "rules" for naming your fantasy team, but who am I to impinge on your right to be sophomoric, disgusting and offensive!?! Have at it!

Instead, I will offer up ideas on team name possibilities, hoping to widen your horizons and bring you into a new era of a more clean, mature, family friendly league standings page. Leave the cuss words and innuendos behind you! Step over into adulthood! Unless you're in a league in which that's highly frowned upon, then carry on.

Here are a handful of suggestions you can mock!

• Don't name your team "(Your name)'s Team." That's lazy. Then again, naming it literally "(Your name)'s Team" is kind of inventive all on its own. ...

• Choose a city/state/region and a mascot as your team name. You want to be a fake NFL general manager? Come up with a fake team name that resembles the NFL teams.

• Feel free to make pop culture references, tied into a player's name. Even if you're digging back to your childhood, these are still fun to consider every year.

• Talk your league's commissioner into choosing a theme for your league, and all team names must have themed names. Some great themes are "Seinfeld," "The Simpsons," "Star Wars" and plenty more that don't start with "S"!

Before we list off some great-ish team names, here are some fantastic team names our readers at The Athletic have offered up in the comments section through the past few years:

• The Dak Side of the Moon – From Aaron S.

• Jurassic Chark – From Daniel L.

• One If By Lamb, Two If By CeeDee – From Aaron B.

• Stafford Infection – From J Kris S.

Fantasy Team Names Based on 2022 NFL Rookies

Here's a list of new fantasy team names based off names of some of the top fantasy rookies entering the league:

Breece Hall
• Breece's Pieces
• Breece is the Word

Drake London
• Drake London Has Fallen
• Drake It 'Til You Make It

Chris Olave
• Olave Garden

Treylon Burks
• The Oregon Treylon

Skyy Moore
• The Rise of Skyywalker
• Skyyfall

Scan here for up-to-date content on TheAthletic.com

The Rest of the Best Fantasy Team Names

1. All Barkley, No Bite
2. Always Sony in Philadelphia
3. Amari Joystick
4. Austin Ekeler: Int'l Man of Mystery
5. Baby Got Dak
6. Bad JuJu
7. Baker's Dozens
8. Bateman Begins
9. Beats By DeAndre
10. Beg, Burrow and Steal
11. Belichick Yo' Self
12. Bend It Like Beckham Jr.
13. The Beverly Tannehillbillies
14. The Big Gronkowski
15. Brady Gaga
16. Can You Diggs It?
17. Catalina Wine Mixon
18. Championship! Lockett Up!
19. Chark Bites
20. Charknado
21. Chubbthumping
22. Christian MingleCaffrey
23. Clyde and Go Tyreek
24. Conner Among Thieves
25. Country Road, Take Mahomes
26. Clam Crowder
27. Dak and Yellow
28. Dak to the Future
29. Dakstreet Boys
30. Dalvin and the Chipmunks
31. Davante Adams Family
32. Davante's Inferno
33. DeShone in 60 Seconds
34. Diggs in a Blanket
35. Dobbins is a Free Elf
36. Edge of Ja'Marrow
37. The Etienne Machine
38. Evans Help Us
39. Fournetteflix
40. Freaks and Zekes
41. Fresh Prince of Helaire
42. Game of Jones
43. Georgia Peach Pitts
44. Godwin Hunting
45. Golladay Inn Express
46. Green Akers
47. Green Eggs and Cam
48. Hangin' With Amari Cooper
49. Hello Kittle
50. Helaire Highwater
51. Here's To You, Allen Robinson
52. Hooked on a Thielen
53. Hot Chubb Time Machine
54. Hot Lockett
55. Hotel, Motel, Golladay Inn
56. How I Kmet Your Mother
57. I Gotta Thielen
58. It Takes Tua to Make a Thing Go Right
59. Jake Fromm State Farm
60. Jalen Hurts When I Do This
61. Joe Burrow, Tiger King
62. Josh Jacobs Jingleheimer Schmidt
63. JuJu Train
64. Judge Jeudy
65. Julio Let the Dogs Out
66. Justin Fields of Dreams
67. Kamara Chameleon
68. Kelce's Heroes
69. Kissing Cousins
70. Kittle Corn
71. Kittle Giants
72. Kittle Litter
73. Kobra Kyler
74. Krispy Kareem
75. Lamar Lamerrier!
76. Lamarvel Universe
77. Lawrence and Order
78. Lights, Kamara, Action!
79. Little Red Fournette
80. Mahomes Depot
81. Mayfield of Dreams
82. McLaurin Order
83. Miracle Miles Sanders
84. The Mixon Administration
85. My Kupp Runneth Over
86. Murray-Up Offense
87. N'Keal a Mockingbird
88. Najee Jose
89. Natural Born Kyler
90. OBJYN
91. One Nation, Under Godwin
92. Peachy Keenan
93. Ridley Me This
94. Roethlisberger Helper
95. Rollin' With Mahomes
96. Rub-a-Dub-Chubb
97. Run CMC
98. Saquonce Upon a Time
99. Saquontum Leap
100. Saved By Odell
101. School of Dawson Knox
102. Shake 'n' Baker Mayfield
103. Sherlock Mahomes
104. Silence of CeeDee Lamb
105. Standup Ekeler
106. Sunday Sermon
107. Super Ja'Marrio Brothers
108. Tampa Brady Buccaneers
109. Terry McLovin'
110. The Tagavailorian
111. The Tannehills Have Eyes
112. That's Amari
113. Thielen Groovy
114. Toyota Kamara
115. Trubisky Business
116. Tua's Company, But Three's a Crowder
117. Tua Legit Tua Quit
118. Tuafinity and Beyond
119. U Fant Touch This
120. UnFournetteable
121. Waddleburger
122. Waiting For Goedert
123. Waller World
124. Wentz, Twice, Three Times a Lady
125. Zeke and Destroy
126. Zeke of Nature
127. Zeke Squad

All the Strategy You'll Ever Need

Dominick Petrillo: How a blind fantasy football expert does his job

By Dominick Petrillo

Dominick Petrillo is a blind fantasy football expert who has written for several outlets. We invited him to share a column on how he does what he does, along with some of the frustrations and limitations of being an analyst for a game he cannot see.

Driving. Becoming a photographer. ... Driving. (I really miss driving.) There are many things I cannot do. I am completely blind. There are many things I can still do, though. Write, answer my own questions when you ask the person I am with — and yes, even opine on fantasy football.

Despite the perception that I am helpless because I am blind, this is not the case. For me and many others like me who are blind, fantasy football and fantasy sports in general are still a big part of our lives. From participating in the Scott Fishbowl for the past five seasons to writing on it for the same amount of time, I love the game. It not only has shown me a wonderful community of like-minded individuals but also — in some ways — has been a savior for me. Fantasy football, and football in general, have given me a mechanism to remain involved in something I love. Sports.

My story

I have been playing fantasy football for more than 20 years. I was in my first league in 1999, the same year I graduated from high school. For the past eight years, entering my ninth, I have continued to play despite my blindness.

On November 19, 2012, my life changed. This is the day I showed up to work and, even with a magnifying glass, I could no longer see the computer. This is the day I went blind. It was, in many ways, the last day I felt whole. I spent many months and even longer wondering: What now? No one would hire me. No one would even give me a chance to write. I was truly lost. But I still had fantasy football, and I still had sports. They saw me through a lot of hard times. They continue to do so.

As my story evolves from blindness to now dialysis and organ transplants, sports are a constant. Something I know will be there. And something I know will not judge me. It has become more than an outlet. It has become a passion and a way to get my story out to help others, something I hope to continue to do here and now. So, what is my process and what are some drawbacks for me and others who are blind? I am glad you asked.

My process

In many ways, my process for playing — and writing about — fantasy sports is the same as yours. Doing research, listening to podcasts and reading articles from my favorite analysts. Podcasts are great, as they put us all on the same playing field. It does not matter if I can or cannot see, because it is not a visual medium. I don't have to figure out graphs and charts in an article or up on a television screen. All I need to do is listen and absorb the information. Something about us blind people — we are great listeners. Otherwise, we would really be in a heap of trouble trying to figure anything out. Is my hearing better than that of others? No. But I know, for some, who have been blind since birth, the answer is a resounding yes. I am able to listen quicker, though. This does allow me to consume more podcasts, as I listen to them at a faster speed than standard.

As far as reading, I can find great nuggets of information just by consuming many different sources. My advice: Don't listen to everyone but find different analysts you tend to like — and read all of their work. Many opinions are great; even differing opinions. It allows you to see both sides and make an informed decision of your own. Never forget, no one is 100 percent right. Christian McCaffrey was the guaranteed No. 1 running back last season. Until he wasn't. Aaron Rodgers was washed up before last season. Oops.

Now, you may ask yourself: "Self, how does he know what is going on in the game and therefore do his analysis?" Simply put, I use the stat sheet. It's as effective as someone who watches film, and in many ways, it is better. For example, I am not mesmerized by the flashy run; one that may have only netted 1 or 2 yards yet made everyone wonder what else that player can do is worthwhile. And when I say look at the stat sheet, I do not just mean the headlines. It doesn't matter to me if I see a running back had 25 carries for 125 yards. Sure, 5 yards per carry is great, but when one run was for 75 yards, 24 for 50 is much less appealing.

The real key to my research — and honestly, anyone's research — should be to do your work completely. A 17-for-25 passing performance for 300 yards is far different from one that's 35-for-55 with 300 yards.

THE ATHLETIC —————————————————— 2022 FANTASY FOOTBALL GUIDE

Do not be beholden to one way of analyzing games. If you're a film junkie, you are missing half the fun. The same goes for those who focus on one position or one team. I do my analysis just as well as anyone else and even better than some. It is done differently, and it may take me a bit longer. But it also makes me more focused on it and conscious of what I am looking at. (No pun intended.)

After the research, the rest of the process for the disabled is relatively the same as for the rest of you. But there are a few challenges I have that you do not. This is where the rest of the story starts.

The challenges

First and foremost, accessibility. This is where it truly starts and ends. Whether it's a case of fantasy research or trying to be in a league, the truth is there are many sites that are not accessible the way we need them to be.

While some websites — namely Yahoo and Footballguys.com — are exceptional when it comes to accessibility, there are many others that, to be nice, are lacking. And this is not exclusive to fantasy football sites. There are a number of popular research sites that are also non-accessible for those who need to use screen readers. There are many people who are working with them or trying to work with them for improvements. Some are willing to listen, and others have said they do not care. Although a shame, it is a reality in a world where money drives decisions. They are making money from their visual customers, so they do not feel the need to make it available to the rest of us. So, what to do?

First off, I have to check out the site and make sure it is able to be used reliably. Part of this is to make sure the entire experience is available to me. Yahoo, as mentioned above, is 100 percent accessible from the draft through the season on its fantasy platform. I would love to see a bit more customization availability, but that is more nuanced and not a challenge.

There are other sites that are accessible for the draft, but the in-season tools are non-functional. These are tricky because you do not know this until you get into the season. Then there are the easiest ones to spot. The completely non-accessible ones.

These are easy to find because, in most cases, you cannot even perform a draft on them. And if you are able to get through that portion, you can only imagine how the rest will go. No thank you. There are, in actuality, only two or three platforms that are successfully able to be navigated from start to finish. There are one or two that are good for drafting, then it falls apart. And there are a litany that do not do either well.

The same can be said about research. Strangely enough, one of the most accessible websites for research is possibly the least accessible for fantasy. There is absolutely nothing that can be done on its fantasy platform, but its main website is wonderful. I do not know what to tell you there. Maybe it should swap department heads for a while to fix things. But until it does, I will strictly be sticking to research on the site.

What is the hardest part of the website challenges? Reaching out to the sites. I have tried over and over to reach out to different personnel at individual sites. Most do not reply. Some reply and tell me they sympathize and will try to work on it. Others still respond back with a simple message: We are not accessible and have no plans to become so. Hopefully, with enough pressure from others, these sites will change their minds and realize the importance of accessibility. If not, it will force the hand of those willing to help to find different platforms to use, thus hurting the bottom line. Only then will things truly start to change for the betterment of all involved.

It takes more than me and my blind colleagues to make a difference. It takes everyone.

Personal message

There are many reasons I continue to play fantasy football. I have always loved sports, and this is a way to stay in the game. It allows me, even though I am usually shy in person, to connect with others with similar interests and stay involved. And it allows me to help others with my stories and actions. My great friend Chris Wesseling, before his passing, said something I truly believe. When people told him they wanted to be a sportswriter, he would ask them why, and the answer would always be the same: to write about sports. His answer would also always be the same: You can do that anywhere. You should want to be a writer for the same reason you should want to do any job. To help others. I have always believed it, and through my friendship with him and others, I have grown to realize this even more.

I am different from you. I am blind. I will be starting dialysis in a few months. I am going to be getting a kidney and pancreas transplant when they become available. But I am also the same as you. I love football. I have a passion for the things I love, and I have the determination to make it if given the opportunity. Those opportunities that you take for granted, I do not get. For every 100 jobs I qualify for, I am immediately

All the Strategy You'll Ever Need

denied consideration for 50 of them because I'm disabled. In my case, of those 50 that are left, I am disqualified for an additional 90 percent because my disability is blindness. These are the facts. For every 100 jobs you will be considered for, I will be considered for five. This needs to change for me and for the younger generation that is still in school and wondering what their lives are going to become. They are the real reason I am going to make it as a sportswriter. To show society as a whole and the disabled community what can be accomplished when an opportunity is given. I tell my story. I struggle. I sacrifice. So the next generation will not have to. At least I am hoping they won't. I am going to leave off with a quote I have come to live by when it comes to my writing and my story:

"Diabetes took my sight. It left me with vision." ▬▬

Maximizing fantasy football draft value by comparing positional scoring over the last 3 years

By Michael Salfino

Every year, I take a three-year sample of the end-of-season actual points scored at each position. This way, I can assess the expected value of, for instance, the TE1 compared with the WR5; and the RB10 compared with, say, the WR10. I used the Pro-Football-Reference database and sorted by half-point PPR scoring. Let's leave quarterbacks out of this because I am strongly opposed to a strategy that seeks to maximize points by drafting quarterbacks early — but more on that later.

The overriding objective when drafting running backs, wide receivers and tight ends in fantasy football is to get the most points, regardless of position. If you're making the 25th pick and 18 running backs have been selected, you probably don't want to take a running back. And if the three tight ends who are in that top tier at the position are taken all in a row before you select, you probably want to cross that position off your cheat sheet and focus somewhere else.

These are the actual averages for the players at each position, ranking by PPR points — all the WR1s, RB15s, TE5s, etc. But this has nothing to do with where the players were actually drafted. So the "RB10" represents how many points the 10th-highest-scoring RB averaged, regardless of where he was drafted. The objective is to know the expected points when you draft the 10th running back in your league. You may have that player ranked higher, of course, but we want to know exactly where the points bar is that you have to beat with that pick, and whether it would be wiser to focus instead on another position.

TE1 matches the expected points of WR5, meaning that a strategy of just waiting on TEs when no one has drafted one and continuing to pound the WR queue after well more than five of those players have been taken — that's leaving expected points on the table. Travis Kelce going around WR5 is perfectly reasonable. I prefer drafting Mark Andrews over Kelce, as Andrews was the No. 1 TE in 2021 and Kelce is over 30. But you probably need an early-round pick to take Andrews after Kelce in the second round when it snakes back to you. Picking fourth, fifth or sixth probably allows you to snake Andrews in Round 2 about 85 percent of the time.

TE5 equals WR30 in points but the fifth TE off the board has been going (according to ADP) where the WR20 typically gets drafted. The play here is to pass on that TE and take the WR. The reason is that you only have to get what you pay for at WR to beat the TE handily, as opposed to drafting the TE5 and hoping he scores much higher than where he's drafted among TEs. We hope all of our players score higher than where we pick them but we want that to be a bonus — we don't want to actually pay for that.

Here's a different way of looking at the data, with the positions and three-year-average point finishes all in one chart:

RB1	407	WR30	189
WR1	391	RB25	169
RB5	270	WR35	177
WR5	285	RB30	153
RB10	231	WR40	162
WR10	253	WR45	153
TE1	289	RB35	139
WR15	237	TE10	153
RB15	207	WR50	143
WR20	225	RB40	123
RB20	193	TE15	133
TE5	188	RB45	107
WR25	209	TE20	115

So with perfect foresight, you would obviously prioritize the No. 1 scoring running back. That's going to be the most valuable non-QB, on average, beating the No. 1 wide receiver by 16 points the past three years, 407 to 391.

But as soon as you think the No. 1 point-scoring running back is likely off the board, you should prioritize wideouts, because the No. 1 receiver is going to beat the RB5, for example, easily (by an expected 120 points). And that continues in the early rounds. The WR5 goes about where the RB10 (or even later) is drafted, and that's about a 50-point expected edge for the WR pick. WR10 beats RB15 by a similar amount. Then, most drafts back off RBs and focus on WRs. (So it's nice to already have your WR studs by then.)

Finally let's look at two different strategy constructions, measured by expected points — just getting exactly what you paid for and not needing to be some great player picker. We'll do 1EliteRB versus RB Heavy.

1EliteRB (meaning you take an elite RB, then focus on WR and TE for your next several picks) — No edge with the first pick since you want that anchor RB just like the RB-heavy team. But then you're taking WR1-5 with pick 2, WR5-10 or TE1 with 3, WR10-20 in the 4th, WR20-30 in the 5th. That's an expected total of 1,360 expected points (330 points +330 + 275 + 225 + 200).

RBHeavy (means you likely go RB, RB, RB, WR, RB) gets you 330 + 237 + 180 + 225 + 140 for a total of 1,110 points.

That's a massacre. But, the RB drafters will say, "OK, but now we get to feast on the higher scoring WRs and you have to draft slug RBs." That's somewhat correct. Add three RBs and a WR in the next four rounds for the 1EliteRB team and three WRs and one RB/TE for the RB Heavy team. That's an expected 135, 135, 135, 150 for the former team (RB, RB, RB, WR) and 150, 150, 150, 135 for the latter (WR, WR, WR, RB/TE).

So the RBHeavy team has picked up about 30 points. But they're still down an expected 220 points through nine rounds. That's a lot. That's 37 touchdowns you have to make up. It's playing decidedly uphill.

This year, structure your selections in a way that optimizes the expected points rather than minimizing them. Keep the chart handy when your pick comes up and you have a dilemma on who to pick, and you could reap the benefits of proper draft construction. ▬▬

Data shows drafting RBs in the second and third rounds is dumb — so why do we keep doing it?

By Michael Salfino

I know drafting running backs is a religious principle in fantasy football. And when there are people like me telling everyone that taking RBs in the second and third round is a bad process, it's treated as heresy. It's not, though; it's math.

This is not a zeroRB article (the style of drafting where you don't take RBs in any early rounds). If you want to draft a running back in the first round, fine. The math supports that. But avoiding RBs in the second, and especially third and fourth, rounds is something you ignore at your peril.

Since 2018, 29 running backs have been drafted in the second and third rounds, according to FantasyPros. Their average ADP is 25.1. Their median point total is 197.6 (full PPR, according to Pro-Football-Reference). Generally, top 36 scorers have at least 200 points, so I consider anything below 170 a bad pick; and the bad-pick rate of these RBs is 30 percent (11 misses out of 37). I consider at least 275 points a boom. The boom rate of these RBs drafted in rounds two and three since 2018 is 16.2 percent (six out of 37).

Now let's do the wide receivers: On average, they have been drafted slightly higher (24.1 overall) but they are also FAR higher ranked on average at their position (since normally nine or 10 RBs are taken in the first round). The median scoring of these 32 wide receivers is 236.8. Their bad-pick rate is 24 percent (11 of 45). Their boom rate is 22.2 percent, not counting one 274.1-point scorer (just under the 275 I demanded of a boom); if I count the borderline 274.1 as a boom, the boom rate grows to 24.4 percent.

So to summarize, if you take a WR over a RB (according to my data over the last few seasons), you should expect 40 more points per pick. You have a significantly greater chance of hitting big (24.4 percent to 16.2 percent). And your bust rate is about 20 percent less.

All the Strategy You'll Ever Need

Now let's fast forward to 2022 and look at NFFC ADP in June (when this column went to print). We have nine running backs going in the second and third round (after seven have typically gone in Round 1). We have 10 WRs going in the second and third rounds (after four have typically gone in Round 1). Should these numbers hold all draft season, Round 1 is significantly less RB heavy than in 2021 (down from 10 RBs to seven) and more WR heavy (up from one to four). But the advantage still holds. You're gaining about 40 expected points for the WRs (or top-two TE, either Travis Kelce or Mark Andrews) you take here after Round 1 versus taking a RB.

Let me add, straight up, that picking running backs in the fourth round and even the fifth round is also minus-EV. I'm focusing on the second and third rounds just because it's here where you will generally hurt yourself the most.

Last year, I heard a defense of this RB-heavy approach from a radio host on Sirius XM's Fantasy Sports Channel. To paraphrase, he cited research that said 91 percent of teams finishing in the top three went RB heavy at the draft. What's wrong with this? The denominator is so large that this data is meaningless. In other words, if 10 or 11 teams (sometimes all teams) go "RB heavy" by some metric at the draft, well, then of course the top three teams in the league will have gone RB heavy; after all, every team basically is doing it. Even if eight or nine go RB heavy, a stat like this is meaningless.

Can you bet against this math? Of course. You need to really believe a back should be drafted in Round 1. But ask yourself why you are so smart in seeing something that the running-back crazed horde is missing?

I'm not even going to talk about the players, arguing for or against any specific back. Just know that if you draft a WR in the second and third round instead of RBs there, you'll have 80 more expected points — 13-plus fantasy touchdowns worth of points. You'll have a much better chance of crushing those picks. And 20 percent less of a chance that those picks really damage your odds of winning.

What's not to like about that? The only religion that you should care about in fantasy football is not "RBs," it's "winning." ▬▬▬

Cognitive bias in fantasy football: Why reading this magazine might actually hurt your process

By Renee Miller

I was obsessed with neuroscience and how the brain works before I was obsessed with fantasy sports, but I was well into both passions before I recognized how they intersected. Decision-making is one of the hottest topics in one of the hottest fields right now, neuroeconomics, but some of the most important principles go back at least a decade to the seminal work of Daniel Kahneman — "Thinking Fast and Slow" — and are equally relatable to fantasy sports decisions.

The basic premise of Kahneman's book is that our highly evolved, efficient brains are wired for shortcuts that enable fast, reasonably good, nearly subconscious decision-making. We are capable of navigating more involved logical and rational neural paths to decision-making, but these are slower and more energy consuming, requiring our full conscious effort. It is not that one is bad and one is good, but that it is important to be aware of how and why we arrive at the decision to draft Player A over Player B in Round 3, or why we're willing to trade away or drop a player we invested in for next to nothing in Week 4 (or conversely, why we endlessly cling to an unproductive investment, refusing to drop him, while demanding unreasonable trade returns for him).

Most of us consider ourselves something of an expert at fantasy sports if we are contributing to, or reading, this magazine. We put in the study time and have a keen interest in strategy that has hopefully paid off in years of fantasy success. But being an "expert" can also be a detriment to learning and studying, which you have likely told yourself is your goal in picking up this magnificent publication. Experts come to the table with ingrained knowledge. You know who you like and why, you have your predictions about the upcoming season ... and you have your biases.

Many cognitive biases that influence fantasy football decision-making arise from the kind of fast thinking in Kahneman's book, using those well-worn, automatic thought highways in your brain. These include those that you are probably familiar with such as recency bias and primacy bias, the biases that cause you to overweight in your decision-making process the most recent and/or the first instance of a parameter. A spectacular debut game — I still remember Matt Forte's 2008 debut or Kareem Hunt's 2017 Week 1 game — or a strong finish to the season — e.g. Amon-Ra St. Brown or Eli Mitchell in 2021 — probably stand out when you evaluate a player. These biases persist because they have generally been beneficial to our survival. First impressions are remarkably accurate, for example, and in many cases, the thing that just happened is very likely to happen again. That's why I emphasize that biases are not necessarily bad, but they can lead to more "auto-pilot" decisions that could be suboptimal.

Another influence is the near-universal novelty bias, in which we overweight and prefer new items. Novelty is met with a surge of dopamine and norepinephrine in our brains, which is a big reason why species from nematodes to humans exhibit this inherent preference for newness. New players haven't let us down (yet) and offer all the promise of their best historical comps — what's not to like? Drafting rookies is a ton of fun, and most of us have done a good job of not reaching too early on them in recent years. If anything, seasons like Ja'Marr Chase's 2021 will test our patience on this season's newcomers like Chris Olave, Drake London and Skyy Moore. Novelty bias is something to be aware of, but I don't recommend avoiding it or trying to overcome it altogether.

It is a fine line between blindly being led through the fantasy season by our ingrained biases and checking or second-guessing everything we're inclined to do. One idea I try to keep handy is the beginner's mind. As a beginner, you are open to knowledge and learning. You have no predisposed notions about how things work or how they should go. You listen to others with grace, try and err as you see fit, and generally think slow. You might make lists of pros and cons when deciding on a trade offer, for example, instead of just going with your gut (which is connected to, and relying on the same fast-signaling neurotransmitters as your brain). When you look at rankings, consider them a range of outcomes, not as set in stone. Tell yourself that past outcomes do not guarantee future performances, good or bad. The tricky part is not giving up on all the information you've gained over the years as an expert player — it wouldn't be very fun to force yourself to ignore everything you've learned about fantasy football, would it? So, aim for balance in using your knowledge while suspecting that some of it might be biasing how you make this year's decisions.

Rankings are probably a big reason you've bought this fantasy magazine, and so are our roundtable discussions that dig a bit deeper into our analyses of certain players as archetypal sleepers or league-winners. These sections of the magazine are likely to give one of your biases a major workout — the confirmation bias. Confirmation bias is when you only consider or pay attention to information that supports an existing belief. This is relevant to the previous discussion about beginner's mind too — instead of ignoring those ranks or blurbs you disagree with, can you take the time to understand the logic behind the writer's opinion? It's hard to admit that you might be wrong or not have all the information you need to make an informed decision about a team or player this year, and it's certainly OK to disagree! But if you just skim the issue looking for those blurbs and headlines that reinforce what you already think is true, you're not learning anything. You might still be in great shape, don't get me wrong, but you might not maximize the potential the magazine is meant to offer. Going back to the highway analogy of cognitive biases, the highway is a good, fast, safe method of travel, but you get a much better idea of the town/country/landscape when you take the side roads. Both might get you to the same place, but who hasn't found a hidden gem of a restaurant or store when taking time to meander down Main Street instead of hitting up the mall?

You can read more about all kinds of other cognitive biases in my ~~outdated~~ nostalgic 2013 ebook on fantasy sports (available from the link in my Twitter bio @reneemiller01). The more you know about the lazy enemy in your brain that can bias your important fantasy decisions, the better you'll be at making the most logical, rational choices you can. ▬▬

Scan here for up-to-date content on TheAthletic.com

All the Strategy You'll Ever Need

A

John Laghezza's
World O' Data Tables

Welcome to our "data" section. What you'll find in here are numbers on numbers... on numbers. We asked our resident data guru, John Laghezza, to sponge up the TruMedia database and create tables of stats he found interesting for each position — his efforts are on the next several pages. Additionally, we reached out to our partners at BetPrep and they shared their "Threshold" data with us (and, naturally, all of you). It's a very cool set of numbers that can help you identify players who consistently score at certain levels every week.

Dive right in! Nerd out! Enjoy! And hopefully this helps you pinpoint some players for your drafts you hadn't been considering yet.

Quarterbacks

Player	2021 QB STAT LEADERBOARD					
	Passer Rating	Pass Att	Pass Comp	Pass Yds	TDs	INTs
Aaron Rodgers	111.9	560	386	4,340	37	4
Joe Burrow	108.3	662	463	5,716	39	16
Dak Prescott	104.2	639	433	4,703	38	11
Kirk Cousins	103.1	561	372	4,221	33	7
Russell Wilson	103.1	400	259	3,113	25	6
Matthew Stafford	102.9	741	502	6,074	50	20
Jameis Winston	102.8	161	95	1,170	14	3
Tom Brady	102.1	810	544	5,916	46	13
Kyler Murray	100.6	515	352	3,931	24	12
Jimmy Garoppolo	98.7	515	344	4,341	22	15
Patrick Mahomes	98.5	780	525	5,896	48	16
Justin Herbert	97.7	672	443	5,014	38	15
Trey Lance	97.3	71	41	603	5	2
Teddy Bridgewater	94.9	426	285	3,052	18	7
Carson Wentz	94.6	516	322	3,563	27	7
Derek Carr	94.0	680	457	5,114	24	15
Mac Jones	92.5	559	376	4,033	24	15
Josh Allen	92.2	708	457	5,044	45	15
Jared Goff	91.5	494	332	3,245	19	8
Matt Ryan	90.4	560	375	3,968	20	12
Tua Tagovailoa	90.1	388	263	2,653	16	10
Ryan Tannehill	89.6	555	372	3,954	22	17

2021 QB STAT LEADERBOARD

Player	Passer Rating	Pass Att	Pass Comp	Pass Yds	TDs	INTs
Davis Mills	88.8	394	263	2,664	16	10
Jalen Hurts	87.2	475	288	3,402	17	11
Lamar Jackson	87.0	382	246	2,882	16	13
Ben Roethlisberger	86.8	649	419	3,955	24	10
Taylor Heinicke	85.9	494	321	3,419	20	15
Daniel Jones	84.8	361	232	2,428	10	7
Baker Mayfield	83.1	418	253	3,010	17	13
Drew Lock	80.4	111	67	787	2	2
Jacoby Brissett	78.1	225	141	1,283	5	4
Andy Dalton	76.9	236	149	1,515	8	9
Justin Fields	73.2	270	159	1,870	7	10
Sam Darnold	71.9	406	243	2,527	9	13
Trevor Lawrence	71.9	602	359	3,641	12	17
Zach Wilson	69.7	383	213	2,334	9	11

2021 QB EFFICIENCY LEADERBOARD

Player	Comp %	DB / Gm	AirYd / Att	Yd / Comp	Comp / Gm	PaYd / Gm	1stDn / Att	TD / Att
Joe Burrow	70.4%	38.0	8.1	12.6	23.2	285.8	38.8%	6.5%
Kyler Murray	69.2%	38.8	7.9	11.4	23.5	262.1	35.8%	5.0%
Aaron Rodgers	68.9%	36.0	7.7	11.2	22.7	255.3	40.1%	7.0%
Dak Prescott	68.8%	41.4	7.7	10.9	25.5	276.6	38.1%	6.2%
Derek Carr	68.4%	41.3	8.1	11.2	25.4	284.1	34.7%	3.7%
Jimmy Garoppolo	68.3%	30.9	7.5	12.7	19.1	241.2	39.0%	4.5%
Tua Tagovailoa	67.8%	32.9	7.0	10.1	20.2	204.1	35.3%	4.1%
Mac Jones	67.6%	33.8	8.0	10.8	20.9	224.1	34.0%	4.2%
Tom Brady	67.5%	44.7	8.1	11.0	28.6	311.4	37.4%	6.0%
Matthew Stafford	67.2%	37.8	8.5	12.1	23.9	289.2	38.8%	6.8%
Jared Goff	67.2%	38.6	6.4	9.8	23.7	231.8	32.8%	3.8%
Ryan Tannehill	67.2%	34.7	7.4	10.5	20.7	219.7	36.2%	4.0%
Matt Ryan	67.0%	36.3	7.1	10.6	22.1	233.4	34.8%	3.6%
Teddy Bridgewater	66.9%	33.7	8.0	10.7	20.4	218.0	34.3%	4.2%
Davis Mills	66.8%	33.5	7.3	10.1	20.2	204.9	29.9%	4.1%
Kirk Cousins	66.3%	38.2	8.2	11.4	23.3	263.8	34.2%	5.9%

Nerding Out

Player	2021 QB EFFICIENCY LEADERBOARD							
	Comp %	DB / Gm	AirYd / Att	Yd / Comp	Comp / Gm	PaYd / Gm	1stDn / Att	TD / Att
Patrick Mahomes	66.3%	44.0	7.3	11.1	26.3	294.8	39.5%	5.6%
Justin Herbert	65.9%	43.5	7.5	11.3	26.1	294.9	38.1%	5.7%
Taylor Heinicke	65.0%	35.9	7.6	10.7	20.1	213.7	33.8%	4.0%
Russell Wilson	64.8%	32.9	9.9	12.0	18.5	222.4	33.8%	6.3%
Ben Roethlisberger	64.5%	40.7	6.7	9.6	24.6	232.6	31.1%	3.6%
Lamar Jackson	64.4%	39.2	9.3	11.7	20.5	240.2	35.3%	4.2%
Daniel Jones	64.3%	37.0	7.3	10.5	21.1	220.7	32.1%	2.8%
Josh Allen	63.3%	41.7	8.2	10.8	24.1	265.5	36.2%	5.6%
Andy Dalton	63.1%	33.4	6.9	10.2	18.6	189.4	35.2%	3.4%
Jacoby Brissett	62.7%	28.8	7.5	9.1	15.7	142.6	30.7%	2.2%
Carson Wentz	62.4%	33.8	7.7	11.1	18.9	209.6	32.0%	5.2%
Jalen Hurts	61.3%	34.8	9.0	11.9	18.0	212.6	33.1%	3.7%
Baker Mayfield	60.5%	34.7	8.7	11.9	18.1	215.0	34.2%	4.1%
Drew Lock	60.4%	21.2	10.1	11.8	11.2	131.2	28.8%	1.8%
Sam Darnold	59.9%	38.6	7.3	10.4	20.3	210.6	30.3%	2.2%
Trevor Lawrence	59.6%	39.3	7.9	10.1	21.1	214.2	29.4%	2.0%
Jameis Winston	59.0%	27.1	8.3	12.3	13.6	167.1	34.8%	8.7%
Justin Fields	58.9%	29.4	9.8	11.8	13.3	155.8	30.7%	2.6%
Trey Lance	57.7%	17.2	9.3	14.7	8.2	120.6	38.0%	7.0%
Zach Wilson	55.6%	34.2	7.6	11.0	16.4	179.5	29.2%	2.3%

Player	2021 QB PACE LEADERBOARD					
	Plays / Gm	Sec / Play	Att / Gm	YPA	YAC / Comp	TD / Int
Lamar Jackson	69.7	27.9	31.8	7.5	4.7	1.2
Dak Prescott	67.8	26.3	37.6	7.4	4.9	3.7
Josh Allen	67.2	27.5	37.3	7.1	4.3	2.4
Tom Brady	67.0	26.6	42.6	7.3	5.2	3.6
Patrick Mahomes	66.7	27.1	39.0	7.6	6.2	2.9
Ryan Tannehill	66.6	29.2	30.8	7.1	5.0	1.5
Justin Herbert	66.4	26.1	39.5	7.5	5.4	2.5
Kyler Murray	66.2	27.4	34.3	7.6	5.4	2.4
Ben Roethlisberger	65.5	26.6	38.2	6.1	5.0	2.2
Sam Darnold	65.1	27.7	33.8	6.2	5.7	0.7

Player	2021 QB PACE LEADERBOARD					
	Plays / Gm	Sec / Play	Att / Gm	YPA	YAC / Comp	TD / Int
Tua Tagovailoa	64.5	27.6	29.8	6.8	4.6	1.6
Jacoby Brissett	64.5	27.6	25.0	5.7	3.6	1.3
Kirk Cousins	63.7	27.0	35.1	7.5	4.9	4.7
Matthew Stafford	63.6	28.2	35.3	8.2	5.3	2.4
Andy Dalton	63.2	28.0	29.5	6.4	5.1	0.9
Jalen Hurts	63.2	27.6	29.7	7.2	5.5	1.8
Justin Fields	63.2	28.0	22.5	6.9	4.4	0.7
Aaron Rodgers	63.1	30.5	32.9	7.8	6.0	9.3
Taylor Heinicke	62.9	28.5	30.9	6.9	5.5	1.3
Derek Carr	62.2	27.2	37.8	7.5	5.3	1.6
Jared Goff	62.1	27.4	35.3	6.6	5.3	2.4
Baker Mayfield	62.0	29.2	29.9	7.2	5.5	1.3
Mac Jones	61.9	28.6	31.1	7.2	5.0	1.7
Carson Wentz	61.9	30.1	30.4	6.9	5.1	3.9
Daniel Jones	61.8	27.1	32.8	6.7	4.7	1.4
Jameis Winston	61.8	28.9	23.0	7.3	6.1	4.7
Joe Burrow	61.5	29.8	33.1	8.6	6.2	2.4
Jimmy Garoppolo	61.5	29.5	28.6	8.4	6.5	1.7
Trey Lance	61.5	29.5	14.2	8.5	7.0	2.5
Teddy Bridgewater	60.9	29.5	30.4	7.2	4.9	2.6
Drew Lock	60.9	29.5	18.5	7.1	5.1	1.0
Zach Wilson	60.9	26.8	29.5	6.1	5.1	0.8
Trevor Lawrence	60.5	26.5	35.4	6.0	4.6	0.7
Davis Mills	59.4	27.8	30.3	6.8	4.7	1.6
Matt Ryan	59.2	27.8	32.9	7.1	4.6	1.7
Russell Wilson	56.1	26.7	28.6	7.8	5.3	4.2

Nerding Out

Wide Receivers

Player	2021 WR2 EFFICIENCY LEADERBOARD								
	PPR PPG	Tgt / Gm	Yds / Rec	AirYd / Tgt	YAC / Rec	Conv%	Tar %	Air %	TD
Cooper Kupp	27.8	11.24	13.0	8.5	5.6	75.9%	32.4%	33.2%	16
Davante Adams	23.0	10.56	12.6	9.5	5.0	72.8%	31.6%	37.1%	11
Deebo Samuel	22.2	7.50	19.0	8.9	10.3	64.2%	26.0%	28.8%	6
Justin Jefferson	20.7	9.82	14.7	12.3	4.5	64.7%	29.2%	45.8%	10
Ja'Marr Chase	18.9	7.53	18.4	12.1	8.6	63.3%	23.4%	37.1%	13
Antonio Brown	18.6	8.86	15.7	12.4	5.4	67.7%	23.1%	30.6%	4
Chris Godwin	18.5	9.14	11.2	7.1	6.0	76.6%	21.2%	19.6%	5
Tyreek Hill	18.0	9.35	11.2	10.0	4.1	69.8%	24.8%	35.2%	9
Diontae Johnson	17.8	10.56	10.9	8.7	4.8	63.3%	27.9%	33.5%	8
Stefon Diggs	17.1	9.65	11.9	11.2	3.2	62.8%	27.0%	35.4%	10
Keenan Allen	16.9	9.81	10.7	8.3	3.3	67.5%	25.7%	30.3%	6
Mike Evans	16.8	7.06	14.0	13.2	3.2	65.5%	16.6%	26.7%	14
Tee Higgins	16.6	7.86	14.7	12.1	3.9	67.3%	23.6%	33.9%	6
Mike Williams	16.2	8.06	14.5	11.9	4.7	58.9%	20.2%	29.6%	9
Tyler Lockett	16.0	6.69	15.6	14.4	3.5	68.2%	24.3%	37.4%	8
Hunter Renfrow	15.8	7.53	10.3	6.7	4.2	80.5%	21.2%	17.3%	9
Jaylen Waddle	15.6	8.88	9.7	7.2	4.2	73.2%	25.2%	26.5%	6
Adam Thielen	15.6	7.31	11.1	9.8	3.7	70.5%	20.4%	26.7%	10
Robert Woods	15.6	7.67	11.7	8.6	4.1	65.2%	21.8%	21.2%	4
Brandin Cooks	15.2	8.31	11.5	10.5	3.9	67.7%	27.2%	39.3%	6
CeeDee Lamb	15.1	7.50	14.9	11.0	6.3	65.8%	20.1%	26.2%	6
Marquise Brown	14.8	9.06	11.1	11.1	4.3	62.8%	26.1%	31.3%	6
DeAndre Hopkins	14.7	6.30	13.6	12.3	3.3	66.7%	20.1%	33.2%	8
D.J. Moore	14.6	9.53	12.4	10.6	4.6	57.4%	28.4%	41.8%	4
A.J. Brown	14.6	8.08	13.9	11.7	4.0	60.0%	27.7%	45.2%	5
DK Metcalf	14.5	7.59	12.9	12.7	4.4	58.1%	27.8%	38.7%	12
Michael Pittman	14.4	7.29	12.3	10.0	3.8	70.2%	25.0%	31.1%	6
Amari Cooper	13.9	6.87	12.4	11.3	3.3	66.0%	18.4%	25.7%	8
Amon-Ra St. Brown	13.7	7.00	10.3	6.3	5.3	75.6%	22.8%	22.8%	5
Darnell Mooney	13.6	11.67	12.7	10.7	5.2	57.9%	27.3%	34.9%	4
Terry McLaurin	13.3	7.71	13.7	13.1	4.1	58.8%	24.8%	42.4%	5
Elijah Moore	12.8	12.83	12.7	12.0	5.0	55.8%	19.1%	30.6%	5
Christian Kirk	12.4	6.06	13.3	11.5	3.2	74.8%	18.5%	27.3%	5

Player	PPR PPG	Tgt / Gm	Yds / Rec	AirYd / Tgt	YAC / Rec	Conv%	Tar %	Air %	TD
Russell Gage	12.2	6.64	12.5	11.2	3.3	71.0%	23.4%	27.9%	4
Corey Davis	12.1	6.56	14.5	13.1	3.7	57.6%	17.8%	28.7%	4
Tyler Boyd	11.7	5.88	13.2	7.8	6.7	71.3%	19.4%	19.4%	5
Jarvis Landry	11.5	7.08	11.0	7.8	5.8	61.2%	24.0%	24.8%	2
Sterling Shepard	11.5	8.83	10.0	7.6	3.1	67.9%	20.6%	19.9%	1
DeVonta Smith	11.3	6.06	14.5	14.2	3.4	62.1%	22.7%	37.5%	5
Chase Claypool	11.3	7.00	14.6	11.7	4.9	56.2%	18.1%	30.0%	2
Jakobi Meyers	11.0	6.71	10.5	9.8	2.8	67.5%	22.3%	28.9%	2
Marvin Jones	10.8	6.94	11.5	12.0	1.8	61.9%	20.4%	30.7%	4
Kendrick Bourne	10.7	3.94	14.4	11.0	6.8	77.6%	13.4%	12.9%	5
Michael Gallup	10.5	7.75	13.2	12.2	3.1	56.5%	16.8%	27.4%	2
Brandon Aiyuk	10.3	5.00	14.8	9.7	6.4	65.9%	18.4%	22.6%	5
DeVante Parker	10.3	9.13	12.9	11.4	2.9	54.8%	21.8%	31.4%	2
A.J. Green	10.2	5.75	15.4	12.2	3.4	58.7%	16.6%	26.9%	3
Cole Beasley	10.1	7.00	8.6	5.8	3.7	73.2%	18.4%	12.9%	1
Van Jefferson	9.9	5.24	16.1	13.5	4.4	56.2%	14.4%	23.2%	6
Tim Patrick	9.8	6.07	13.5	11.2	3.8	62.4%	18.0%	25.6%	5
Cedrick Wilson	9.6	15.25	14.9	10.0	4.5	73.8%	10.1%	11.9%	6
Allen Lazard	9.5	5.00	12.4	10.5	3.8	66.7%	12.8%	19.0%	8
Emmanuel Sanders	9.4	5.54	14.7	14.9	2.1	58.3%	14.4%	24.4%	4
K.J. Osborn	9.3	10.25	13.2	10.6	3.1	61.0%	14.2%	17.7%	7
Courtland Sutton	9.2	6.13	13.5	15.4	2.3	59.2%	18.3%	30.6%	2
Odell Beckham	9.2	6.83	12.1	11.9	3.1	53.7%	17.9%	26.5%	5
Jamison Crowder	9.2	17.75	7.0	7.5	3.3	70.4%	16.5%	16.7%	2
Marquez Callaway	9.1	7.64	17.0	13.7	2.9	54.8%	18.7%	30.7%	6
Rashod Bateman	8.9	16.75	8.4	9.3	1.6	68.7%	16.0%	17.4%	1

2021 WR2 EFFICIENCY LEADERBOARD

Nerding Out

Player	PPR Total	Routes	Tgt	Rec	Rec Yds	Air Yds	Rec%	YAC	Rec 1stDn	TD
						2021 WR2 STAT LEADERBOARD				
Cooper Kupp	472.5	625	191	145	1,947	1,641	73.0%	846	49	16
Davante Adams	368.3	551	169	123	1,553	1,609	72.8%	613	84	11
Deebo Samuel	356.0	408	121	77	1,405	1,029	64.2%	698	44	6
Justin Jefferson	352.4	623	167	108	1,616	2,071	64.8%	482	72	10
Ja'Marr Chase	320.6	579	128	81	1,455	1,617	64.0%	651	49	13
Tyreek Hill	306.5	575	156	110	1,237	1,647	71.2%	443	63	9
Stefon Diggs	291.5	643	165	103	1,225	1,841	62.4%	326	66	10
Diontae Johnson	285.4	504	142	87	949	1,437	61.3%	420	47	8
Keenan Allen	269.8	641	157	106	1,138	1,310	68.9%	337	63	6
Hunter Renfrow	269.1	296	74	63	649	833	85.1%	267	30	9
Mike Evans	268.5	628	114	74	1,035	1,484	64.9%	239	56	14
Chris Godwin	259.4	560	127	98	1,103	931	76.6%	586	46	5
Mike Williams	258.6	505	114	64	927	1,497	56.1%	302	42	9
Tyler Lockett	256.4	500	107	73	1,175	1,567	68.8%	277	37	8
Jaylen Waddle	249.8	579	141	104	1,015	1,017	73.7%	439	57	6
D.J. Moore	247.5	622	163	93	1,157	1,727	57.1%	426	60	4
DK Metcalf	247.3	499	129	75	967	1,636	58.1%	328	48	12
Michael Pittman	244.6	555	129	88	1,082	1,189	67.8%	348	50	6
Brandin Cooks	243.8	528	134	90	1,037	1,410	67.2%	355	45	6
CeeDee Lamb	241.8	432	96	62	925	1,233	64.6%	391	43	6
Marquise Brown	236.3	625	146	91	1,008	1,631	62.3%	388	41	6
Amon-Ra St. Brown	233.3	279	74	58	598	840	78.4%	307	31	5
Tee Higgins	232.1	482	110	74	1,091	1,327	67.3%	290	53	6
Darnell Mooney	231.7	521	115	68	842	1,480	58.0%	320	35	4
Terry McLaurin	225.5	582	130	77	1,053	1,717	59.2%	317	47	5
Christian Kirk	210.6	379	64	77	627	1,189	73.4%	151	26	5
Amari Cooper	208.5	502	102	66	824	1,145	64.4%	214	39	8
Adam Thielen	202.8	446	95	67	726	903	70.9%	239	33	10
DeVonta Smith	192.6	491	100	64	901	1,448	62.0%	210	42	5
A.J. Brown	189.9	347	105	63	869	1,217	58.3%	248	41	5
Jakobi Meyers	187.3	513	120	77	822	1,109	65.0%	220	39	2
Tyler Boyd	186.8	341	70	67	661	728	71.4%	336	29	5
Marvin Jones	183.2	599	117	73	808	1,422	59.8%	128	41	4
Kendrick Bourne	181.5	106	19	52	230	551	84.2%	108	8	5
Brandon Aiyuk	174.3	471	84	56	826	865	66.7%	357	37	5

Player	PPR Total	Routes	Tgt	Rec	Rec Yds	Air Yds	Rec%	YAC	Rec 1stDn	TD
					2021 WR2 STAT LEADERBOARD					
Russell Gage	171.0	243	66	66	550	871	66.7%	147	23	4
Chase Claypool	169.6	392	88	59	714	1,202	55.7%	242	30	2
Van Jefferson	168.2	536	84	50	739	1,199	54.8%	204	30	6
A.J. Green	162.8	310	51	54	507	1,119	64.7%	112	22	3
Cole Beasley	162.3	302	75	82	448	630	69.3%	190	22	1
K.J. Osborn	158.5	234	38	50	290	855	57.9%	67	10	7
Tim Patrick	156.4	436	75	53	633	995	62.7%	179	34	5
Courtland Sutton	156.2	517	96	58	767	1,509	59.4%	133	35	2
Marquez Callaway	154.8	305	60	46	561	1,060	55.0%	95	25	6
Cedrick Wilson	153.8	143	23	45	209	575	60.9%	63	9	6
DeAndre Hopkins	147.2	325	64	42	572	788	65.6%	140	32	8
Mecole Hardman	145.9	280	56	59	397	612	71.4%	307	21	2
Allen Lazard	142.5	350	46	40	383	653	67.4%	119	23	8
Elijah Moore	141.2	183	49	43	330	899	53.1%	129	13	5
Robert Woods	140.2	319	69	45	556	563	80.0%	198	17	4
Robby Anderson	138.5	555	104	53	494	1,156	48.1%	160	25	5
Kalif Raymond	138.4	382	59	48	533	725	69.5%	248	25	4
Jarvis Landry	138.0	321	87	52	570	686	59.8%	299	29	2
Emmanuel Sanders	131.7	479	67	42	572	1,077	58.2%	83	28	4
Antonio Brown	130.1	95	30	42	346	734	73.3%	119	19	4
Odell Beckham	129.1	360	70	44	482	1,092	57.1%	125	24	5
Gabriel Davis	128.9	147	29	35	204	838	44.8%	53	11	6
Laviska Shenault	128.0	295	64	63	419	554	62.5%	258	20	0
Byron Pringle	127.8	98	16	42	175	641	87.5%	47	11	5

Nerding Out

Running Backs

Player	2021 RB EFFICIENCY LEADERBOARD								
	PPR PPG	Att / Gm	Yds / Att	Tgt / Gm	Yds / Rec	1stDn / Rush	3rdDn Conv%	Rush / TD	100+ RuYd
Derrick Henry	26.0	27.4	4.3	2.5	8.6	22.4%	75.0%	21.9	5
Jonathan Taylor	24.0	19.5	5.5	3.0	9.0	32.2%	64.5%	18.4	10
Austin Ekeler	21.9	12.9	4.4	5.9	9.2	22.8%	12.5%	20.0	1
Alvin Kamara	19.0	18.5	3.7	5.2	9.3	14.6%	18.2%	151.0	3
Leonard Fournette	18.7	12.9	4.5	6.0	6.6	25.3%	73.3%	21.4	2
Joe Mixon	18.6	18.2	4.1	3.0	7.5	21.1%	36.4%	20.5	3
Najee Harris	18.4	18.1	3.9	5.5	6.3	20.0%	61.1%	47.5	3
Christian McCaffrey	18.2	14.1	4.5	5.9	9.3	20.2%	66.7%	99.0	0
James Conner	17.2	13.5	3.7	2.6	10.1	23.4%	57.1%	19.3	0
Dalvin Cook	16.9	19.2	4.7	3.8	6.6	22.9%	36.8%	41.5	4
D'Andre Swift	16.6	11.6	4.1	6.0	7.3	14.6%	30.0%	30.2	2
Nick Chubb	16.5	16.3	5.5	1.8	8.7	26.8%	50.0%	28.5	5
Elijah Mitchell	16.4	18.8	4.7	1.8	7.2	22.3%	0.0%	44.8	5
Josh Jacobs	15.6	14.5	4.0	4.3	6.4	20.2%	50.0%	23.1	2
David Montgomery	15.6	17.3	3.8	3.9	7.2	24.7%	47.1%	30.7	2
Aaron Jones	15.5	11.4	4.7	4.3	7.5	21.6%	87.5%	42.8	1
Ezekiel Elliott	15.2	13.9	4.2	3.8	6.1	21.8%	71.4%	26.9	2
Damien Harris	15.1	13.5	4.6	1.3	7.3	27.2%	69.2%	13.5	5
Cordarrelle Patterson	15.0	9.6	4.0	4.3	10.5	21.9%	66.7%	24.0	1
Antonio Gibson	14.9	16.1	4.0	3.2	7.0	25.8%	60.9%	31.0	2
Kareem Hunt	13.8	9.8	4.9	3.4	7.9	27.5%	54.5%	16.0	0
Darrell Henderson Jr.	13.6	12.4	4.6	3.3	6.1	26.8%	35.7%	25.4	0
Rashaad Penny	13.4	11.9	6.3	0.8	8.0	28.7%	0.0%	15.7	4
Duke Johnson	13.0	14.2	4.6	1.0	10.2	26.9%	28.6%	22.3	2
Melvin Gordon III	12.9	12.7	4.5	2.4	7.6	23.6%	70.0%	25.4	3
James Robinson	12.8	11.7	4.7	3.3	7.2	23.7%	55.6%	21.7	1
Clyde Edwards-Helaire	12.6	11.9	4.3	2.3	6.8	17.6%	100.0%	29.8	2
Javonte Williams	12.5	11.9	4.4	3.1	7.3	26.5%	59.1%	53.8	2
Chase Edmonds	12.3	9.7	5.1	4.4	7.2	27.2%	80.0%	103.0	1
Chris Carson	12.3	13.5	4.3	1.5	4.8	20.4%	80.0%	18.0	0
Devin Singletary	11.8	11.1	4.6	2.9	5.7	22.6%	50.0%	25.3	1

Player	PPR PPG	Att / Gm	Yds / Att	Tgt / Gm	Yds / Rec	1stDn / Rush	3rdDn / Conv%	Rush / TD
Jonathan Taylor	408.1	332	1,811	5.5	51	40	360	20
Austin Ekeler	349.8	206	911	4.1	94	70	647	20
Najee Harris	312.7	307	1,200	4.0	94	74	467	10
Joe Mixon	297.9	292	1,205	4.3	48	42	314	16
Leonard Fournette	261.6	180	812	4.3	84	69	454	10
Ezekiel Elliott	259.1	237	1,002	4.1	65	47	287	12
James Conner	257.7	202	752	3.4	39	37	375	18
Alvin Kamara	246.7	240	898	3.5	67	47	439	9
Cordarrelle Patterson	240.6	153	618	4.3	69	52	548	11
Antonio Gibson	239.1	258	1,037	4.1	52	42	294	10
Josh Jacobs	234.0	217	872	4.0	64	54	348	9
Aaron Jones	233.0	171	799	4.7	65	52	391	10
Nick Chubb	231.3	228	1,259	5.5	25	20	174	9
Damien Harris	227.1	202	929	4.6	20	18	132	15
Dalvin Cook	220.3	249	1,159	4.7	49	34	224	6
D'Andre Swift	215.9	151	617	3.3	78	62	452	7
Javonte Williams	211.9	203	903	4.4	53	43	316	7
Derrick Henry	208.3	219	937	4.3	20	18	154	10
Melvin Gordon III	207.1	203	918	4.5	38	28	213	10
David Montgomery	203.0	225	849	3.8	51	42	301	7
Devin Singletary	200.8	188	870	4.5	50	40	228	8
Darrel Williams	199.0	144	558	3.9	57	47	452	8
AJ Dillon	186.6	187	803	4.6	37	34	313	7
Elijah Mitchell	180.0	207	963	4.6	20	19	137	6
James Robinson	178.9	164	767	4.7	46	31	222	8
Myles Gaskin	174.6	173	612	3.2	63	49	234	7
Tony Pollard	165.6	130	719	5.5	46	39	337	2
Darrell Henderson Jr.	163.4	149	688	4.8	40	29	176	8
Michael Carter	158.4	147	639	4.6	55	36	325	4
Sony Michel	153.3	208	845	4.2	33	21	128	5
Saquon Barkley	152.6	162	593	3.5	57	41	263	4

2021 RB STAT LEADERBOARD

Nerding Out

Tight Ends

Player	RecYds	Rec	Tgt	Tgt / Gm	Yds / Rec	100+ RecYd"	TD
	2021 TE STAT LEADERBOARD						
Mark Andrews	1,361	107	154	9.1	12.7	5	9
Travis Kelce	1,125	92	134	8.4	12.2	4	9
Kyle Pitts	1,026	68	110	6.5	15.1	3	1
George Kittle	910	71	94	6.7	12.8	3	6
Dallas Goedert	830	56	76	5.1	14.8	2	4
Dalton Schultz	808	78	104	6.1	10.4	0	8
Rob Gronkowski	802	55	89	7.4	14.6	3	6
Mike Gesicki	780	73	111	6.5	10.7	1	2
Zach Ertz	763	74	112	6.6	10.3	0	5
Noah Fant	670	68	90	5.6	9.9	0	4
Darren Waller	665	55	93	8.5	12.1	2	2
Cole Kmet	612	60	93	5.5	10.2	0	0
Hunter Henry	603	50	75	4.4	12.1	0	9
Tyler Conklin	593	61	87	5.1	9.7	0	3
Dawson Knox	587	49	71	4.7	12.0	1	9
T.J. Hockenson	583	61	83	6.9	9.6	0	4
Jared Cook	564	48	83	5.2	11.8	0	4
Tyler Higbee	560	61	85	5.7	9.2	0	5
Pat Freiermuth	497	60	79	4.9	8.3	0	7
C.J. Uzomah	493	49	63	3.9	10.1	0	5
Gerald Everett	478	48	63	4.2	10.0	0	4
David Njoku	475	36	53	3.3	13.2	1	4
Evan Engram	408	46	73	4.9	8.9	0	3
Dan Arnold	408	35	52	4.7	11.7	0	0
Foster Moreau	373	30	44	2.6	12.4	0	3
Durham Smythe	357	34	41	2.4	10.5	0	0
Austin Hooper	345	38	61	3.8	9.1	0	3
Albert Okwuegbunam	330	33	40	2.9	10.0	0	2
Mo Alie-Cox	316	24	45	2.6	13.2	0	4
Jack Doyle	302	29	43	2.5	10.4	0	3

Who are the most consistent fantasy performers? BetPrep's "Threshold" data has some interesting answers

(all data via BetPrep)

One of the more underrated elements of fantasy sports is consistency. When we look at end-of-year stats, we may see a player who scored a lot of fantasy points, but that final number hides what could have been a season full of frustratingly inconsistent peaks and valleys. Further, if we're looking to pinpoint a possible 2022 breakout, this set of "Threshold" data can help identify the players who did the most with limited playing time.

Take AJ Dillon, for example. In the 16 games Dillon played the last two seasons, he reached the 10-point plateau in standard scoring (non-PPR) in 25 percent of his games played; he scored 15 points 18.75 percent of the games, and had 20 or more points in 12.5 percent of his games. And he's gotten 15 or more rushing attempts just five times, while starting (according to Pro-Football-Reference) just twice.

What follows is a series of leaderboards from BetPrep, using the Threshold data, for QBs, RBs and WRs, from the 2020 and 2021 seasons.

QUARTERBACKS
(minimum 5 games played)

Player	Games	18 FPPG
Aaron Rodgers	32	84.38%
Patrick Mahomes	32	81.25%
Deshaun Watson	16	75.00%
Kyler Murray	30	70.00%
Josh Allen	33	69.70%
Tom Brady	33	63.64%
Russell Wilson	30	63.33%
Lamar Jackson	27	62.96%
Justin Herbert	32	62.50%
Dak Prescott	21	61.90%

Player	Games	27.5 FPPG
Josh Allen	33	36.36%
Tom Brady	33	30.30%
Kyler Murray	30	30.00%
Patrick Mahomes	32	28.13%
Lamar Jackson	27	25.93%
Justin Herbert	32	25.00%
Russell Wilson	30	20.00%
Dak Prescott	21	19.05%
Aaron Rodgers	32	18.75%
Deshaun Watson	16	18.75%

Player	Games	30 FPPG
Josh Allen	33	30.30%
Kyler Murray	30	23.33%
Patrick Mahomes	32	21.88%
Dak Prescott	21	19.05%
Deshaun Watson	16	18.75%
Tom Brady	33	18.18%
Lamar Jackson	27	14.81%
Justin Herbert	32	12.50%
Joe Burrow	26	11.54%
Tyler Huntley	9	11.11%

NOTES: Jalen Hurts finished 11th in the second "Threshold" table, scoring 27.5 FPPG in 17.24 percent of his games. ... While Aaron Rodgers may be your choice if you're looking for a floor of 18 FPPG, he gets a little more inconsistent as you aim for that 27.5 FPPG level, dropping from first to ninth (he's 12th when we adjust the Threshold to 30 FPPG).

RUNNING BACKS
(minimum 7 games played, scoring is standard/non-PPR)

Player	Games	10 FPPG
Alvin Kamara	28	85.71%
Christian McCaffrey	10	80.00%
Austin Ekeler	26	76.92%
Najee Harris	17	76.47%
Derrick Henry	24	75.00%
Jonathan Taylor	32	75.00%
Dalvin Cook	27	74.07%
Nick Chubb	26	69.23%
Aaron Jones	29	62.07%
James Conner	28	60.71%

Player	Games	15 FPPG
Christian McCaffrey	10	70.00%
Alvin Kamara	28	64.29%
Jonathan Taylor	32	56.25%
Derrick Henry	24	54.17%
Nick Chubb	26	53.85%
Dalvin Cook	27	48.15%
Elijah Mitchell	11	45.45%
David Montgomery	28	42.86%
Chris Carson	16	37.50%
Joe Mixon	22	36.36%

Player	Games	20 FPPG
Derrick Henry	24	41.67%
Joe Mixon	22	36.36%
Nick Chubb	26	34.62%
Christian McCaffrey	10	30.00%
Dalvin Cook	27	29.63%
Alvin Kamara	28	25.00%
Jonathan Taylor	32	25.00%
Rashaad Penny	13	23.08%
David Montgomery	28	21.43%
Austin Ekeler	26	19.23%

NOTES: This is essentially a list of the elite RBs three times, but it's interesting to see Elijah Mitchell surface as a reliable 15 FPPG scorer and Rashaad Penny have such a large volume of 20 FPPG games in non-PPR formats after playing just 13 games the last two seasons. ... This should also serve as a reminder of how dominant Christian McCaffrey can be when healthy. ... Just missing the 20 FPPG list were a bunch of interesting names: Najee Harris, Jeff Wilson Jr., Josh Jacobs, Kareem Hunt, Rhamondre Stevenson and Ezekiel Elliott all come in at just above 15 percent of games with 20 or more fantasy points. Stevenson may be the player to keep an eye on here, as he's only played 12 career games and had 10 or more rushing attempts in just seven of them. In his three games with 15 or more carries, he's gone over 100 yards twice.

WIDE RECEIVERS
(minimum 7 games played, scoring is standard/non-PPR)

Player	Games	10 FPPG
Davante Adams	30	70.0%
Deebo Samuel	23	69.6%
Justin Jefferson	33	63.6%
Will Fuller V	11	63.6%
Mike Evans	32	62.5%
Calvin Ridley	20	60.0%
Tyreek Hill	32	59.4%
Ja'Marr Chase	17	58.8%
Stefon Diggs	33	57.6%
Joe Mixon	22	36.36%

Player	Games	15 FPPG
Davante Adams	30	46.7%
Tyreek Hill	32	40.6%
Cooper Kupp	32	37.5%
Will Fuller V	11	36.4%
DK Metcalf	33	36.4%
Ja'Marr Chase	17	35.3%
Deebo Samuel	23	34.8%
A.J. Brown	27	33.3%
Antonio Brown	15	33.3%
Adam Thielen	28	32.1%

Player	Games	20 FPPG
Davante Adams	30	33.3%
Tyreek Hill	32	25.0%
Ja'Marr Chase	17	23.5%
Tyler Lockett	32	21.9%
Elijah Moore	11	18.2%
Deebo Samuel	23	17.4%
Cooper Kupp	32	15.6%
Calvin Ridley	20	15.0%
A.J. Brown	27	14.8%
Adam Thielen	28	14.3%

NOTES: It's a little crazy to think that in every third game, you can basically count on Davante Adams to score 20 fantasy points per game in non-PPR scoring. ... Cooper Kupp missed the 10 FPPG threshold because he only went over that total in 53.1 percent of his games. ... Will Fuller is a force when he's healthy.

Quarterback is king in cards: Value in Zach Wilson, how rubber bands destroyed Johnny Unitas and more

By Michael Salfino

Projecting quarterbacks in fantasy can help you win your league; but projecting them in reality can help you make serious money — in the football card game. Let's take a look at the market as of June 2022 for last year's crop of first-round quarterbacks. And then we'll dabble in a little vintage (pre-1970) card speculation with the quarterback who pretty much gave birth to the belief that it's by far the game's most important position.

First the 2021 draftees.

The only quarterback who had success as a rookie was Mac Jones, who was the last of the five rookie first-rounders drafted, at No. 15 overall. Trey Lance, the No. 3 overall pick, barely played. Trevor Lawrence — the No. 1 overall pick widely viewed as a generational prospect — and No. 2 overall pick Zach Wilson were largely done in by their poor environments, though it's also clear they did not remotely rise above their circumstances. No. 11 overall pick Justin Fields also struggled mightily for the undermanned Bears, who subsequently fired their coach (like the Jaguars did Lawrence's).

The values of their Panini Orange Prizm rookie card (limited but not autographed) has little to do with their draft order. In the card game, it's how you're playing right now in the NFL that determines the value of a rookie card. So it's Jones' card that, in a perfect "10" grade from PSA, fetches the most money, about $250 in recent eBay sales. Then Lawrence at $210, followed by Lance (about $150-$175), Fields ($125) and Wilson bringing up the rear ($110).

(Important note: Please check prices in the market before you buy anything and make sure you are comparing the same card in the same grade from the same grader. These prices are available in eBay search, 130Point.com or on the PSA site. The modern card market is constantly fluctuating.)

Let's compare the card prices to MVP odds in June. This is not to say that a second-year QB is remotely likely to win the award. But it does show the bookmakers' sense of the upside that each quarterback has at this moment. We'll go in the order of best odds to longest:

- Trey Lance: 5000/1

- Mac Jones: 5000/1

- Trevor Lawrence: 6000/1

- Justin Fields: 15000/1

- Zach Wilson: 15000/1

One thing it does tell us is that the oddsmakers have not lost their faith in Trevor Lawrence being a generational prospect (even though he performed about as poorly, by most objective measures, as Wilson). But are we really capturing the ceiling of these players in the near term, or are the MVP odds just a proxy for team wins? It could just as easily be the latter than the former, though of course there is a chicken-egg issue with team wins and QB upside (i.e. — the expected wins may be a reflection of the perception of how the QB will play). How can this really be the case with Trey Lance, however, who didn't play enough last year for us to have any sense of how the Niners will fare with him at the helm? I think this model is interesting, but I would not bet it. It's just too close to the team over/under totals.

The player most out of whack with consensus opinion pre-draft and going into his sophomore year is obviously Wilson. He seems to be the one screaming value given he is the cheapest card and was universally viewed as being worthy of the No. 2 overall pick in a draft with maybe the best QB prospect ever at No. 1. It wasn't controversial where the Jets drafted Wilson. It was chalk.

But Wilson was just so bad, generally. What if we look at other top 5 overall QBs who performed similarly as rookies in yards per pass attempt (for me the stat that is most uniform through time), to see if any in their age 22 or younger seasons (Wilson played at age 21 in 2021) struggled like Wilson did? We also want them to be underwater in TD/INT ratio. Other than Lawrence, here were the QBs with a YPA of 6.0-to-6.5 (Wilson's was 6.1) with more interceptions than TDs (Wilson had nine TDs and 11 picks, though he ran for four scores). We also require a minimum 10 starts, according to Pro-Football-Reference.

That generates the following rookies, in order of year:

- Norm Snead (1961)

- Bob Griese (1967)

- Peyton Manning (1998)

- Matthew Stafford (2009)

- Blake Bortles (2014)

Note that Josh Allen was just over 6.5 per attempt so he did not make the list, but he had more picks than TD passes, too. If you want to include him, that's reasonable.

I was around for 1998 Peyton Manning and no one thought he was disappointing as a rookie, I can assure you. But he certainly was nothing like the Manning he would become. The other Hall of Famer on the list is Griese. Matthew Stafford is a good comp to Wilson as rookies (stats-wise) and Stafford had inner-circle Hall of Fame WR (eventually) Calvin Johnson. Norm Snead was a four-time Pro Bowl passer (three more than what Stafford has earned thus far in his career). Obviously, Wilson could end up being another Bortles, too, though even Bortles went to a championship game and had a profitable sell window. But these historical comps indicate Wilson still has very good odds of being a good player, probably no different than he had going into his rookie year.

Josh Allen's Orange Prizm is about $1,000-$1,500 in top grade now. In June following his rookie season, it was $25 in a PSA 10. No one thought much of Allen after his rookie year, even after his second season, when the card in June of 2020 was selling for about $200 (he made the playoffs in the interim).

We wish that Wilson's PSA 10s were trading for $25 like Allen's. But cards were $8 to grade then and are now about $90 — that's most of the difference. (The workaround is to buy raw for steep discounts and get the grade when you think it's time to sell.)

Maybe Stafford is the better comp. Stafford was a No. 1 overall pick but would have been No. 2 to Lawrence, hypothetically, too. Despite only one Pro Bowl, his rookie card reached $400 right after his Super Bowl win. It's now about $275 (you need to sell on the news in modern cards). In August of 2021 (after he was on the Rams), it was about $100 (these are PSA 10 prices).

Bottom line: Wilson's supporting cast has been massively upgraded via free agency and the draft and he's in his second year in a Shanahan system that has been very kind to quarterbacks and generally maximized their performance.

Fields is another worthwhile play. He has elite traits of course, with his arm and running ability. The environment in Chicago has not been upgraded, as is the case for Lawrence and especially Wilson. Fields' supporting cast is still terrible. And he was only an 11th overall pick, so far less draft capital than Wilson. However, he was viewed by numerous scouts of being worthy of a top-three pick. While his current card price for the Orange Prizm that we're looking at is not the bargain that Wilson's appears to be, it's still a bargain.

Finally let's look at a vintage-era player whose cards seem to be undervalued. We're looking at PSA 6 prices with Johnny Unitas, focusing on his rookie card through his 1962 Topps card, which has black borders and is thus very condition sensitive. Like his Topps cards of 1959, 1960, 1961, it's the first numbered card in the set, which means it was sorted that way by most collectors, being the first card on a stack held together with a rubber band, getting pressed against the edge of a box, being exposed to more sunlight and handling, etc. This limits the supply of cards in the excellent-to-near-mint condition we're seeking in a PSA 6. (You can confidently buy vintage cards graded by SCG in a "6" grade, too, and often get discounts relative to PSA.)

We've looked at the most recent average price paid in the EX-MT grade for Unitas cards relative to their book prices. Remember there is a premium for well-centered cards in every year. If you can find a graded centered card for the book price or the price of average recent sales, you should always buy it.

- 1957 (rookie card): 97% book ($1,140)

- 1958: 100% book ($200)

- 1959: 103% book ($180)

- 1960: 240% book ($120)

- 1961: 90% book ($80)

1962: Not enough sales but $175 for reasonably centered is great, though it could go for as much as $250. This is a very low sales/pop card; a very tough card. The book

Trading Cards Crossover

price of the 1962 Unitas is thus very unreliable and, I would wager, too low. 1962 Topps football is one of the hardest sets for condition in the hobby given those black borders, across all sports.

I bought a 1961 Fleer PSA 8 Unitas in 2020 for $175 and it's not moved — however there have been no sales post-pandemic. There is a very recent sale of a PSA 9 that was 26% over book. That would put today's expected value of a PSA 8 at also 26% over book: $252. (Extrapolating the value of the most recent sale to the book value for that grade to the grade you're buying is a reasonable way to assess the current value of the card in question.)

Bottom line: Unitas was the NFL's first superstar, who basically invented the quarterback position, and played in the championship game that first made the league a television phenomena. He will always be an iconic figure in the sport. Plus his cards are generally more rare as he was given the honor of being the first card in the set for his peak seasons. You can buy ALL of his earliest, non-rookie cards all in EX-MT condition for well under $1,000. I have a hard time seeing how, over time, this can be a losing investment. And I expect it will be a winning one. ▄▄▄

XVII. Glossary

Fantasy football: Glossary of commonly used terms

By Brandon Funston

As you peruse the many fantasy football columns offered by The Athletic leading up to and throughout the upcoming NFL season, you are likely to come across many of the terms listed below. Definitions of these commonly used terms have been provided in case their meanings are unfamiliar to you.

aDot — "Average depth of target" in terms of air yards the football travels per pass attempt. In 2021, Russell Wilson led all qualified QBs in aDOT at 10.2 yards. Marquez Valdes-Scantling led all receiving targets in aDot at 18.2 yards. The stat was created by fantasy legend Mike Clay.

ADP — Indicates a player's "average draft position" based on an aggregation of fantasy football drafts.

Air yards — Refers to the distance a pass travels in the air before it is caught or incomplete.

Auction — A fantasy draft format in which every team manager is allotted a certain amount of "money" to bid against the other teams in the league for players. Teams must fill out an entire roster with the allotted budget. It is the preferred method of drafting for those who believe every team should have the option to try to obtain any player they wish to roster.

Bell-cow RB — A running back who is the clear majority leader (in terms of touch volume) in an NFL team's backfield.

On the comeback — After making a pick in a serpentine-style draft, the "comeback" is when the draft works its way back to your next pick.

Double-tap — A team that has back-to-back picks in a serpentine-style draft. For example, "I landed Jonathan Taylor with the first overall pick in the draft, then double-tapped wide receiver on the comeback."

Dynasty — A fantasy football format that allows managers to maintain their rosters year over year, more closely aligning with how real-life teams are run.

Dynasty draft — An annual draft held by a dynasty league's team managers to select the incoming NFL rookie class and any other un-rostered players.

FAB — Also commonly referred to as "FAAB," which stands for "free-agent (acquisition) budget," the amount of "money" you have to use for bidding on players in your league's free-agent pool.

Go-to WR — The wide receiver who is the main target option for an NFL team. Sometimes referred to as the "Alpha" receiver.

Half-PPR — Fantasy football scoring format in which receptions are counted as 0.5 points.

Handcuff — Typically referring to a backup running back who is the next-in-line option should the team's starting RB miss time. For example, Minnesota's Alexander Mattison is Dalvin Cook's handcuff.

Keeper — A scaled-down version of a dynasty format, a keeper league allows for a limited number of players (three to five is fairly typical) to be "kept" and carried over to next year's fantasy roster.

League winner — A player who has a heavy influence on a fantasy team's success. A player can be a league winner by vastly outperforming their ADP and/or by going on a prolonged hot streak through the fantasy football playoffs.

Picking at the turn — A team that picks first or last in a serpentine-style draft. With the exception of the first and last picks of the draft, teams picking at the turn get to make two picks in a row during the draft process (the last pick of a round and the first pick of the following round).

Platoon — Typically referring to an NFL team backfield in which volume is distributed equitably between multiple running backs. For example, the 2021 Denver backfield (Javonte Williams/Melvin Gordon).

PPR — A fantasy football scoring format in which players are awarded one point per reception.

QB1 — For fantasy football purposes, a starter-level QB. Typically based on a 12-team fantasy league, a QB1 is the equivalent of a top-12-scoring quarterback in fantasy points.

RB1/RB2/RB3 — For fantasy football purposes, a top-level starting RB. Typically based on a 12-team fantasy league, an RB1 is the equivalent of a top-12-scoring running back in fantasy points. An RB2 would fall into the top 13-24 range at the position, an RB3 in the 25-36 range and so on.

Redraft leagues — Unlike keeper and dynasty leagues, redraft leagues make all players available to be drafted at the start of each new fantasy football season.

Red zone — The area inside the opponent's 20-yard line.

ROI — "Return on Investment," in reference to how a player performs relative to where they were selected in a fantasy draft.

Sleeper — A player who possesses more upside potential than they are being given credit for within the fantasy football community.

Snake draft — A serpentine-style fantasy draft format in which the order in which teams select players in Round 1 is reversed for each subsequent round.

SuperFlex — A league format in which QBs can be used in a starting Flex lineup spot in addition to the standard Flex options (RB/WR/TE).

Target — A pass intended for a particular player. In 2021, Cooper Kupp led the NFL with 191 targets.

TD-only — Fantasy football scoring format that only awards points for touchdowns.

TE-premium scoring — A fantasy football scoring format in which tight ends receive a higher value for receptions than the other positions.

Third-round reversal — A serpentine-style draft with a twist. In a third-round reversal draft, the order in which teams select in Round 1 is reversed for Round 2, with Round 3 following in the same order as Round 2. Round 4 and each subsequent round revert to the typical serpentine process. This draft method is thought to help level the playing field for teams picking late in Round 1 that don't have an opportunity to select the most elite draft options.

Tier — A denotation of where gaps in expected fantasy value exist within a group of players, be it by position or in overall rankings.

Touch — Either a rushing carry or a reception. In 2021, Najee Harris led the NFL with 381 touches (307 carries plus 74 receptions).

Volume — For quarterbacks, volume refers to pass attempts. For running backs and receivers, volume refers to touches. In fantasy football, "volume is king" is a common refrain.

WR1/WR2/WR3/WR4 — For fantasy football purposes, a top-level starting WR. Typically based on a 12-team fantasy league, a WR1 is the equivalent of a top-12-scoring wide receiver in fantasy points. A WR2 would fall into the top 13-24 range at the position, a WR3 in the 25-36 range, a WR4 in the 37-48 range and so on.

YAC — "Yards after contact" when referring to a rusher. It can also be "yards after catch" when referring to a receiver's additional yards gained after securing possession of a pass.

YPA — "Yards per attempt" for a quarterback, calculated by dividing the total passing yards by the number of pass attempts.

YPC — "Yards per carry" for a rusher, or "yards per catch" for a receiver. (It can also be referred to as YPR, "yards per reception.")

zeroRB — A drafting methodology in which a team manager avoids the running back position in the early rounds of a draft.

zeroWR — A drafting methodology in which a team manager avoids the wide receiver position in the early rounds of a draft.

Scan here for up-to-date content on TheAthletic.com

Fantasy Football Roster

Team Name: _____

Round	Pick	Position	Player Name	Team	Bye Week
		QB			
		RB			
		RB			
		WR			
		WR			
		WR			
		TE			
		FLEX			
		SUPERFLEX			
		DST			
		K			
		BN			
		BN			
		BN			
		BN			
		BN			
		BN			
		BN			